GENESIS

By Daniel Berrigan

Prose

The Bride: Essays in the Church
The Bow in the Clouds
Consequences, Truth and
Love, Love at the End
They Call Us Dead Men
Night Flight to Hanoi
No Bars to Manhood
The Dark Night of Resistance
America Is Hard to Find
The Geography of Faith (with Robert Coles)
Absurd Convictions, Modest Hopes (with Lee Lockwood)
Jesus Christ
Lights On in the House of the Dead
The Raft Is Not the Shore (with Thich Nhat Hanh)
A Book of Parables
Uncommon Prayer: A Book of Psalms
Beside the Sea of Glass: The Song of the Lamb
The Words Our Savior Taught Us
The Discipline of the Mountain
We Die before We Live
Portraits: Of Those I Love
Ten Commandments for the Long Haul
Nightmare of God
Steadfastness of the Saints
The Mission
To Dwell in Peace: Autobiography
A Berrigan Reader
Stations (with Margaret Parker)
Sorrow Built a Bridge
Whereon to Stand (Acts of the Apostles)
Minor Prophets, Major Themes
Isaiah: Spirit of Courage, Gift of Tears
Ezekiel: Vision in the Dust
Jeremiah: The World, the Wound of God
Daniel: Under the Siege of the Divine
Job: And Death No Dominion

GENESIS

Fair Beginnings, Then Foul

DANIEL BERRIGAN

ROWMAN & LITTLEFIELD PUBLISHERS, INC.

Lanham • Boulder • New York • Toronto • Oxford

ROWMAN & LITTLEFIELD PUBLISHERS, INC.

Published in the United States of America
by Rowman & Littlefield Publishers, Inc.
A wholly owned subsidiary of The Rowman & Littlefield Publishing Group, Inc.
4501 Forbes Boulevard, Suite 200, Lanham, Maryland 20706
www.rowmanlittlefield.com

PO Box 317
Oxford
OX2 9RU, UK

British Library Cataloguing in Publication Information Available

Library of Congress Cataloging-in-Publication Data
Berrigan, Daniel.
   Genesis : fair beginnings, then foul / Daniel Berrigan.
     p.   cm.
   Includes bibliographical references.
   ISBN 0-7425-3192-9 (pbk. : alk. paper)
   1. Bible. O.T. Genesis—Commentaries.   I. Title.
   BS1235.53.B48   2006
   222'.1106—dc22   2005017111

Printed in the United States of America

♾ ™ The paper used in this publication meets the minimum requirements of
American National Standard for Information Sciences—Permanence of Paper
for Printed Library Materials, ANSI/NISO Z39.48-1992.

To John Dear
William Hart McNichols
Stephen Kelly
Benjamin Jiminez—

Beloved brothers
whose courage
turns foul dayszl to fair.

Contents

Foreword

Daniel Berrigan is not an academic Scripture scholar searching for an (always elusive) "original meaning" of the text. His concern is for the significance of the text to us—in the here and now. This does not mean that he is unaware of the results of biblical scholarship. He frequently notes the contribution of Yahwist, Elohist, and Priestly traditions. He is not, however, interested in identifying, like an archeologist, the different layers of tradition in the book of Genesis.

Daniel does not seem to be particularly enthusiastic about the scribes and, near the end of his reflections, he asks who is "a modern equivalent of the scribe, perhaps an academic theologian? But hardly a mystic or prophet or martyr." Daniel is no more writing as an academic theologian than as a biblical scholar. But is he writing as a mystic, prophet, or martyr?

Daniel doesn't strike me as a mystic, though certainly he is a man of prayer, thoroughly informed by the Ignatian *Spiritual Exercises*. This is seen over and over again in his reflective participation in the narrative from Adam and Eve to Joseph and his brothers. This prayerfulness is related to his being a poet, concerned with images, imagined reality—Ignatius of Loyola's "composition of place" among other things, as well as entering into the psychology, the thought processes, of the patriarchs and their predecessors.

Daniel Berrigan has long been known to be a prophet, someone who courageously speaks out God's will for our sinful warring world. The great prophets of the past engage in symbolic actions for which they were often punished or even killed. Because of these actions, prophets often become martyrs. Daniel has engaged in many such actions, for one of which he spent two years in Danbury Prison, after which he never recovered his former state of health. Many times in the course of his present reflections on Genesis he relates the text to recent martyrs—his brother Philip, Steve Kelly, and several others by name. For Daniel Berrigan, Genesis speaks to our time and our world.

But Genesis speaks not only to our time and our world but also to the New Testament. John and Paul are frequently introduced as commentators or completers. The two testaments form a unity in a way that transcends time and place. Perhaps Daniel's commentary will do the same. Recently, I studied some texts from the late fourth century that dealt with the image of God in human beings (Gen 1:26). According to those venerable church fathers, we are God's image when we rule over the subhuman world with intelligence, justice, compassion, and love—in other words, as God rules. It occurred to me that although this interpretation was addressed to men and women sixteen hundred years ago, it is extremely relevant to our age with its ecological concerns. Likewise, Daniel Berrigan's commentary, addressed to our present time and world, may well have unforeseen relevance for future ages with concerns that are not yet ours. Whether or not this proves to be the case, Daniel's present reflections have great relevance for our age and our concerns.

Welcome to a great spiritual adventure!

Robert Carter, S.J.

Preface

For seven years I have pondered this—our sublime, notorious, at times noxious—Book of Beginnings. Pondered, read, dug, dunged, planted. The text became a kind of background music in my life, now a low hum, again a furious cacophony. I was enduring (and sometimes even managed to celebrate) membership (it could hardly be dignified by the noble word citizenship) in these United States. Enduring barely, as multitudes of innocents across the world were dying under American sanctions and bombs.

Seven years. A number of friends, together with members of my immediate family, were standing in draconian courts and prisons. I went on, a more or less presentable Jesuit. Tasks, some blessedly quotidian, some less so, occupied my days—teaching here and there, leading retreats, writing. I also was arrested constantly, as U.S. interventions blundered on with ungovernable force—Central America, Bosnia (with NATO), and at present writing, Afghanistan and Iraq.

And, to our story of beginnings, I was searching in Scripture for a version of ancestry which would shed a measure of light on dark days. A version of cosmic, primordial beginnings. What were we humans like at the start, what went right (for awhile), what in short order went drastically wrong? And above all, what of this deity who purportedly (if one can credit a Jewish-Catholic pulse) had set things in motion, all manners of being—intelligent, living, inert—a veritable cornucopia of variety and beauty?

The book of Genesis, I thought, was by no means an "objective" biography. As the story developed through Exodus and on to Kings, the image and behavior of the God, I concluded, were strongly colored by the ideology of the imperial sycophants, especially of the Davidic and Solomonic era. In the hands of court scribes and priests, the deity of the realm emerged as a projection, useful to the designs of the empire. He chose this people over all comers. His ethic curiously resembles that of his powerful sponsors. He was pleased with punctilious worship, especially when it preceded military forays; the two were closely joined, a prosperous outcome guaranteed by intercessions.

Such themes lie of course in the future, outside the purview of Genesis. Still, a hint shadows the text—the malfeasance of patriarchs, the betrayal

xiii

and murder of brother by brother, the bickering and envy and deceit, the sacrifice of principle in favor of pride of place. The lengthy story of Joseph is particularly instructive and disturbing; sweet innocence yields to experience of a certain kind. Power beckons, enchants, and corrupts.

These themes hit home, and hard, distressingly contemporary. Power corrupts. We are the woeful citizens of a world power in the images of Joseph's Egypt, of his pharaoh and of a transformed Joseph—no longer the provider, now a tyrant on the move. War ravages. It destroys the civilized skills, so long and laborious in the making, of give and take, mutuality, respect, love of the creation.

Someone has said it well; the barbarians are no longer at the gates—they are running new Egypt.

Acknowledgments

These seven laborious years would have turned Sisyphean, had not family and friends lent strong support.

I am much blessed (as is each member) in my New York Jesuit community.

Among Scripture scholars, I've benefited by savants—Walter Brueggeman, Norman K. Gottwald, Robert Alter, and the late John L. McKenzie. Elegance, plain talk for commoners, insights bringing the Word to life, are their gifts to me.

Thanks to Katie Lane for her meticulous, skilled editing.

In December 2002, my brother Philip died. In a dark time, when hope becomes hard, the loss is beyond calculating. Let me pause and salute that leonine heart, stilled.

HOPE AGAINST HOPE

You, gone.
A world, vanished
I'd claimed for my own.

"Claim it!"
Your love urged,
Conferring grandly
As a lord ascendant.

Now is never.
Unreconciled
To ghostly music,
To myriad faces,
To earth in travail
And witnessing stars—

Where shall I turn?

Introduction

What is at issue with respect to the Scriptures is not what lies behind the text in the form of an (always elusive) original meaning, but what lies in front of it where the interpreter stands. The Bible always addresses itself to the time of interpretation. . . .

If the text does not apply to us it is an empty text. . . .

We take the text in relation to ourselves, understanding ourselves in its light, even as our situation throws its light upon the text, allowing it to disclose itself differently, perhaps in unheard-of ways. (Gerald L. Bruns, "Midrash and Allegory," in *The Literary Guide to the Bible*)

"Turn the Scripture and turn it, for everything is in it." (Kabala)

1:1 So to our beginnings.

"In the beginning, God created," or "At the beginning of God's creating . . ." Momentous, majestic.

The Hebrew word for "create," *bara,* is used here as elsewhere, for a properly divine action. And in the first verse of all, "created" sums up the entire process.

We are in the realm of poetry, in this sense at least—the author(s) "imagine reality." Images are offered, an answer (better, a hint of an answer) is proposed to the questioning mind, as the "first week" unrolls.

It is as though the author knew that one day a question would be raised—how can it be that all things are? Further, how can it be that prior to a "point of time" (including time itself), all things were not? And who, or what, made the momentous difference, who brought to pass the time of all things, time included?

Raising such questions implies, hints at an answer. Does not creation stand in a queasy balance, between an indubitable existence, and the inability to contain or explain existence here and now?

✦ ✦ ✦

Metaphysics were not the strong suit of our ancestors in the faith. Questions of creation and origins were of another realm; they were grist for the mill of the arts. Specifically, for the art of storytelling.

Let us tell a story then, of a "first week." Let us sing it aloud, recount it to children, celebrate it in various sanctuaries. And let us do this long before "the story" and its consequence were made official, codified, centralized, (and to that extent) set in stone in the Jerusalem temple–palace era.

Prior to that, we are free to imagine a "liturgy of the start of things" taking different forms, local and folk in character, here and there in the two kingdoms. In other words, it would seem more fruitful to ponder (and celebrate!) the source of traditions, rather than setting ourselves a prosaic task, for instance, calculating the date of their setting down in the pages before us.

✦ ✦ ✦

These vaulting images of all things tumbling into being, flora and fauna and finally we humans, created in the image of great God—they were told and told again. They created song and dance and, eventually among Christians, fresco and mosaic and statuary and poetry and opera. . . .

How did the images come to be? And more, how did they become so fruitful as to create endless forms and variations, images born of images?

One theory of sources seems plausible. The first stories took form out of a sense of helplessness, of limits reached. Of limits that once reached, must then be breached. Every generation was beckoned to enter the awesome cave of the past and there "imagine the images."

But mere prose was helpless to encompass the stupendous *magnalia Dei*, the holy Wonders, beginning with the divine nod—all things, come forth!

Poetry then, the ineffable imagined!

And a process was underway. Liturgy and its accompanying arts and cycles of feasts and fasts, mourning and celebrating, made of the year a cosmic wheel of light. The community mounted and rode the turning wheel, improvising, ever so gradually codifying what was seen and undergone and remembered. Summon the images of a palpable world. Know what to make of it, make ever more of it—see, hear, touch, feel!

The wonders of the first week emerged—and the consequence thereof.

In time, given the likes of David and Solomon, the localized images, rooted in memory and kinship, grew questionable and of questionable value to the grand enterprise. Inevitably, grossly, one thinks. Solomon was building stone by stone, a very kingdom of necessity. Local shrines and cults, rooted in ancestry and long custom, became the enemy of the imperial ideology of centralizing and control, the jeweled fingers closing to a fist, the claim, the cult, stupendous and dismal at once, of "bigger is better."

What followed was unutterably tragic. The imperial spirit prevailed—where required, by force of arms. (Armed force was invariably required.) Thus we read of an imperial Hebrew form of the later Greek horror, the unification under Solomon foreshadowing the unification by mad Antiochus.

This dream of the imperium, a spurious sterile unity. And it was all up with local traditions; scuttle them!

We sense an awful inevitability, the heavy hand, the long reach of the imperial arm. Prophets? Where they dared speak, they were persecuted. An imposed "clarity" touched everything with a frosty wand. Temple rubrics were set down, and in the social and economic realms, class and status were staked off and closely guarded. Alienation and concealment were the weapons. The real issue of course was—control.

Israel was emerging as a kind of early "security state." Religion, along with other structures, must bow before the prevailing ideology. Cult and moral code, everything understood as *torah*, the law, must issue from headquarters, from the priests and Levites of Jerusalem.

A parallel suggests itself.

Celtic liturgies in the time of St. Patrick were unselfconsciously local in language and style; in authority they were egalitarian. Women had a large part in leading the communities and their liturgies.

The Romans for their part sensed a distant rival, and recoiled. The Celts must be "Romanized" in every cultural, cultic, legal aspect. So it was done, and an entire Celtic tradition was submerged.

A like case could be made for the Orthodox traditions. We are told of a disgraceful bickering, culminating at the turn of the thirteenth century in the "mutual excommunication" of the warring patriarchs. A wound long suppurating—then ever so slowly, and with what pain, healing.

1:1   "In the beginning, God created."
We all have memories of these wondrous images of the start of things. I recall the series of "creation windows" in the old St. Andrew's church on Block Island, Rhode Island. My dear friends, Katharine and Frederick Breydert, created folk drawings that reproduce, in direct lines and primary colors, Blake's "garden of innocence." Pure yellows, greens, blues at first; then these yield to darkness and the world we walk, a "garden of experience."

Imagine then—the dawn of all things—including light and darkness, water and land, bird and beast. And ourselves! Placed last as we are (and apparently lords and mistresses of all) on the scale of the momentous first week—how greatly we humans are magnified!

Other tales than ours sought to explore, illumine, edify the faithful of other cultures with images of "first things." And it remains remarkable that not one of these resembles Genesis. We hear stories of chaos and combat, of gods and demons battling for sovereignty over things—to-be and humans-in-the-making.

Nothing of this here. Setting the clocks of the planet, God is serene and sovereign from the start.

And even as the tasks of time multiply, God dwells in the great savannah we name eternity.

Creation. No great effort, no war in heaven or on earth. A mere majestic word "Let there be . . ." and all things spring into being, in time and place.

chapter one

"In the beginning . . ."
(1:1–28)

1:1–4

The "Priestly tradition" is credited with the first verses of the song of creation. If indeed priests are responsible for this glory, one thinks in gratitude, more power to them!

They will, in fact, rarely repeat so audacious and gracious a song. Perhaps codified after the exile, Priestly verses of Genesis will lose their weightlessness, will fall to earth and plod along, with heavy implications and multisyllabic words; the transcendence and self-distancing of the Creator.

The priests will give us the law, with a vengeance, and (God help us) the whole of Leviticus.

✦ ✦ ✦

Let us then rejoice, and doubly, for the present glorious lifting poems, chapters 1and 2. Let it be said once more. That the priests could sing at all, or induce others to sing a tune of transcendent glory, seems nothing short of miraculous.

Perhaps in time, the song gene proved recessive. In any case, the gift seems to have yielded before a clerical combustion of status and rank. And by the era of ineffable Solomon, all goes ill. The priests stand high and mighty in prosperous estate, serving both the temple god and the godling of the imperial palace. They are named in royal account books, part of the multitude of imperial employees.

✦ ✦ ✦

The Priestly part in the traditions presupposes both the Yahvist and Eloist elements. The priests will build on these, in accord with their own view of God and the world (and, need it be added, their preeminent place in the imperial system). They make much of dates, lists, genealogies; a veritable Priestly industry tidies up the earlier writings.

Much is made too of legal matters; the "rest of *Jawe*" as the final day of creation, the covenants with Noah and Abraham and the rite of circumcision.

✦ ✦ ✦

Treating of the great First Week, Thomas Aquinas offers a useful heading. On the first three days occur the "works of division"—light from darkness, upper from lower waters, seas from land and vegetation. On the latter days, the fourth to the sixth, the "works of ornamentation" are celebrated. On day four, sun, moon, and stars appear. Day five, birds and fish. And day six, animals and the "first parents."

✦ ✦ ✦

We will forebear discussion of the cosmology offered here. "Archaic . . . poetic . . . a storybook tale . . . a bard's verses . . ."; these tags are not always attached in admiration.

"Scientism," that shibboleth, a catchword omniscient as a telescope in space, dismisses out of hand our hebdomad and the ingenious forthcomings of that first week.

Still, a question lurks. Does a culture of technique match the grandeur and assurance of "in the beginning, God . . ."?

✦ ✦ ✦

At stake here, for the author(s) of Genesis and the believing community as well, is something other than probing and dissecting the creation, for sake of whatever scientific "secrets" might be thought to lurk there. At stake was faith, and its task—fidelity to the God of creation, the God who willed to be known primarily through creation.

For Christians as well, a celebration is implied, of the grand "analogy of faith," tribute paid to the Pauline "Mystery"; to that One Whose measure immeasurably surpasses the seeking mind.

✦ ✦ ✦

1:2

> But the earth
> became
> chaos and emptiness,

and darkness
came over

the face
of the deep. . . .

Yet the Spirit
of God
was brooding

over the surface
of the waters. . . .

We follow a minority opinion here, to be sure. The Hebrew rarely uses the verb "to be." Where it is found, a finger passes over the text, underscoring. A point is being made.

The point here? A suggestion of the Fall. The original creation was reduced to a ruin. "Chaos and emptiness," it would seem, are not the original images for the "nothing" out of which came all things. They express rather the wreckage through sin, of the fair face of things already in place.

The "brooding" of the divine Spirit over the waters, "*ruah Elohim*" (otherwise "a mighty wind," or "breath of God"), points to the divine power of restoring the ruination. A pre-Pentecost image?

✦ ✦ ✦

1:3–4 The first day.

To "divide, separate" light from darkness, seems on the face of it, a moral as well as a creative act. So immediately:

God
saw

light
was
good.

It will be a constant refrain, a slight but penetrating drumbeat, or a heartbeat—the "goodness" of all things.

Let us doubt not. Doubt not, though fair creation be changed to "chaos and emptiness," be pillaged and degraded and rendered all but unrecognizable, far from the original hope.

From the start, goodness–beauty is the attribution and glory of all things.

Their vesture, their inmost being is conferred and confirmed. And all proceeds from the original Goodness–Beauty.

✦ ✦ ✦

We dwell on Act and Actor, we give thanks. And we persevere in this, against mammoth odds. In our lifetime the principalities seem hell-bent on destroying, enervating, rendering ghastly and death ridden, the sublime works of the beginning. Thereby dishonoring the Author of all. For if the creation is doomed to death, slow or sudden—how shall we name God rightly as God of Life?

✦ ✦ ✦

> If wars of self-determination and other kinds of local and regional mayhem multiply and run out of control; if the wealthy and powerful use globalization to systematize and exacerbate exploitation of the poor and powerless; if the poor and powerless react with terrorism and other forms of violence; if the nuclear powers insist on holding on to and threatening to use their chosen weapons of mass destruction; if more nations then develop nuclear or biological or chemical arsenals in response and threaten to use them; if these weapons one day fall, as seems likely, into the hands of terrorists; and if the United States continues to pursue an Augustan policy, then the stage will be set for catastrophe. (Jonathan Schell, *The Unconquerable World: Power, Nonviolence, and the Will of the People*)

✦ ✦ ✦

In a prosaic sense, light can hardly be "divided" from darkness, nor can darkness be said to contain or imply light. To stay consistent with the images of this cosmology, light would have to be created (as is done here, ex nihilo, presumably) and darkness is simply let be, in shadow, background, and contrast.

However poetic or primitive the science, it bears repeating that more is at stake than images drawn from physics. To "separate, divide" light from darkness would imply a moral act—and an instruction as well.

The implication—the Creator urges a like work on us. The "dividing" is exalted; it becomes a vocation. Light is not darkness, the two are not confounded or mingled in a kind of moral twilight, whether in conscience, personal behavior, ideology, or structure.

✦   ✦   ✦

The light–darkness theme is dear to the Gospel's fourth evangelist. From the prologue, he lingers over it in contemplative delight.

John sees this divine intervention, not as a simple "division" on the part of God's raised arm; rather as a drama, and a tragic one at that.

The drama engages God, up close—the Word. The action proceeds within time (one almost said, within every time). Again and again, it must cope with a creation that has gone terribly awry, that is plunged in darkness.

We are not to miss the point. A promontory holds John attentive, a pilgrim on a headland. The first "division" of the Hebrew Bible becomes the first of the Christian. What is presented in Genesis as a matter of power over nature (together with the implication noted above), in the Gospel becomes an explicit moral matter.

For John the theme is unutterably daring; the powerlessness of God, in face of the human wound, our radical moral scission—the Fall, and ourselves the Fallen.

The darkness in which humans stand dazed and lost cannot bear the scrutiny, the light of God. Schizophrenia wins the day; rather, the night. Such a world! Every effort is exerted—of improvisation, technique, politics, the military, world-devouring economics—that the supernal Light be snuffed out, that "the world" prevail in its self-appointed, self-destructive way; power, domination, pride of place, sin and darkness and death.

Our lifetime, one thinks, surpasses the malignancies of the past. We mourn the monstrous weaponry, the wars, the sanctions (the terroristic hubris), the death of the unborn, of children and the aged, the contempt shown life and the living. And the vengeance taken against the oppressors; the multiplied deaths on 9/11 in New York, Virginia, and Pennsylvania.

✦   ✦   ✦

In Christ, God enters the Creation lists, and the conflict sharpens, light in contention with darkness.

And what of the outcome? The evangelist seems unwontedly somber, unsure. On the one hand:

> The light
> shone
> in darkness
>
> and the dark
>
> could not

extinguish
the
light. (John 1:5)

And yet:

The Word
was
the true light

that enlightens
every human;

He came
into the world,

the world
was made
by Him

and the world
did not
know Him.

He came
to His own
and his own

did not
receive
Him. (John 1:9–11)

The Lightbearer entered the world. He held a gift in hand, a grace, a proffer of enlightenment.

"I
am the light
of the world.

Whoever
walks
with me

will have
the light
of life

and
will never

walk
in
darkness." (John 8:12)

Alas, malice prevails. The noble One is halted in His tracks, the Light is extinguished.

But the outcome, death, is hardly ultimate, hardly invalidates the Vocation, whether of Christ or ourselves; quite the opposite. It places the One Made of Light and ourselves as well, and our darkness, at the center of a drama. In Christ, to be human is to be protagonist—in a tragic drama, to be sure—and the tragedy befalling not solely the rejected Holy One. Befalling humans, and indeed all creation.

But this tragic outcome is hardly to be thought the last act.

These notes are set down in Holy Week. Each year, we Christians recall the passion of Christ. Day after day the coil of drama is tightened. Lightning plays around a silent, central Figure. In secret and public, base decisions are contrived. Then rejection, denial, betrayal, scorn, torment, and death.

And these are revealed as working unto an eventual good. The word of God places the scions of darkness under a merciless public light. Humans cower there, facing judgment.

It becomes unbearably clear (that Light again!); disciples, family members even, officials of church and state—these (and by implication ourselves) willy-nilly are thrust into the drama.

A harsh mercy is at work; we are not allowed to wash hands of the crime and walk away—into the dark.

Seeking as we do a cover of spurious innocence, ignorance, nonaccountability—we stand nonetheless in the harsh light of judgment, we the Fallen.

In the drama of the Lightbearer, a further irony comes to bear.

The roles of protagonist and antagonist are summarily reversed. Humiliated, put to naught, the Lightbearer casts off His bonds and mounts the podium. A far different Judge!

And lo, Pilate the wily apparatchik stands in the dock. The truth is out. Judgment is at hand.

Before John's eyes the drama unrolls—light and darkness—an image of the life of faith in a Fallen universe. The darkness–light theme is pivotal; it will emerge again and again, questioning our distemper, a drama of healing. "Know yourselves in this clash and conflict, come to knowledge of your true condition"; this is the start.

Who are the blind, who the seeing?

John delights in reversing expectation—and this chiefly among the Olympians. In his time and ours, a few claim life-and-death power over others. They wage war, mount sanctions against the innocent, huckster a savage economic system throughout the world.

Suddenly these, together with a vast presumption of "God on our side," are placed in radical question. Bluntly the Olympians are informed: your high estate is an utter deception.

✦ ✦ ✦

And what of outsiders, the excluded and exploited, lepers, women, sinners, the Samaritans of this or that culture?

Come! They are beckoned into the circle of light. Hands are laid on them, their dignity, withheld or larcenously stolen, is restored. They belong; they are the beloved, the "sightful" ones—the "seers."

These are liberated from the wiles of the world, from the dark ones intent on rewarding wickedness and punishing the "little ones" (John 9).

✦ ✦ ✦

1:4, 10, 12, 18, 21, 25, 30   We note again the constant refrain as creation emerges, the "goodness" of all things.

A skillful polemic is implied. Countering Canaanite and Mesopotamian myths, the phrase denies the existence of an "equal principle of evil" at work in the universe, challenging the Creator.

Our text allows for no such contest. Upon all creation the divine favor rests, goodness mirroring back the Good.

✦ ✦ ✦

> Life in its unfathomable depths is so wonderfully good. . . .
> And if we just care enough, God is in safe hands with us
> despite everything. . . .
>
> You cannot help us, but we must help You, and defend Your
> dwelling place inside us to the last. . . .

You see, I look after You and I bring You not only my tears
and my forebodings. . . . I even bring You scented jasmine,
and I shall bring You all the flowers I meet on the way. . . .
I shall try to make You at home always. . . . (Etty Hillesum,
en route to the death camp)

✦ ✦ ✦

1:6–7 Second day, second "division"; the "waters above from the waters beneath." Or this: waters of "the vault," from waters "here below." The
sky, as a kind of vaulted dome. (Or as others would have it, the "salt waters
from the fresh").

In any case, to a people dependent on water for refreshment and the
prospering of crops, this would appear another crucial "division." Lowly
water, source and sustainer of life, is paid lofty tribute.

✦ ✦ ✦

A town long vanished from sight, its name hovering uncertainly in
learned tomes, is named variously and euphoniously Sichem, Sachara,
Naplous, Askar. The place is rich in biblical history.

Little matter the names; the uncertainty serves to underscore the ancient
mystery. In that place Abram, the proto-holy one, received the Promise and
built an altar (12:6). There too, Jacob bought a field and raised an altar
(33:18–20). And Jacob, dying, willed the same territory to Joseph (48:21–22).

Christians have seized on the place, its rich history, for a midrash, a borrowing. Meekly, the waters of Genesis await a further blessing, a "raising
up."

We pause at an episode in the time of Jesus. Venerable Sichem was an
enclave of Samaritans. Its people were considered pariahs, heretics, and
worse; by Jews they were detested more heartily than pagans. (And let it be
added, they survive to this day, a little knot of invincibles.)

In a deadly insult, his adversaries call Jesus "a Samaritan" (John 8:48).
Hardly a credential, the insolence. And more; from the rejected, rejection. En
route to Jerusalem (Luke 9:52), Jesus is refused hospitality by a Samaritan
village.

It is as though the "well of Jacob" were transformed, heated to a steam-
ing geyser, an apt symbol of long simmering hostilities.

Then the waters cool. There occurs a momentous encounter. At the ancient well, Jesus encounters a woman. Even among these outcasts, she is a
pariah.

And a further blessing is conferred on the waters of Genesis. Now they are declared holy, a "living water." Like a temperate current in an icy stream, these Waters flow from their Fountainhead through time and place. Toward all—toward even such as this woman. Toward such as ourselves. Drink, and live.

The disciples are absent from the scene (except one thinks, for one among them). And the portal of mystery opens. The encounter is majestic and quotidian, both. "Jesus," John reports laconically, "had to cross Samaria." It is noon, He pauses, thirsty, and asks for a cup of water.

The woman for her part is astounded; does a Jew speak to her? Yes, and more; He enlarges on the theme of water:

> Whoever
> drinks
> of this water
>
> will
> thirst
> anew.
>
> But
> the one
> who drinks
> of the Water
>
> I
> shall give,
> will thirst
> no more.
>
> The water
> I
> shall give
>
> Will
> become
>
> a
> fountainhead
>
> welling
> up
>
> to
> life
> eternal. (John 4:14)

The promise, the gift, the grace of gracious God, of God with us! The mystical is also supremely practical; the water flows free, unfailing and abounding, refreshing the parched pilgrim. Grace.

And the image is offered ourselves as well; in a parched world, a moral wilderness, we are granted goodness, water, grace.

The "bread yes, but roses too!" The "over and above" mere stodgy, arid survival—the "roll, the rise, the carol, the creation."

✦ ✦ ✦

That One stands at our side. He does not dither between "yes" and "no"; nothing of the kind, no vacillating. He is "never anything" but "yes" (2 Cor 1:19)—Christ. The Source.

He sought a boon of water from the woman's vessel. She for her part was curious, then concerned, then urgent. Please, give me Your waters and their holy quenching.

But He puts her off, He turns grave, accusative; and surely this too is part of the revelation. First things first; she must go and fetch her spouse.

She has no spouse; her domestic ties are tangled. She has had a series of husbands, and the man she lives with is not her husband.

Mercy within mercy, granted without mercy. Her life is disordered; how can she drink from the well of Life?

(How can we?)

She drinks nonetheless. Refreshed, even emboldened by His words:

> The woman
> put down her water pot
>
> and went back to the city,
> to tell the folk there;
>
> "Come,
>
> have sight of a man
> who has told me
> all the story of my life.
>
> Can this be the Christ?"
>
> So they
> left the city,
> and came out

to
find
Him. (John 4:28–30)

Unnamed, she is like a prelude, she is sister of the women of the empty tomb. Of another outsider:

Mary Magdalen
brought news
to the disciples,

of how
she had seen
the Lord,

and He
had spoken
thus

to
her. (John 20:18)

✦   ✦   ✦

1:9–11   The third day of Genesis, and more tasks await; the amassing of waters, and the "separation" of land from sea.

The Word
was present to God
in the beginning.

Through Him all
came into being,

and
apart from Him
nothing
came to be.

Whatever
came to be,

in Him
found life.

He was
in the world,

and
through Him

the
world

was
made. . . . (John 1:2–4, 10)

Thus an original (in more senses than one!) text is classically corrected or completed or clarified—or perhaps something of all three. And we are cast forward to the time of "new creation."

As far as sea and land are concerned, and the setting of the boundaries of each—an Event, modest yet stupendous, an Event which from the dawn of creation, is "to come."

And it is granted us to know; the Event has come to pass.

Which is to say:

The Word
became
flesh

and
made

His
dwelling

among
us. . . . (John 1:14)

He has walked our earth, north and south across the land. Thereby the ground is rendered holy, and perennially our own. It is written:

The next day,
Jesus

wanted
to set out

for
Galilee. . . . (John 1:43)

As
the Jewish Passover
was near,

Jesus
went up

to
Jerusalem. . . . (John 2:13)

. . . He
left Judea

and
started back

for
Galilee. . . . (John 4: 3)

Later,
on occasion
of a Jewish feast,

Jesus
went up

to
Jerusalem. (John 5:1)

And so on, and so on, the peregrinations!

Land and water and their original boundaries, the one for walking and harvests, the other for refreshment and cleansing.

But for the Word made flesh, the things of nature are changed utterly. We are told how shifty waters grew solid and upheld him. As He walked the land, He walked the waters of our world. Or so it is written:

> As evening drew on, His disciples came down to the lake. They embarked, intending to cross the lake toward Capernaum. By this time it was dark. . . .
>
> Moreover, with a strong wind blowing, the sea was becoming rough. Finally, when they had rowed three or four

miles, they sighted Jesus approaching the boat, walking on
the water.

They were frightened, but He told them, "It is I, do not be
afraid. . . ." (John 6:16–20)

✦　✦　✦

According to John's strong implication, the famous "laws of nature" established in the Great Week (permeable water, solid land, and the "separation" of one from the other), those laws simply do not apply.

Waters and land; we respect the difference, as a simple matter of prudence. We also respect (as a matter touching on faith?), in the story of the
Wonderworker, the boundaries and differences dissolved.

(Or the episode of "walking on water" to be thought a "parable about
Jesus," an analogy of analogies so to speak, as we have "parables by Jesus"?
Some would have it so. Perhaps. Then again, perhaps not.)

He, it is said, makes the waters firm for His footing. As indeed, He makes
unsteady times firm (at least relatively—go slow here), for the feet of the
faithful.

And as for the soil of earth, He takes it in hand, mingles it with spittle,
and composes an unguent that heals the blind (Mark 8:22–26).

✦　✦　✦

1:13

Evening followed,
morning came,

the
third
day.

And the waters were watery, and the land solid. The waters flowed and
gave of themselves largehandedly, drenching the land. And a living rainbow of greenery and multicolored fruits and flowers sprang forth.

✦　✦　✦

"Evening followed, morning came"; overnight there appeared blossoms,
buds, then a burst of fruit. It was outrageous, all but instantaneous, as
though spring, summer, and autumn tumbled into the light, one upon another. As though an Alaskan summer burst the bonds of winter; or as
though the majestic northern lights denied darkness its regimen.

Not to be wondered, God saw that it was good! The white light of divinity was fractured like a bundle of sticks across the knee, to make a fire. Or this; as though under a prism, the divine imagination blazed abroad "over the bent world."

Everything bespoke in multitudinous metaphor, everything was "like" and "alike," the plumage of a bird of paradise.

Or like (sic) brother to sister or sister to brother, things were "unlike." To be sure, contrast, opposition. And yet, and yet—look, brother and sister bear like (sic) features!

✦   ✦   ✦

What God was doing on the third and following days, what inmost meaning would arise, we were not to know as yet. No wonder of course, since "we" did not yet exist.

Let me try. What God was doing was something akin to this. Beyond count, as though sowing the sky with stars, or an autumn field with wild flowers, God was—multiplying metaphors!

The Creator moved like a sower sowing seed, multiplying—possibilities, nuances, footprints, burst of music, implications. Take note, take note! This resembles that, this stands in contrast to that . . . poetry, the music of things.

Musicians and poets and artists of every kind, gazing on this vade mecum of beauty, this angelic accompaniment, would be moved to declare, "Why, it is like . . ." or "It is as though. . . ."

We remember. It was written, eons later, by John:

> . . . the Word
> was in God's presence,
>
> and the Word
> was God.
>
> He
> was present to God
> in the beginning.
>
> Through Him
> all
> came into being,
>
> apart from Him
> nothing came to be.

Whatever came to be
in Him
found
life. . . . (John 1:1–4)

✦ ✦ ✦

Now we have it (perhaps, we have it). This Word was (is) with God, from
the beginning. And not only that—as though that were not enough—
through the Word all things come to be.

And more and more; through Him all are rightly named; thus far in our
first week, land, water, flora.

✦ ✦ ✦

We have the "Now," and the stage, the setting. Only let the Word walk
the earth. And lo! it is as though he treads a Persian carpet, strewn with
woven flowers, trees and vines, verdure and fruits of all kinds.

Only let His imagination flow free, and we shall see. The Word explodes
(too noisy a word)—it is like that first week. On its magical third day "evening came and morning followed." And in a few hours, entire seasons came
and left their noble trace, a cornucopia vast as a world. All silent, they left
their riches behind, and departed.

✦ ✦ ✦

The Word is made flesh.

He imagines reality, summons metaphors, extends, explores, playing,
improvising, a music glorying in a theme, a dancer in a dance, likeness, un-
likeness, parable, the imagination that upends stolid suppositions (things as
they are), in fervent, sure, skilled favor (things that might be, shall be).

Like this. Hold a seed, hard and cool, close in the hand. Shall the seed be
perennially itself, only a seed? By no means;

He spoke to them
in a parable:
"a farmer
went out
to sow some seed. . . ." (Luke 8:5)

He said to the crowds,

"When you see a cloud
rising in the west,

you say immediately;
'rain is coming';
and so it does . . .

you hypocrites!

if you can interpret
portents of earth and sky,

why can you not interpret
the present time?

Why do you not judge
what is just?" (Luke 12:54–57)

Jesus spoke this parable;

"A man had a fig tree
growing in his vineyard,
and he came out

looking for fruit,
but did not find any. . . ." (Luke 13:6)

✦　✦　✦

And so on, and so on.

Our story has touched only the flora. Creation goes forward—and so does that "second creation" of which the Gospel tells.

By way of likeness and contrast, what images does the creation awaken in Christ, what the animals and fish—what we humans?

There will be no end of stories. An end of stories would mark the end of humans. It is that simple, that awesome.

Jesus has opened the storehouse; and it will never close. The evangelist John declares so, in a hyperbole unwonted and heartening:

". . . yet
if (the deeds)

were
written about
in detail,

I doubt

there would be
room

in the entire
world

to hold
the books
to
record
them." (John 21:25)

✦ ✦ ✦

1:14–19   The fourth day. The hand of the Creator widens its swath. The gestures grow ever more beneficent, the images more daring.

Here also, ideology enters the text. And in a double sense; the planets are set in place, designed to mark dates and religious celebrations:

> . . . to show
> the time
>
> when days,
> years,
>
> and
> religious festivals
>
> begin. (Bible of Jerusalem)

And—danger. The two "major and minor" planets that separate day and night, are not so much as named (though the Good News Bible, in a major faux pas, names them!)

To the contrary, this note of the Bible of Jerusalem is instructive, and correct:

> "The names are omitted by design; the Sun and Moon, which neighboring peoples revered as gods, are here merely lamps placed in the heavens to light the earth and mark time."

And McKenzie:

> The heavenly bodies, which were the seats of deity in Mesopotamia as well as the means by which the will of the gods was ascertained, are here reduced to means of telling time. (John L. McKenzie, *Dictionary of the Bible*)

✦   ✦   ✦

Images of light! Christ is self-declared, our Light:

> "I
> am
>
> the light
> of the world.
>
> No follower
> of mine
>
> will ever
> walk
> in darkness.
>
> No,
> that one
>
> shall
> possess
>
> the
> light
>
> of
> life." (John 8:12)

And a moral reflection, drawn from common sense, on the same theme:

> "One who lights a lamp
> does not put it
>
> in the cellar
> or under a bushel basket,
>
> but rather
> on a lampstand. . . .
>
> The eye
> is the lamp
> of your body.
>
> When your eyesight
> is sound,

your whole body
is lighted up,

but
when your eyesight
is bad,

your body
is in darkness.

Take care then,
that
your light

be
not
darkness. . . ." (Luke 11:33–35)

✦ ✦ ✦

The light, the Light!

Has cultural darkness ever been more encompassing, or the light of faith more crucial, than in our own times?

Light, in a place of absolute darkness. Four friends, including my brother Philip and my fellow Jesuit Stephen Kelly, on the last Sunday of Advent, 1999, entered the Warfield National Guard base in Essex, Maryland, poured their blood over the engine of two A-10 Thunderbolt bombers, also known as "Warthogs." They were of course arrested, jailed, tried, and convicted. Philip wrote (in part):

> Attack a village with an A-10 Warthog and leave a trench.
>
> Attack a village with an A-10 Warthog firing depleted uranium and leave a poisoned graveyard—the people dead, plants dying or sterile, the earth eternally toxic.
>
> The A-10 is an aircraft built around a gun. . . . This criminal plane fired 95% of the depleted uranium deployed by the US during the first Gulf war. . . .
>
> Sanctions (a crime against humanity) and depleted uranium (a war crime) have killed 1 million Iraqis since the

war's end. . . . (Statement of Elizabeth Walz, Philip Berrigan, Stephen Kelly, S.J., Susan Crane)

✦ ✦ ✦

Philip died on December 6, 2002. I can summon no greater tribute; the truth was on his lips.

✦ ✦ ✦

1:20–23 The fifth day, the day of birds and fish. And of fabulous monsters said to roam the deep—though on land or sea never seen by mortal eyes. (Nevertheless, was not our Jonah swallowed by one such, and disgorged on a far shore, unharmed and chastened?)

And more wonderful yet, did not Christ, in scorn against his detractors, draw on the fishy tale, imagining it anew, showing how fabulous events may enlarge and enhance a truth? Indeed, He did.

Hidden in that dark mammalian gullet and its human prey, a light was struck:

> Some of the scribes and Pharisees then spoke up, saying, "Teacher, we want to see you work some signs."
>
> He answered; "An evil and faithless age is eager for a sign! No sign will be given it but that of the prophet Jonah.
>
> Just as Jonah passed three days and three nights in the belly of a whale, so will the Human One pass three days and three nights in the bowels of the earth." (Matt 12:38–40)

✦ ✦ ✦

And He beckons the birds of the air into the orbit of "good" things, that we be charmed and instructed, both:

> He proposed
> another parable.
>
> "The reign of God
> is like a mustard seed,
> which someone took
> and sowed in his field.

It is the smallest seed
of all,

yet when fully grown
it is the largest
of plants;

it becomes so big
the birds of the sky

come
and build
their nests

in
its
branches." (Matt 13:31–32)

✦ ✦ ✦

1:24–25 The fifth day, the day of "cattle, creeping things, and wild animals of all kind." Insects and lizards and serpents, great lions and vast ponderous elephants, these came forth.

And we are well advised not to omit from our bestiary the two monstrous marvels celebrated by the God of Job, the hippopotamus and crocodile:

"See, beside you
I made Behemoth. . . .

He came
at the beginning
of God's ways,

and was made
the taskmaster
of his fellows. . . .

Can you lead about
Leviathan
with a hook,

or
curb his tongue

with
a
bit? . . ." (John 40:15)

✦ ✦ ✦

And thanks be to this God—Who for reasons best known to Himself created gnats and lice. Let them too be sung! We are told in the briefest of poems, how from the beginning, these afflicted our humankind:

> Adam
> had 'em.

And not to forget; thanks also to the God of Daniel, who saved his servant from the den of the ravening roaring ones!

> The king ordered Daniel to be brought and cast into the lions' den. . . .
>
> The king rose very early the next morning and hastened to the lions' den. As he drew near, he cried out to Daniel sorrowfully, "O Daniel, has the God whom you serve so constantly been able to save you from the lions?"
>
> Daniel answered, ". . . My God has sent his angel and closed the lions' mouths so that they have not hurt me. . . ." (Dan 6: 16, 19–23)

✦ ✦ ✦

1:26–31 Evening and morning, the sixth day.

And what shall we name it, the momentous climax sung by harpists, told by storytellers and scribes (all of whom might be thought somewhat affected by parti pris!).

No wonder God takes counsel, whether within, or perhaps with the Word, "through whom all things came to be."

> "Let Us
> make
> humankind
>
> in our image,
>
> after
> our
> likeness. . . ."

"Image"; very physical. And "likeness," further defining the "image," by way of excluding equality. (As if one were to say something like, "yes, the son much resembles the father, but. . . .")

In any case, the human is implicitly defined; mirror of the divine, created by Another. The Divine, the human—like and unlike, each insisted on, as the inspired (in more senses than one!) author breathes deep and gains confidence (5:1).

The term is borrowed anew, as Adam begets a son Seth (5:3) and the "divine resemblance" is passed from father to progeny, like a common DNA.

And an ominous note. The Fall, then the fratricide wrought by Cain. And it is as though that murderous wound were never to be stanched or healed. This is our history. Blood continues to flow, as though secretly, under a closed door. Blood will have blood:

> If anyone
> sheds
> human blood,
>
> by a human
> shall his blood
> be shed;
>
> for
> in the image
> of God,
>
> have humans
> been
> made. (9:6)

The note of the Bible of Jerusalem (BJ) is curious, cautious, and let it be said plain—wrong. This, astonishingly: "All blood belongs to God. But eminently, God will avenge the blood of humans, made in the image of God" (4:10).

He (sic) delegates humans to this task. A general formula legitimates the punishment of the guilty by the justice of the state, and execution by the relatives of the victim, the "vengeance of blood" (as in Num 35:9; Deut 19:12, etc.).

The scholarship has gone awry, at least in this; it ignores the midrash offered by Christ.

"My command
to you
is:

Love
your enemies,

pray
for
your persecutors. . . ." (Matt 5:44)

And again:

". . . Put up
your sword

where
it belongs.

Those
who use
the sword

are
sooner
or later,

destroyed
by
it." (Matt 26:52)

First the command, one notes, then the principle. And the general rule ("the destroyer destroyed") is not to be thought merely a counsel of prudence, as though the law of talion were being vindicated.

Jesus is no tactician. He is master of spirit, its boundaries and behavior. Here we have, writ large, a law of soul. Destruction of the swordsman follows on drawing of the sword. To kill another is to die. To wield the blade, no matter the prevailing or walking free, is to die within.

✦   ✦   ✦

Today, bloody today. Will we ever have done with the violence, the affliction?

Yes—the curse of Cain at long last is lifted. The blood of "the Lamb who was slain" exacts no blood, not a drop. It is freely given, to cleanse enmities and end scapegoating (Rev 5:6).

✦ ✦ ✦

"Let us create. . . ." Who was it, one asks, who overheard the divine One, pondering aloud?

Perhaps the Word,

> . . . Who
> was
> present
>
> to God
>
> in
> the
> beginning. (John 1:2)

✦ ✦ ✦

1:28 We have a much-discussed, even vilified text:

> God
> blessed them
> and said;
>
> ". . . Be fruitful
> and multiply
>
> and fill the earth
> and subdue it;
>
> and have dominion
> over the fish of the sea
>
> and over the birds of the air
> and over every living thing
>
> that moves
> upon the earth." (Revised Standard Version)

✦ ✦ ✦

> ". . . Be responsible for it!
> Watch over . . .

all the living things
on the earth!" (Inclusive Language Bible)

✦   ✦   ✦

". . . Have dominion
. . . over all living things
that move
on the earth." (New American Bible)

✦   ✦   ✦

". . . Hold sway
over . . .
All the beasts
that rove the earth." (Bible of Jerusalem)

✦   ✦   ✦

Confusion compounded. What make of it, this apparent invitation to rape and pollute the fair earth?

Various solutions, some ingenious, none satisfactory. Even the editorially cautious Inclusive Language Bible (ILB) admits (as do none of the others): "Unfortunately, the actual Hebrew is even more brutal, prompting traditional translations to soften the language somewhat."

Then the argument for the defense: "But the charge immediately follows the statement that we were created in God's image—that is, to be like God—so surely the idea of stewardship and care taking, not violation and destruction, is inherent in that calling."

This god, in other words, is ecologically correct. Or so it is adduced—and this in spite of the Fall—and the god of the Fall, who in due time will urge wars of extermination and ecological ruin.

Do we have here an effort to cleanse the text, tidying up this rampageous god (sic), in accord with modern sensibility?

Nothing for it, he (sic) grows wild and wilder.

✦   ✦   ✦

Other editorial notes are equally ingenious, if equally unsatisfactory. BJ chooses to see no difficulty in the text, and keeps mum.

The New American Bible (NAB) is more venturesome—if not plain wrong. This comment: "Man [sic] is here presented as the climax of God's creative activity; he [sic] resembles God primarily because of the domination God gives him over the rest of creation."

Thus wonderfully, "in our image, after our likeness" is granted no weight as to the source of divine resemblance. Astonishing.

One could go on and on. The text stands there, a scandal. And part of a larger scandal; the permeating violence of the god of the Hebrew Bible.

✦ ✦ ✦

On the subject, Walter Wink is worth quoting at some length:

> There are 600 passages of explicit violence in the Hebrew bible, 1000 verses where God's [sic] own violent actions of punishment are described, 100 passages where Yahweh expressly commands others to kill people, and several stories where God kills or tries to kill for no apparent reason.
>
> Violence, Schwager concludes, is easily the most often mentioned activity and central theme of the Hebrew bible. . . .
>
> This violence is the beginning of a process of raising the scapegoating mechanism to consciousness, so that these projections on God can be withdrawn. . . .
>
> The God whom Jesus reveals, refrains from all forms of reprisal and demands no victims. . . .
>
> Jesus' message reveals that those who believe in divine violence are still mired in Satan's universe.
>
> To be God's offspring requires the unconditional and unilateral renunciation of violence. The reign of God means the complete and definitive elimination of every form of violence between individuals and nations. (Walter Wink, *Engaging the Powers: Discernment and Resistance in a World of Domination*)

✦ ✦ ✦

In any case, the imagery, the "dignity of origins," one day will be greatly enhanced and deepened.

Words all but fail—even so sublime a rhetorician as Paul.

As words all but fail ourselves, beckoned as we are from grace to glory. By gracious gift, the faithful enter the new creation, are made "in the image of," come to "resemble," the Word made flesh.

> We know that God makes all things work together for the
> good of those who have been called according to His [sic]
> decree.

> Those whom God foreknew, are predestined to share the
> image of God's Son, that the Son might be the firstborn of
> many brothers and sisters. (Rom 8:28, 29)

Paul's pen falters over a reality too vast. And a kind of juridical abstraction takes over. Best perhaps to stay with the original analogy, which speaks of the genetic resemblance of son to father. Seth resembles Adam; who would have thought otherwise? It is all quite carnal, and to that degree helpful in approaching the mystery.

✦   ✦   ✦

The "Mystery," period. According to Paul, the Reality admits of no plural. It is unique—and all-inclusive. Capital, It touches on us, this Gift of gracious God. We "come to resemble" Christ. Through the initiative, lead, impulse, beckoning of Another—the Gift is bestowed. His and ours, Himself, ourselves.

There must follows another matter also, of behavior in the world.

✦   ✦   ✦

A correction is in order; strike the "also." Does not the behavior follow on the invitation—in the deepest sense, palpable, dramatized, visible—that we become human?

Or—to admit both plight and opportunity—that we submit to the plight of the Fallen, and reject the proffered recovery. And are stuck among the inhuman.

✦   ✦   ✦

We note with horror how blood courses under the closed door, how the spirit of Cain prevails, socializing and normalizing violence and death. Death is regarded simply, brutally, as the preeminent solution of human conflict.

Rid of those "others," the objectors, the deviants, those who clamor for rights human and civil, for a decent life, for their own cultural and political forms—air to breathe, water to drink—rid of such as these, along with the unproductive and indigent—and lo, we are rid of the problems.

Is the world and ourselves thus to sink bodily into hell?

Looking in the faces of the guards one day, I have never been so frightened in my life.

I sank to my knees with the words that preside over human life; "And God made humankind after God's likeness."

That passage spent a difficult morning with me. (Etty Hillesum)

✦   ✦   ✦

There must arise those who say nay—the vocation of the believing community. These are called to exorcize the curse. With onerous labor, at risk of good repute, freedom, of life itself. Knowing how a culture of death would claim us for its surrogates and justifiers, its nid nodding exterminators.

Surely this is a painful business, bringing grace to bear in the world, interfering with "death as usual." Painful, hardly to be thought rewarding to lust or greed or pride of place. Likely rather to bring in its wake punishment and scorn.

Those who violate the law of the land in protection of the innocent and endangered shortly come to know the price. As the Plowshares communities know, enduring year after year the courts and prisons of the land.

U.S. GETS JUSTICE, NUNS GET PRISON

Under his punctilious demeanor, Judge Robert Blackburn was plainly exasperated. The three elderly women before him were incorrigible. Dressed in black with black veils, black socks and shoes, they were engaged in a silent protest, responding to his questions with simple nods of the head. They smiled beatifically and their lawyers read to the court their messages of love. One of the lawyers even called them "human angels."

What should the judge do with these blasted women?

Carol Gilbert, Ardeth Platte and Jackie Hudson are convicted felons. They're also Dominican nuns who pray for the judge every day. They don't fit the standard profile of habitual offenders in US District Court. But when Assistant US Attorney Robert Brown read their considerable criminal

records . . . into the record . . . it was clear that at least under
the law of the land, they qualify.

It's the law of the land they don't accept.

They do accept responsibility for their symbolic acts,
though. They snipped through a chain-link fence surrounding a Minuteman missile site in northern Colorado,
spilled their blood in the shape of crosses, banged on the
facilities with small hammers and chanted prayers.

They admit they did it. They just refuse to say it was wrong.
(Diane Carman, *Denver Post*, July 27, 2003)

✦   ✦   ✦

A century has ended, a new millennium is underway. And sound reason
has run amok. It is as though perverse purpose would ravel and wreck the
fabric of creation itself.

The litany of loss is all but endless: Vietnam, Cambodia, Laos, Panama,
Granada, Nicaragua, Salvador, Guatemala, East Timor, South Africa,
Northern Ireland, Iraq, Cuba, Kosovo. And the monstrous counterattack
against the World Trade Towers and the Pentagon. And now, Afghanistan,
Iraq. And, if one can credit the warmakers, more to come.

Nothing for it, we must hope on, against hope. Which is to say, walk
steady, whether on earth, water—or air.

Persevere in works which repair and console, cherish and protect.

✦   ✦   ✦

IF

If I am not built up
bone upon bone
of the long reach and stride of love—

if not of that
as stars are of their night;
as speech, of birth and death; thought
a subtle paternity, of mind's eye—

if not, nothing.

A ghost costs nothing.
Casts nothing, either; no net,
no fish or failure. No tears like bells

summoning across seas
the long reach and stride of love
dawning, drowning those black waters.

(DB)

chapter two

"In the Divine image . . ."
(1:27–4:24)

1:26 A momentous breakthrough; the first humans. Man, woman emerge from the shadows and walk the stage of the world. A triumph! Each is gifted with intelligence and will. In this is their dignity; knowing and choosing, they resemble their Creator. Imagine, images of God!

And images of those to come, one and all.

✦   ✦   ✦

Thus a biblical anthropology is announced, a theory (and by implied instruction, a practice) of the human. Judge rationally then, and freely choose! Rationally, freely choose? What a long tormented path our two beloved ones will tread, protagonists and progenitors of weal and woe! (And we in their wake; and I setting down these words, I in their image, to be sure; unto another millennium, and ourselves raw, tormented, tedious—we too, progenitors and protagonists of weal and woe.)

✦   ✦   ✦

They put foot to earth, noble, untried as children in a nursery. Will they mature and grow skilled in virtuous behavior? Will they embrace the good? Instruction along these lines, their place in the scheme of creation, will shortly be issued. But here, for a start God speaks, "Let it be so. . . ." Humans respond and arise. And love has entered the world.

For all divagation to come, for all crime and the shortfall of hope—still, love will never depart. In this conviction we stand. Losing it, we fall anew—as of old.

✦   ✦   ✦

We shall shortly learn much of divagation and crime, perhaps a great deal more than we desire. The parents wreak the Fall, a recalcitrant human family increases and multiplies. Woe upon woe, a deluge of woe. And yet, moral greatness too flames on the dismal horizon, patriarchs and prophets, great women and men alike.

In the world of the Fall, societies develop. Under David and Solomon, the "chosen" rise to the height of glory. Then, as though by force of gravity, the chosen fall down and down, into corruption and idolatry.

What then of God, in such a world? According to Ezekiel, God cannot abide the great temple and its odious idolatries.

God departs the scene, affronted. From such a world, God is forced out, an "undocumented" Deity, an exile:

> The glory of God
> left the threshold
> of the temple
>
> and rested
> upon the cherubim. . . .
>
> The glory of God . . .
> rose
> from the city,
>
> and took a stand
> on the mountain
>
> which is
> to the east
>
> of
> the
> city. (Ezek 10:18, 11:23)

✦   ✦   ✦

In the culture of Jesus, a like image is implied. God is a Samaritan—barely tolerated and, occasion requiring, virulently despised. And finally, as Roman and Jewish principalities summon the "law of the land," He is capitally disposed of.

Once and for all disposed of; so goes the supreme fiction and fustian of that "law of the land." To this day, the law would dispose of the Christ and His works. And of those as well who dare perform His works. So goes the fiction. And the Christ, and His works, go on.

✦   ✦   ✦

One Samaritan is never quite done with:

> Because he wished to justify himself (the lawyer) asked, "And who is my neighbor?"
>
> Jesus replied,
>
> "There was a man going down from Jerusalem to Jerico who fell among thieves. They stripped him, beat him, and then went off, leaving him half dead. A priest happened to be going down the same road; he saw him but continued on. Likewise there was a Levite who came the same way; he saw him and went on.
>
> But a Samaritan who was journeying along came on him and was moved with pity. He approached him and dressed his wounds, pouring in oil and wine. He then hoisted him on his own beast and brought him to an inn, where he cared for him. The next day he took out two silver pieces and gave them to the innkeeper with the request, 'Look after him, and if there is any further expense, I will pay you on my way back.'
>
> Which of these three, in your opinion, was neighbor to the man who fell among robbers?"
>
> The answer came. "The one who treated him with compassion."
>
> Jesus said to him, "Then go, and do the same." (Luke 10:29–37)

How lucid and piercing, the self-understanding of Jesus! He imagines Himself aright; He himself is the Samaritan of the story. And He knows well what the status entails in suffering and rejection.

He knows ourselves as well, our complex, often devious role in the world. In the same story, we are the victim struck down "on the road," the half dead bundle of anguish in a ditch.

Or let us make a best case of us. We are the priest or Levite, religious folk of a certain stamp, with agenda of our own. Hardly impelled to linger on a road notorious for brigandry, for sake of a compassionate deed. We view the victim (how can we not?), perhaps we even approach close. And—no great matter here! Or—no concern of ours! We scurry off the page.

What a biography! Save for this inglorious interlude, the story deprives both priest and Levite of name and history. No more mention of them; incident closed.

Thus our "religion" and its errands in the world are held up to the scorn of the thoughtful. Grace is neglected or despised. No blood or mire on the sandals! Fearful and footloose, these ornaments of the temple flee, in favor of their sorry errands. Free, for what it might be thought worth, of a contaminating pity.

It all goes together. Perhaps the word "Samaritan" sprang to the lips of these religious officials. Perhaps it became known that one such had paused and succored a victim (by implication at least, Jewish) in the ditch. What a curl of the lip, what a drawing close of phylacteries!

By way of contrast (shocking contrast, given the Storyteller) the Samaritan has no religious status worth mentioning. He guards no altitudinous rank, has no pressing "religious" errand to speed him from the unwelcome scene, no pulpit to mount, no theories or theology to expound.

He knows one thing; the answer to the question posed by the lawyer. He knows it in a vital, immediate, tactile, dramatic, costly way—who his neighbor is.

✦   ✦   ✦

Indeed, given another rabbi than Jesus, the lawyer's question might have brought a merely tribal or forensic response. My neighbor? Why, a Jew to the Jews, a Samaritan to Samaritans.

No! The question brought this Samaritan into being. Whether in the flesh such a compassionate one existed, he exists now—for all time, for all peoples—this consummate human being. Who because he received and succored an alien, someone of forbidden and forbidding access—for this he himself is received and succored. Whose name is transformed—from unmentionable to beloved. The beloved of Jesus, and of the ages. Jesus loves him as He loves Himself. And why not? The Samaritan is an image of Himself.

✦   ✦   ✦

Perhaps, implies our story, this unlikely one has traveled the same dangerous road before, and came on others in a distressful plight. In any case, he knows what must be done, and proceeds swiftly.

This too we observe and ponder. The Storyteller knows what must be done; therefore he recounts each step, with finesse and detail. The healer binds up the wounds, pours in oil and wine, brings the afflicted one to an inn, pays the innkeeper, assuring him of further moneys if needed.

We learn of those skills of Jesus from other, startling episodes of healing—the recovery of sight or limb, even of life. The Teller of the tale has walked the perilous walk, Jerusalem to Jericho, has lived the tale. So his Samaritan, quite simply and modestly, does what he can. In sum, it seems plausible that we have in hand a quite wonderful midrash, enlarging the original creation tale.

Jesus gives Himself away, merging with the unlikely hero. We know who He is, we know His guise in the world; even in the eyes of "His own" he is an outsider, a "slave" (so Paul dares name him)—a Samaritan. In such guises the Divine One slips into time and creation.

The guise, the disguise, the protective coloration, how stunning. . . . And dangerous too! This is the form love has assumed.

One thinks it is the only guise that makes sense in a Fallen world, that gives hope, brings order amid the socialized insanities huckstered by the principalities, whether of that time or our own.

Thus the "kenosis" Paul speaks of—the diminishing, the outpouring of Divinity into the frail vessel of our humanity:

> He
> did not deem
> equality with God
>
> something
> to be grasped at.
>
> Rather
>
> He
> emptied Himself
>
> and took the form
> of a slave,
>
> born
>
> in
> human
> likeness. (Phil 2:6–7)

He is
"the Word

that was present
to God
from the beginning.

Through Him
all things
came into being. . . .

He was
in the world,

through Him
the world was made,

and without Him
was made

nothing
that
was
made. . . ." (John 1:2–3)

In Christ, the apotheosis—and under the yoke of law, the nadir—of the
human. Him the full range of exposure to malice and the law, to the vagar-
ies of the mighty, their vengeance and exactions.

✦   ✦   ✦

Paul hymns a paean to the ironies of life, contradictory, striking sparks,
yet strangely complementary. These touch him, wounding and healing,
both. Stretched on the rack of life, all but broken, Paul is not broken; lo, he
is strangely renewed:

We are afflicted
in every way,
but not crushed;

perplexed,
but not despairing;

persecuted,
but not forsaken;

struck down,
but not destroyed;

always
carrying

in our bodies
the death of Jesus,

so that the life of Jesus

may also be manifested
in our bodies.

For
while we live,

we are always
given up to death

for
Jesus'
sake. . . . (2 Cor 4:8–11)

✦ ✦ ✦

And the apotheosis of our creation story. "On the sixth day, evening and morning. . . ." What glory—to be followed by what dolor!

The ancestors enter time and the garden. The only world, the world they know—a paradise. For the present, magical and diaphanous, a Golden Age.

✦ ✦ ✦

1:29–30 To humans, every seed-bearing plant and fruit-bearing tree is given for nourishment. And for the animals, green plants for food. All is harmonious, all proceeds as ordained.

Do questions nag, whether of life and death, contention and survival? They do not. Out of sight and mind they lurk, far from the radiant page. Far from paradise.

✦ ✦ ✦

And whether from dread or nostalgia or a sense of bitter actualities, we long that the shadowless scene might continue, in a peerless high noon of nature and grace, with no serpentine interference or human bungling, no cracks in the crystalline scheme of things!

✦ ✦ ✦

The first creation account, and the second shortly to follow, is plausible, beautiful, enticing. But alas and alack, the scheme and dream of innocence cannot long last.

✦   ✦   ✦

We know it, and not solely from the text at hand. We know it; our chagrin and sorrow are self-generated. We too have partaken of the fruit. For dark consequence we were unready. We were adolescents, grasping untimely at adulthood. We were warned, but neglectful of the warning. Unready, then stunned amid the wreckage of the sweet schema of life. Death, loss, guilt, sin, a dark quaternity, lodged in our bones, close as a marrow.

Still, as Christians believe, relief is granted. Hope has not died on the vine, in the sheaf. Christ remains, "our sweet reprieve and ransom." Through the life and death of One among us, the principalities are kept at bay.

✦   ✦   ✦

We have been offered a well-ordered, day-by-day account of the creation, a tribute, we are told, to a strengthened "Priestly" tradition in the late exilic period.

To the culminating scene then; quick, give it place! It will not last, it is a sun at zenith. Humans walk the earth, along with other living beings. All are lovingly, providentially cherished under the vault of heaven.

But, but. How quick comes the night!

✦   ✦   ✦

2:3 First, we learn of a Grand Respite, the Seventh Day, on which God rests from what might be thought considerable labors:

So

God
blessed

the seventh
day,

and
made
it

holy.

Made holy, by God and no human—a Sabbath instituted by the Creator—and for our sake, as the Priestly tradition insists. That we too may rest from the "works of resemblance," deeds of compassion and justice. Rest awhile; for rest too is declared godly.

And we all but hear the caveat of the homilist–priest. Well and good the rest. But no interruption from godly attitude and impulse, from compassion toward one another, toward the "widow and orphan and stranger at the gate."

No rest from these, any more than the Creator rests from care of us, or the heart takes sabbatical from its beat.

✦ ✦ ✦

2:4 A perplexity arises. Why a second account of creation, a story more ancient by some 450 years—and greatly in contrast with the first?

The tale is set down in a time of glory, the reign of Solomon. And "glory" of a certain kind is the symphonic note of the story. Imperial longing is in the air, and pride of place; a sense of pride, the prevailing of the chosen amid the nations.

So. A national epic is called for. The tale as told is a literary equivalent of say, a grand pyramid, a Babylonian frieze, a Roman arch. Or a St. Peter's Basilica.

✦ ✦ ✦

Sources of the imagery are easily come by, and of no great moment as to spirit and instruction. Mesopotamians also had their "garden of delight," a dreamlike landscape and crystalline streams, a "paradise" in which the gods consorted, and as often combined, with mortals.

The traditions internal to our story are vastly more important. Clearly but subtly, another voice is making itself heard. As though under the leading gestures of a great maestro, we are passing from the "Priestly" account of creation to the "Jawist."

The name bestowed on the Deity falls on our ears like the arc of a baton, the crash of an opening chord. The Name above all names, "Lord God"—is all but unique to these chapters.

✦ ✦ ✦

2:4–6 We sense at the start a certain hesitancy, a breath held. The climax is sure; do we not have the music by heart?

And on the cusp of a moment, the crowning chord is delayed. Why, what to say of our composer? Omniscient, skilled, a Beethoven, a poet laureate of

Solomon's court. A noble assignment honors his skills, even as it serves for warrant and credential.

His pen is sure, and his eye.

He is privy, he feels to his fingertips, to his stylus (to his baton), the apt, the surprising imagery (that chord again!).

✦   ✦   ✦

Water is the theme, as befits a torrid environment. If no rains fall, no grasses or shrubs or crops flourish. And most important of all, no humans "to till the soil."

Naming humans and simultaneously declaring them absent is a stroke of genius. The landscape opens before us like an empty stage—a tease, a hint of things to come; only wait, someone stands in the wings!

Also absent (but sure to come) are plants, herbs, rainfall. But not to worry; there is water after all, an underground stream surfaces:

> A stream
>
> welled up out
> of the earth,
>
> and watered
> all
>
> the
> surface
>
> of
> the
> ground. (2:6)

So. In the sere landscape—a breathing space, an oasis.

✦   ✦   ✦

2:7 The moment has come. From the humble earth, like a skilled potter God takes clay in hand and fashions the first human.

He is "adam," which is to say, from the earth, *adamah*. Like a clay figurine, he stood erect, a simulacrum, an inert form. He, it, lacks everything of soul, breath, life.

Then the "breath of life" issues. Into his nostrils passes the Spirit of the Lifegiver:

Lord
God

breathed
into his nostrils

the breath
of
life,

and
the man

became

a
living
being.

✦   ✦   ✦

In a stupendous metaphor and midrash, the creation is saluted by prophet Ezekiel. In vision, the seer stands in an ancient battlefield, littered with the bones of fallen warriors. The Spirit passes over; the casualties are shaken into life:

Thus says
Lord
God

to
these bones:

"See,
I will bring

spirit
into you,

that you
may come
to life. . . ."

I
prophesied
as God
told me,

and
the spirit

came
into them;

they
came
alive

and stood
upright,

a
vast
army. (Ezek 37:5, 10)

And the resuscitation of the dead invites a larger metaphor:

". . . These bones
are
the whole house
of Israel.

They
have been saying,

'our bones
are dried up,

our hope is lost,
we are cut off.'"

Thus
says

Lord God:

"O
my people,

I
will open
your graves

and
you

will
rise. . . ." (Ezek 37:11–13)

✦   ✦   ✦

We Christians too know something of the like, a "second creation."

We are told how a breath of life once touched the broken community, the coven of former disciples.

"Former" is the operative word; it shows in hangdog looks and mute shame. The scandal of the cross has ground them fine, dry bones and less; a powder of purpose fled.

Then,
suddenly
from up
in the sky

came a
noise

like
a strong driving wind,

heard
all through the house

where
they were seated.

Tongues
as of fire!

These
parted

and came
to rest
on each.

All
were filled

with
the
Holy
Spirit. . . . (Acts 2:2–3)

The fiery descent and seizure is saluted also by Paul. His phrase all but defies translation:

> . . . who gives life
> to the dead,
>
> and calls
> mere nothing
>
> into
> existence. . . . (Rom 4:17)

✦ ✦ ✦

An "Eden," a "garden," a "paradise." Pristine, it stands "toward the east" and the rising sun, the dawn of the long day of our story. Adam is placed there, a child in Blake's "garden of innocence."

The setting, seductive to the senses, includes all manner of fruit trees, "delightful to eye and delicious to taste." And at the center of this munificent circle, the "tree of life."

And presumably somewhere near, another; the "tree of the knowledge of good and evil."

✦ ✦ ✦

It is suggested that the "tree of life" is a later addition to the text; this seems plausible. We are being subtly told of the gift of immortality. Later (2:17), the same tree no longer commands attention. It stands there, one among many in the wondrous orchard, while the text focuses on the "tree of choice."

All things, including the two trees, are "good," as was insisted in the first creation account. Why then the planting of the fateful tree(s)? An ethical summons, a boundary, a taboo, a testing? A hint that death lurks, even in paradise? Perhaps all of these.

In the seductive way of great poetry, the text is like the footprint of an angel, a track of hints and innuendos—and we follow.

Go further, stay with it!

✦ ✦ ✦

And what of the Creator, what role in the developing drama?

Far from simple. The creative role is at least triple; and in many respects it stands in contradiction to logic.

God astounds us; who is to make sense of the Holy? This eminence cannot be wrapped in categories.

God appears first as the molder of a "something" that shortly becomes a "someone." Dead, blind, deaf, speechless, senseless—clay to start. Then lo! the "it" is breathed upon, a kind of supernal mouth—to-mouth summoning of life.

Then a second function; the God draws from the asexual, inclusive "human"—from a spare rib of the "Adam"—a woman. She who was named in the first account as an equal partner, an equally noble "image of God," is here reduced to a kind of appendage, an afterthought.

And we wonder. Are the two accounts, inherently contradictory, placed side by side by a redactor whose skills are foreign to nuance? Or does something escape us?

Is the scribe of the first week less aware than ourselves of style and its disciplines, of the notorious collision and contradictions of the double account? Possibly not. (One could venture that the redactor[s] were as intelligent, as aware of "collisions and contradictions" as our modern selves!)

Why then include two accounts (This is it. No, that is it!) concerning woman, her status, her function?

✦ ✦ ✦

The first portrayal, that of equal "image of God," will be dramatized in the women of the Bible who seized the reins of personal or social destiny. Women of the quality of the midwives Shiphrah and Puah, of Ruth, Deborah, Judith, Rebekkah, Tamar, the nameless clairvoyant of Endor, Michal, Abigail. Such as these moved veritable mountains of prejudice and pettiness, contrived brilliant ruses, won the day.

The second account might well reflect a postlapsarian, male-dominated culture. Within it, women are subject to males—even at times, to male violence. Women's status gives rise to reductive, even demeaning images: She is "a fruitful vine in the corner of your house" (Psalmist). And so on.

✦ ✦ ✦

But to our account, its literal reading:

"And while the earth creature [the 'adam'] slept, God took one of its sides [or possibly, 'ribs'], and closed up the flesh in its place. Then our God made the part which was taken from the 'adam' into a woman, and bought her to the 'adam.'"

The generic being of our second version, now divided in two, becomes properly "a man." And the woman?

"If the earth creature is without gender before woman is created, then surely it becomes gendered when the split takes place . . ." (ILB).

✦   ✦   ✦

3 Finally, awfully, the lapse, the falling away from grace.

And the Creator takes a third role—the antagonist. God evicts the pair, condemns the woman to painful childbearing, the man–cultivator to meager harvests, and both to eventual death.

✦   ✦   ✦

Does God love the work of creation, or does God regret the work of making the doll–man and spouse?

Genesis speeds into Exodus, patriarchs yield to kings and prophets. And in Jawe we shall have massive evidence of a double mind, of moods and mental skirmishes, of a loving hand and heart and a recoiling, damning hatred.

An Omnipotent Enigma, pondering and weighing, pummeling, raging, threatening—then turning, turning about, heart on high, heart an emblem of all things—a God like a mother cradling her children, a God ecstatically in love.

✦   ✦   ✦

And let us be warned. Let no one, not the greatest among humans, presume to summon a council of the profane, to contrive a final word concerning the Holy. God is God. "*Procul este!*, Keep your distance!" is the thunderous command from Sinai.

Distance indeed.

History unrolls, a scroll stained with blood and tears; God and ourselves, fated and mated, bride to groom. As if one flesh, consummated—then cast off. The Deity in love with us, the Deity stuck with us. It is uneasy, fretful, awful, unspeakably grand—this to–fro of the pendulum slung from heaven, the divine and human, lethal and inhuman rhythms.

Events tumble from time's womb. The Deity ponders the work of Her hands. Humans seem madly intent on chaos and rebellion. And God withdraws to a mood of regret and recrimination, setting in motion a mechanism of catastrophe.

But falling short of total. At times, the Deity yields to another mood. A song of songs rises to God's lips. Once more we humans are bride of the holy One, the bride Isaiah and Hosea celebrate, the fallen and forgiven one(s).

Once more, in the Song of Songs, the two are united in a garden of delight. Jawe lingers, lost in love.

✦   ✦   ✦

Some elements of the Genesis story hang untidily, like clumsy grafts on the tree of life. That tree is no sooner planted in the mind than it is left where it stands, a static symbol.

The eye roves elsewhere. Did the man and woman eat its fruit, thus assuring immortality—or did they not, since death is shortly threatened? We are told nothing of this.

Also a rather curious antiquarian interest surrounds the river that refreshes Eden. It branches into four streams, we are informed—as if the detail mattered. And more, and evasive of any discernable point, precious metals are to be found in one of its tributaries.

Why all this? Perhaps drawing on a local geography of the time, or plunging the garden deeper in imagination—or something of each?

✦　✦　✦

The drumbeat slows, the day darkens. There follows the notorious episode of the "Fall" (never so named in the text, be it noted).

No passage in Hebrew scripture has so flooded the landscape of history, touching all shores and ages; such oceans of ink expended, such multitudinous furrowed brows, pondering, stopped short upon the meaning of this tale.

What point attaches to the fateful eating of the fruit of the "tree of knowledge of good and evil"? Perhaps a powerful symbol of otherwise unspecified, sinful activity?

Is one or other (or all) of the following implied in the image? Loss of the human measure, preemption of divine foreknowledge, seizure of power over life and death, manipulation of nature to selfish ends—yielding to dualism (knowledge of good and evil) in place of the unity of all (tree of life). And so on and so on.

✦　✦　✦

The text urges us. What form might the offense take today? Perhaps a scientism intent on genetic engineering, or the creation of ever-more-hideous weapons of mass destruction?

✦　✦　✦

The apostle Paul seized upon the catastrophe, construing a thunderous midrash, a powerful resume of history, a convoluted, detailed play of analogies and contrasts.

A curse is uttered in the garden, and a cycle of death and depravity is set

in motion. The eye of Paul rests with a kind of narrowed, ominous hope on
Adam:

> that type
> of the Man
>
> to
> come. (Rom 5:15)

The first human has earned a larger scope, has become an analogue,
through a mighty summoning of contrasts. Through Adam, the human vocation fell down and down—to dire necessity, our steps set on the wrong
road.

And then, a stupendous turnabout. Through a "second Adam," all is restored and healed, the genetic misadventure corrected, the curse canceled:

> Just as
> through one man
> sin entered the world,
>
> and through sin
> death
>
> (death thus coming
> to all
>
> inasmuch as
> all sinned) . . .
>
> I say,
> from Adam to Moses
> death reigned,
>
> even
> over those
> who had not sinned . . .
>
> as Adam sinned,
> that type
> of the Man to come.
>
> But the gift
> is not
> like the offense.

For if
by the offense
of one

all
died,

much more
did the grace
of God

and the gracious gift
of one man,
Jesus Christ,
abound

for
all.

In the first case,

the sentence
followed

upon one offense
and brought
condemnation.

But
in the second,

the gift came
after many offenses,

and brought
acquittal.

To sum up then;
just as
a single offense

brought
condemnation
to all—

a single
righteous
act

brought
acquittal and life
to all.

Just as
though one human's
disobedience

all
became
sinners,

so
through
one human's obedience,

all
shall
become
just. (Rom 5:12–19)

✦　✦　✦

What a majestic, complex symphony, and what assurance! Paul's is a
new word, unheard before. No mention of these in the prophets; the meaning of the "tree," the nature of the "sin," doctrine of the "Fall," of "original
sin"—these come tardily.

His insight must be accounted unprecedented. He takes ancient history
as his mind's prey, and lo, fashions it anew. Adam and Christ are the pivotal
figures of our tribe; sin and grace, guilt and forgiveness the polarities.

Daring Paul! He reconstitutes the Genesis episode, a story of the one and
the many; of Adam's sin, followed by a multitudinous history of sin.

Adam is stricken by lightning and reels into the outer world, mortal and
afraid. There, off-kilter, he falls and falls. And he is hardly alone in his predicament. He is preeminently the First of Many. All who descend from him
inherit the dereliction, a legacy of utmost dolor.

To this day and hour, and even as these notes are set down. Or so it is
declared, and so the sorry evidence mounts.

✦　✦　✦

What to make of the following? Is a modern woman denying the Fall, or
is she asserting the power of the Analogy?

There is no one here but us chickens, and so it has always been; a people busy and powerful, knowledgeable, ambivalent, important, fearful and self-aware; a people who scheme, promote, deceive and conquer; who pray for their loved ones, and long to flee misery and skip death.

It is a weakening and discoloring idea, that rustic people knew God personally once upon a time—or even knew selflessness or courage or literature—but that it is too late for us.

In fact, the absolute is available to everyone in every age. There never was a more holy age than ours, and never a less. (Annie Dillard, *For The Time Being*)

All inherit the curse—all but One, Christ. One escapes; escapes both crime and consequence, the lusting after power and dominion, the "one" crime, the "original."

But Christ must nonetheless inherit, if not the sinful proclivity, still, the history of sin. He is like an Aloysius, innocent, tormented, and holy—this youth, a lightbearer among the vulpine Gonzaga clan.

So with Christ. All but weighing Him under is the Davidic ancestry, a deluge of idolatry, lust, betrayal, fratricide. . . .

But He is also "from above"; divine origin escapes the crime of origins. His life, His works strike free. So living, He dies, throttled by the noose of the law of the land. And of the temple as well.

The imagery falls short. We ponder the start of things, of one "sin," compressed and symbolic, and of the ancestor–sinner.

In due time or undue, Adam and his consort die. And the darkened story lurches along, crime spawning on all sides. And God grows wrathful. In redress of grievance, a wild, universal deluge is summoned.

And Christ confronts it, a wall of waters, of death. Grace must be that tragic and costly, that strong. His portion is scorn and condemnation and death. Undergoing, going under.

And this must be, if anything in favor of ourselves, these "least sisters and brothers," is to be, if death is to be evicted from the *ekumene*, the human dwelling.

+ + +

What a vocation, what a weight to shoulder aloft! The cross, He hefts it. Finally, barbarically, He is fastened to it.

In a world given over to death (only look about you! Paul urges)—such self-giving is the clue, the hint of relief. And though the terror of the world mounts and multiplies—that wall of water!—still the hint abides.

✦ ✦ ✦

QUEBEC, ROADSIDE CROSS

He was irremovably there, nailing down the landscape,
more permanent than mountains time could bring down
or frost alter face of. He could not be turned aside
from profound millennial prayer; not by birds

moved mournfully to song on that cruel bough,
not by sun, standing compassionate at right hand or left.

Let weathers tighten or loosen the nails; he was vowed to stand.
Northstar took rise from his eyes, learned constancy of him.
Let a cloudburst break like judgment, sending harvesters homeward
whipping their teams from field, down rutted roads to barn—

still his body took punishment like a mainsail
bearing the heaving world onward to the Father.
And we knew nightlong; in the clear morning he will be there,
not to be pulled down from landscape, never from his people's
hearts.

(DB)

✦ ✦ ✦

The role of Eve in the crisis has spilled seven seas of ink—most of it one thinks, fruitlessly (sic). The story is clear as to her quality; she is sharp of mind, alluring, resourceful, skilled in crafts of parrying. She invites a comparison hardly to the advantage of her rather shifty, muddled spouse.

✦ ✦ ✦

Controversy has swirled about "the woman," mostly aimed at her belittling. (Such must be accounted a plank in the eye of exegetes, usually male, and unconscious of the bone-deep bias of their craft.)

Male mastery over the woman is presented as postlapsarian. Perhaps male domination too is a sign of a broken covenant with Jawe; equality will be restored only when the couple is reconciled with God.

Or so it is ventured. But what a long time must we cower under the heel, how multitudes groan while theologisers "explain" (or obfuscate) the plight!

✦ ✦ ✦

3:1–5 The conversation with the serpent is guileful and witty, on both sides. He (sic) leads her on sinuously, denying with a dollop of covert contempt, the validity of the divine prohibition; eat not of this. Pooh, pooh; did God threaten they would die if transgression fell? Sinuous, he waxes indignant, his glittering head wags. Why, nothing of the kind!

Then he unveils a promise—of his own contriving, to be sure. At odds with the divine threat, the serpent offers the attentive couple nothing short of an apotheosis. Only imagine; an apotheosis. Transgressing, they will become godlings!

And (by way of a smart flick of implication), is this not the source and root of the prohibition—fear on high? Shall not the status of the two rise and rise, shaking the throne of heaven?

Arrogating thereupon the name of the "tree of knowledge of good and evil," the wily one hugs it to breast, strictly for his own ends. That "likeness to the gods" which is the pleasant fruit of the tree, will consist in this—you will know good and evil.

✦ ✦ ✦

Now both sides have spoken. To all evidence, each understands the mysterious pivotal phrase, the name of the forbidden tree and the name of the dangling fruit,

> . . . pleasing
> to the eyes,
>
> desirable
>
> for
> gaining
> wisdom. . . . (3:6)

And as well, each has grasped the drift of the promise—the fruit, so to speak, of a languid appetite and the merest effort toward appeasement. Why (guilefully) you have only to extend an arm, pluck the fruit, eat. Then presto!

> ". . . knowing
> good and evil,

you
shall be

as
gods. . . ." (3:4)

Or so it is promised.

✦   ✦   ✦

The promise is false, but not manifestly so.

Every Eden, it would seem, spawns an adversary—against the good, against the Author of good. And the outcome of the contest? It will hardly be limited to the portals of the garden. Monstrous repercussions will shape (better, misshape) time and the world. In *saecula saeculorum*.

Unto our day, and its pervasive darkness. And beyond.

✦   ✦   ✦

The story holds, firm, true, awful. We have lost them, the original humans. Lost sight of them, even of deep kinship with them. What remains of them and their garden is a shambles, the world a shack thrown together in the teeth of furious weathers.

The man and woman, once accounted stable, permanent, original, are no more. The peerless are Fallen. And so are we, banished outsiders. A sense shadows our days, it cannot be shaken off or shrugged aside; we are not what we were, not what we are called to be. We are not where we were originally placed, we are evicted tenants, undocumented. The weathers, the landscape are altered at core. And so are we.

✦   ✦   ✦

The story, the story! A primordial calamity reverberates through time and place. We cannot know it directly, it can only be told of in images shifty and obscure. It contradicts every theory and effort and the sweat and strain of genius bent to the creation of whatever utopia, whatever "ideal state," a community of "No Fall," "No Failure," "No Sin" or "No Selfishness," "No War."

The story turns idealists to stone.

It also pummels ethical children into maturity, this bitter dose of a medicine labeled "After All, The Fall; And Who They Were, Is Who We Are. Alas."

✦   ✦   ✦

Foundations are shaken; the noble work of the First Week suffers a devastating quake.

And the creation, disfigured and rent, receives the banished duo, it is a forbidding, throttling embrace. Throughout these first eleven chapters, "The Saga of Beginnings," the theme is explored. From the day of disobedience in Eden, humans suffer deterioration of impulse and act, of behavior personal and social.

Thenceforth we are disposed—genetically it would seem—to malice. The families grow in skills of husbandry and tilling, they offer sacrifices of mitigation—and for all that, suffering and sin proliferate.

That "knowledge of good and evil" sticks, the clue. The parents were created in harmonious union with God and creation. The "tree of life" signified the gift, the glory.

A serpent offered a far different fruit; let them only taste, they would know good and evil. Which is to suggest how alike they are. At the least, they would be a schizoid people, torn with contrary urgings; wisdom and folly, grace and death in contention, friendship and hatred toward God and one another.

✦   ✦   ✦

4:1–25 Onward—and downward, to the Abel-Cain episode.

The story is clearly a compilation of various traditions. Its era is uncertain, despite a text that would make the protagonists sons of the first parents.

Important details indicate a fully formed society. A cult is in place, and a tribe.

Cain slays his brother. Some would wreak vengeance on him, others would protect him.

Events worsen, "the center cannot hold." A deluge is decreed, nearly making an end altogether of matters human. The tower of Babel stands unfinished, the tribes of earth grow witless, scattered like chaff in a high wind.

And what of the deity? Repeatedly, provocatively, the author forbids us our logic. We are not to crib, cabin, and confine the supernal one. Countering the stories of violence and retribution and disgust with humankind, a second grand theme goes pari passu; mitigation from on high. Time and again, in midcourse of a horrid decree, Jawe entertains saving second thoughts, intervenes, puts the brake to disaster, prevents the worst.

Thus. Even as the first parents are ejected, God clothes them in "leather garments" against the rigors of life in the raw.

God forbids capital punishment against Cain. The Deity likewise spares the first of many "remnants." Noah is drawn from the flood, unlikely as a Jonah regurgitated.

And after the collapse of the tower of folly, Abraham is summoned, in view of a momentous choice. The choice will fall like a ray of dawn on every page of the Story of Night.

✦ ✦ ✦

Originally the place of the Shekinah was in the lower regions (of earth). When Adam sinned, It ascended to the first heaven. When Cain sinned, It ascended to the second. . . .

This is a way of teaching that the wicked drive It away from the human abode. . . .

In contradistinction, righteous men arose and made It descend. . . . (Abraham Cohen, "God and the Universe," in *Everyman's Talmud: The Major Teachings of the Rabbinic Sages*)

✦ ✦ ✦

4:1 Why this story of fratricide, immediately following on the Fall and eviction from paradise? Instructive. In a new world, the "outside," two brothers are born. One is an innocent, countering the Fault. In the soul of the other, the Fault lies deep. His brow is a midnight, his soul a tightened spring of envy.

And shortly, the sin of the parents begets another, and a worse.

✦ ✦ ✦

ABEL

One blood veined us, stem and fruit
weighing our mother Eve.
"Brothers,"
said her burning eyes; "See, hand
must lock in hand, fingers root
in no rock than this other. Abel
in Cain, younger in his brother."
"Mother, the worm that raveled Eden
tents in the parent tree.
"New lambs
sniff and shy at my blood.

"Go, red fleece
teach death to my mother."

(DB)

✦ ✦ ✦

We are at the beginning of time; yet in the story of the brothers, we are in subsequent, Mosaic time. Abel offers first fruits, in accord with (a far later) law. For this lyric leap of fealty, he wins divine approval.

His name is a word game; Cain, "the acquisitionist," is a child of his era—but like his brother, not of the first era. His offering is humbler, fruits of the earth. Yet, as would seem, the rub is other than the quality of his proffer to God. This, the faith of Cain is less vibrant than his brother's.

✦ ✦ ✦

The author of Hebrews is harsh. Cain compares badly with his brother.

By faith Abel offered God a sacrifice greater than Cain's. Because of this he is attested to be just, God himself having borne witness to him on account of his gifts. . . . (11:4)

The letter of John goes even further, is all but implacable:

We should not follow the example of Cain who belonged to the evil one, and killed his brother.

Why did he kill him? Because his own deeds were evil, while his brother's were just. (1 John 3:12)

How far scapegoating has gone! The flat statement, "belonged to the evil one," would consign Cain once for all to Gehenna. And this, though Jawe of the Thunderbolts proves merciful to the delinquent.

✦ ✦ ✦

Indeed the Hebrew Bible has no monopoly on rancor. The epistle of Jude (1:22) is inflammatory, a diatribe. As an ancestor of false teachers in the community ("so much the worse for them!"), the memory of Cain is summoned. He is a very progenitor of wickedness:

"They have taken the road Cain took!" (Jude 1:11)

These fathers in the faith, how self-assured they were, surrogates of the final Judge!

✦   ✦   ✦

4:8–11   Fratricide, the first "war on earth" is also a "war in heaven," as will be underscored in episodes that follow. The book of Revelation will verify the truth (12:7–9).

And what of God, as murder most foul is consummated? The Deity, we are told, witnesses the crime, but does not intervene. The implication would seem to be; let the worst proceed; let freedom (of a sort) ring.

Prior to the catastrophe, God strove to stay the hand of Cain, lending him a second thought or two. (Still, one wonders; is the God also subtly pushing matters, egging Cain on?)

There follows an extraordinary encounter, a monologue with no response, only a question and a reflection, dying on the air.

God speaks:

Why
these
dark looks?

If
your intention
be good,

you
can hold your head
high.

But
if not,

sin
is a demon

lurking
at the door.

His urge
is

toward
you;

none the less,

you
can

master
him. (4:6–7)

✦   ✦   ✦

Second thoughts keep jarring. The deity, for good or ill, is closer to the
bloody outcome than his probing might suggest.

Good faith or bad? Is ignorance feigned? Surely he knows what the author knows, and reports:

> The Lord looked with approval on Abel and his offering,
> but on Cain and his offering he did not.
>
> Cain greatly resented this, and was crestfallen. (4:4–5)

✦   ✦   ✦

In any case, and whatever the game, at length the God intervenes. On
the face of it, he offers a sound psychology, along with paternal advice. The
Deity senses the purpose taking form, and questions the morose countryman. All in vain. The weapon falls; murder most foul.

What then of Cain, and his fate? He will not walk immune. He stands
under judgment, the verdict of a God who could not, or would not prevent
the crime. A God who, as the blow is struck, is unexpectedly powerless—or
inexplicably absent.

Whatever the case, to the divine logic mercy befits.

✦   ✦   ✦

And what of Abel, we wonder, the innocent, the first of a countless multitude of victims? And what of the "voice of his blood," crying out from the
ground?

Haunting. The author of Hebrews again:

> By faith Abel offered to God a better sacrifice than Cain,
> through which he obtained the testimony that he was righ-
> teous, God testifying about his gifts.
>
> Therefore although Abel is dead, he still speaks. (11:4)

✦   ✦   ✦

The psychology of guilt and repentance, in the dialogue that follows, is
remarkable. This time only, Cain responds. Arrogance has evaporated. No

more denial; in effect, he was his brother's keeper. He admits to the noble charge, and his violation.

And God, for his part, refuses to exact vengeance unto death. This is the judgment—Cain is condemned to live on. Retribution takes a strange form; he must live on in the world. With this stipulation, he will carry on his body a name, an indelible stigma. Cain. The world will know him.

✦ ✦ ✦

Innocent blood ran, and the body of Abel lay uncovered, an abomination. So Cain is forbidden his landholding, is cut away from soil and livelihood. How can he turn up the earth or plant crops when the soil is stained with his brother's blood? Will he not hear a cry from the earth; Nefas, what you have done!

That sentence of God, it goes against all conventional "systems of justice," even the least draconian. Cain must not perish, nor is he to be locked away from his own kind.

Quite the opposite, he is condemned to wander everywhere and dwell nowhere, a gyrovague about the earth, a nomad. A marked man, and shunned.

He will be stigmatized, but not primarily as a mark of shame. A bizarre twist of the decree proves in fact a mercy. The "mark of Cain" will protect him. Not only is he not condemned to death; he cannot be killed with impunity.

By command of God, Cain belongs to a protected tribe. The decree falls with the solemnity of a death (or birth) knell:

> If
> anyone
>
> kills
> Cain,
>
> Cain
> shall
>
> be
> avenged
>
> sevenfold. (4:15)

✦ ✦ ✦

We flounder about, in deep and bitter waters. The sentence uttered against the parents has struck home. And for dramatic shock, the narrative sharply syncopates history. The blow of Cain strikes his brother close in time after the Fall; in the next generation.

✦ ✦ ✦

What greater sorrow, one thinks? The parents live on, to witness the murder of a son.

Death has entered the world. We had thought (perhaps we had been led to think, our author is a genius of indirection and innuendo)—we surmised that the first death would befall the parents, gently and in course of nature.

Not to be. Death arrives like a thief in the night. The parents are horrified witnesses of violence and its consequence. Worst of all, the murder is fratricidal.

The first family of our tribe, and horridly dysfunctional.

✦ ✦ ✦

4:17–24   We have here a mishmash of traditions regarding the line of Cain. Whence indeed, we marvel, did he come on a wife?

The wanderer and his mark cannot quite be done with; time and again, a revenant, in this or that tradition he stalks the page.

Sometimes the account is consistent with the judgment laid on him. Thus he is said to beget wandering sons—a shepherd, a musician, and a smith.

And again the account contradicts the divine judgment, he settles in and founds a city!

✦ ✦ ✦

And a question. Does every tradition, whatever branching bloodline, require a murder, and a murderer, at the start?

We come to a fifth (or so) generation of Cain, to a certain Lamech.

As though unable to countenance the horror, the author lingers over a single episode. It is wrapped close as a rotten fleece about a criminal life.

Against this monstrous one, no moral judgment is pronounced. The narrative speaks for itself. We have simply a verse, perhaps from a drinking song. We imagine it bellowed by the lout, in face of a captive audience—his two wives?

Is he an abuser of women, are they being warned?

> ". . . Wives of Lamech,
> listen
>
> to
> my utterance:

I
have killed
a man

for
wounding me,

a child
for bruising me.

If Cain
is

avenged
sevenfold,

then
Lamech
Seventy-sevenfold!" (4:23–24)

The stakes of violence have risen and risen.

This is the last mention of the clan of Cain. The curtain falls, with the above echo, wild, mocking, mordant, of his legacy and line.

But if this is all, if such as Lamech are allowed to ravage the moral universe, to seize center stage—what hope remains?

✦ ✦ ✦

In the Bible, an unbearable, uncouth wickedness requires a halt, a counterpoint. The likes of Lamech cannot bellow the last word, a brutal manifesto that hope itself has been put to death.

This, the counter. Jesus summons the excessive "7" of avenging Lamech, to a far different end; that of reconciliation—the perennial, wearying quest, the heart of His humanism, and ours:

Peter came up and asked Him: "Lord, when my brother wrongs me, how often must I forgive him? Seven times?"

"No," Jesus replied, "not seven times. I say seventy times seven times." (Matt 18:21–22)

chapter three

"God blessed them and named them 'Humankind' . . ."
(4:25–9:6)

4:25

> Adam knew his wife again
> And she bore him a son . . . .

In the preceding story we leapt ahead smartly, to the era of awful Lamech. Now we are briefly back with Eve, in the first generation.

And a question arises—why this violation of linear time?

Time, that mysterious, even ferocious angel! In a clumsy circumlocution,
Augustine wrote of time as a perceived movement of planets,

"the measure of motion, according to that which is before and after."

A weighty definition indeed, if not an imponderable, leaving us more or
less where we were.

In Genesis, time is something other than the whirring of planets in their
course. From the start of creation, biblical time is thrust at us, indifferent if
not hostile to Augustine's planets and their ineluctable, majestic wheelings.
Biblical time is bent to theme and purpose, a kind of prime matter of religious history.

Time will tell, as the saying goes; but in the historical books, time is constantly subverting expectation. God acts and acts again, but the interventions are bewilderingly inconsistent.

No "perfect" Olympian, this god! Another being entirely. A God of
moods and whims, of virulent hatreds and inexplicable preferences—fierce,
disdaining, beyond apprehending, One who refuses to be cornered, defined,
spoken for.

This God functions in biblical time—a difficult, all but impossible landscape. In Exodus and the following books, the Deity creates crises and ec-

static moments, draws the human tribe laboriously up mountains and through desert wanderings, upbears humans and stops them short.

And Jawe brings to being every type of our kind—kings and criminals, saints and rascals—and sometimes the two in one skin.

The Deity's gaze enters time—and time brims with crime and consequence, with the clairvoyance of prophets and the heroism of martyrs.

Human origins and their multiple shocks and surprises, humans unpredictable, brutal, tragic, holy—we follow the festering unfolding, the worst and the noblest of our kind.

✦ ✦ ✦

And a question keeps recurring—a conundrum, a box within boxes, a torment, a koan. It is never done with. Who are we humans, whither bound—if anywhere—and under what aegis?

That "aegis" is of point. In our stories, time has its peak moments. God commands Abraham to perform a bizarre sacrifice, Moses is rapt on the mount, Jacob must wrestle nightlong with a mysterious assailant. Then such points of ecstasy and crisis yield to other rhythms, perhaps to a quotidian plod.

And a Purpose emerges, above and beyond human resolve or conniving. It takes the form of a Promise.

At the start, all is clear, including the god's purpose in creation. For our part, humans are created free. Then, through the primal sin, clarity falls to thwarting, delay, paralysis of purpose. The point of the divine venture in our regard grows woefully obscure. The landscape dims under a crepuscular, eerie half-light. The hope of God is halted in blood, is rejected, taken for granted, erased through lust, greed, violence. It is shamed or bartered away or derided in foul act.

And somehow, by a gift never totally withdrawn, the divine purpose persists. It haunts us, leads us on, makes eventual sense of senseless events— even after deluge or wildfire all but make an end of our sorry kind.

✦ ✦ ✦

How tell of that interfering, denouncing, forgiving God, now a fury unleashed, now a maternal breast bared?

Perhaps through the method of our author(s)—a sober foreboding taken for sensible mood—expect the worst, be grateful for mitigation and mercy.

And disrupt, at times chaotically bend time, backward, forward. And ourselves pitched along, as though time were a wild colt and we the half-thrown rider, seeking somehow to stay aboard the story.

Thus our tales, a wild ride through time.

Now and again, priests intervene, and we have a sobersided linear account—pieties, abstractions, formulas, commands, niceties of temple worship. The style is devoid, or at least minimally expressive, of the torrid and arctic moods of love.

Thus the biblical question, and by strong implication, an answer. Is time a mere "measure of motion"? If that were all of it, love and hatred would have fled the planet.

They have not; they turn the pages to fire and ice. We must walk there.

Early in Genesis our ride on the wild side gets underway. Generations tumble one upon another. No strict guidelines or rubric of time and place. We careen forward, from Adam and Eve and the Fall to the death of their son, and on and on—to a criminal descendant of the fifth generation.

Then abruptly back to Eve, and her loss—Abel is murdered.

Still, she is consoled; another child born to her. And in two breathless verses, son Seth races into parenthood, begetting his son Enoch. *Eccolo*, a newborn grandson of Adam, and given (so there!) a Hebrew name! And that is that, the shortest of genealogies.

But wait, lest we think surprises and complications are done with, Enoch, we are told, is the first mortal to confer on God a new name, "Jawe." An assertion that other stories will contradict flatly; according to these latter stories, until the time of great Moses, no one addressed God by this name.

Which is to infer perhaps once more that the writer or compiler is uninterested in numbers as such, or the date of such and such an event or influence. His intent is other; to shake up our "ordinary time," and thereby, ourselves.

The implication presses home. Time as mere sequence cannot convey the larger callings and renegings, the sins, disruptions, and interventions that have shaped and misshaped our past—and inevitably, our present.

The deep truth, deep as the maw of hell, noble as the vault of heaven, the truth that shakes our souls—we are sons and daughters of Adam and Eve. The implication is vast, ominous.

The original Fault brings in its wake a horridly magnified next phase. We have seen it, and pondered—the first parents beget a murderer and a victim. And Cain the fratricide must be marked for life; "for life" in more senses than one; marked, "guilty"; marked, "divine mercy."

Rudely, the story shoves him from shadows to center stage. His shadow grows; it falls over peoples and generations. He flees, he cannot escape. Again and again he arises, a night-browed protagonist in the human drama.

If the truth of things, the truth of our plight is to be made plain, he is a crucial ancestor. Cain's other names are Guilt, Confusion, Remorse, Shame, I Flee. He brought death, and he cannot die. Hatred and love pursue him. Everyone claims him, everyone shuns and despises him.

Such contradictions roil the pages! We note the hatred, the shoving aside, the implication—I am not like that. Or: we are not like that, as we daughters and sons—of whom?—strain with might and main to deny the affinity, the implication.

This too—a covert half-shamed admiration, a mimesis—the vast socializing of the spirit of Cain through generations, tribes, nations. In wars unending, murderous behavior is accepted and adopted. The abhorrent, the abnormal—normalized. Including, for surfeit of horror, our own century and lifetime.

Everyman? Say, his name is Warrior, is—Cain the fratricide.

But for a crucial Intervention, which Christians name Incarnation, Cain's story is our own, and our only one. Cain, the weapon falling and falling, the brother disposed of, again and again. Multitudes of brothers, in the vast generational denial of blood affinity—the crime we name war—the attempt at all and any cost, to deny through bloodshed that we are who we are—sisters and brothers of one another.

Cain, a denial of blood bond, a cliché written in blood.

✦   ✦   ✦

Cain has even become—pious, religious. He occupies a Christian pew; he appears worshipful and wears a Sunday face. See him in us. Leaning to him, we Christians turn our backs and close our ears against the austere words and actions of Christ.

Only give us time and occasion; the occasion being a Constantinian concordat, in whatever form. The cosigner of the pact is Cain.

Thus again and again, the community of believers shows the world a bizarre, schizophrenic ethic.

In time, there arise "peace churches," a notable redundancy, but perhaps a necessary one, since there will also arise "churches of Cain," with their ethic of allowable killing, of murder beyond accountability—wars necessary, just, befitting. Wars approved of a certain god, whose provenance is known to pagans as well—Mars.

✦ ✦ ✦

The image of Abel too will emerge again and again through the ages; necessarily, one thinks, this brother–victim.

Cain's weapon falls and falls; and lo! Abel the innocent is also socialized. A multitude of Abels are born in our lifetime, the brothers whose innocence and uprightness are a deadly affront, a provocation, a source of bilious envy. Walk carefully, Abel!

✦ ✦ ✦

In every generation there will be executioners, victims, and more or less guilty bystanders. Including, as in the original crime, a divine bystander.

And no breakthrough, no "third way"?

Yes, for Christians a Someone, a Breakthrough; for every Constantinian Christian, a Christ. For the god–bystander, the noninterfering god—the incarnate Son, submitting to the sword of Caesar. One Who also sternly forbids violent reprisal among His own. "Peter, put up your sword."

✦ ✦ ✦

We have marveled how the Abel-Cain myth proliferates and contradicts and raises doubts. Does Cain the fratricide gain a fixed abode? He does. Does he wander the earth? He does. Is he one or many? He is both one and many.

Cain, a presence undeniable, is denied place, a shadow upon our soul, communal and personal, the shadow across generations, exemplar and icon of a certain view of life. The majority view, to be sure. Let the minority admit it, lifelong. And never give up—

"the right to fail, which is worth dying for." (W. H. Auden)

✦ ✦ ✦

To this degree, the spirit of Cain takes hold; murder will become the common currency of the tribe. Terrifying, verifiable in our own culture, unto our century.

Still, we confess and take heart. Cain does not own or exhaust the story. Though he lays heavy claim to it.

✦ ✦ ✦

4:17–24   In the pages of Genesis, the progeny of Cain are given short shrift, concentrated. It is as though disdain lies heavy on the page, the chronicler cannot have done with him quickly enough.

But a harsh instruction is implied. Cain cannot be done with. It must be known how the miasma spreads, how murder proliferates. No avoiding it, this dark subtext of the lore of the tribe. No avoiding finally a Lamech and his brutish braying.

And we are left with that. Except that we are never left with that.

✦   ✦   ✦

Write it again, linger over it, the saving bitterness. The biblical account of the line of Cain trails off; his method and madness abide. He has defined war, once for all he has dramatized it—the killing of brother by brother.

Of no small moment, this piercing biblical insight. A truth contemned throughout history, denied in practice, above all through war itself.

Does a brother stand in the gunsights? No. An enemy stands there.

An enemy has appeared; he must be done away with. By whatever means, let the unwanted or unprofitable or despised cease to exist. By racism, sexism, homophobia, abortion, capital punishment, and "assisted suicide."

✦   ✦   ✦

4:25   There follows another rupture in the time sequence. We return to Eve, and her muted sigh of joy. A new child!

It is as though Abel and Cain recede to the shadows; the one to Sheol, the other to scouring the earth for relief and recourse.

And the mother appears, bearing a newborn, purchased with her tears. How poignant! She holds the child before our gaze and announces his name, Seth:

> ". . . offspring
> in place
> of Abel,
>
> because
> Cain
>
> slew
> him."

✦   ✦   ✦

6:1–4   A tale within the Story, so to speak.

Let us take it as a fragment of ancient lore (everything in these few verses is rightly introduced with a "perhaps").

So. Once upon a time, vast mythological beings descended into time and this world, and coupled with mortal daughters. And the offspring were unlikely children indeed, treading uneasily the thin tegument of our planet, born of mortals and immortals!

The species were known as the "Nephilim," Titans who left traces of their passing in the ruins of huge megalithic structures.

Our ancestors viewed these, when centuries later they invaded Canaan, and paused in awe before the towering relics.

But Jawe, viewing these interplanetary proceedings, was hardly amused.

Clearly, mere creatures were abandoning all sense of limit, of taboo. Men and women, clay molded by his hands, by his allowance the longest-lived of all creatures—these were playing havoc with high heaven, were mimicking the god!

"The spirit of God," the *ruah* giving breath to the living, differentiating them one from another—that spirit also set limits. Moral behavior was defined; instructions promulgated—as for example, the notorious Primal Instruction Regarding Harvesting and Eating.

And despite all, *eccolo*, suddenly boundaries are overvaulted. Spirits dared couple with mortals, engendering a race of arrogant demigods!

The Great Instruction went unheeded. The dangerous fruit was passed on, woman to man, parent to seed. And worse followed—primal restraints were down. The *ruah*, the breath that granted these mortals a quasi-endless life—this was fast becoming the breath of scandal itself.

Therefore a judgment. We shall cut short the breath of life. Hereafter they shall draw it with effort, and briefly.

Did the tactic succeed? Did a briefer span engender less impudent subjects? In light of what followed, it would seem not.

The diagnosis of the human condition offered in Genesis 6:5 is dire indeed. The first stratum of consciousness is rife with guilt. Sin, it is confessed, has come to dominate humankind.

Like lightnings unspent, catastrophe hangs on the air. Then the bolt falls. A decree; extinction of the living is decreed.

✦ ✦ ✦

On reflection, the biblical realism here is astonishing, worlds apart from conventional veneration for the "founding fathers" of this or that era. Commonly, cultures are hotbeds of such mythology. Ancestors are icons of virtue, clairvoyant, protean, incapable of ill deeds.

And something follows from the myth of "immaculate conception" of this or that nation. The puffing of the founding fathers lends credence to the perennial myth of virtuous national behavior.

Thus the reasoning, the dupe—our beginnings were the work of paragons of wisdom and compassion. How then, inheritors as we are of such virtue, can our conduct in the world be other than wise and compassionate?

✦   ✦   ✦

6:11   The story of the Flood is a striking example of ancient myths turned to religious instruction.

Sources tell of a series of floods, devastating the Mesopotamian area. In the stories, this or that inundation (and each was in fact quite limited) is widened to an ungovernable catastrophe. By decree of the gods, whether malicious or arbitrary, the living perish.

Still, at least in one such story, all life does not go under. Through the subterfuge of one among the deities, the hero of the Gilgamesh epic is snatched from the depths.

✦   ✦   ✦

In our Genesis and its skilled chroniclers, an ancient tale is burnished anew, transformed to a story of crime and punishment—and of mercy as well.

Two traditions converge, each with its own spirit and style. The Yahvist version is charged with verve and color; the Priestly is reflective, precise, somewhat dry.

In certain details the story clashes, the contrasts and contradictions are charming. Thus, what number of animals were herded into the ark, and what was the chronology of the disaster? Let two voices tell us, not one; and by all means, let small differences be.

✦   ✦   ✦

We note as well the first of many awakenings of the deity to moods contrary, fiery, shocking to a conventional eye.

The god repents having lent breath to this unmanageable tribe. Has a plenary failure issued from his hand? Shall the Creator be confounded, hu-

miliated? Was it for sake of demeaning outcome that the garden of delights
was created?

And what, by way of amelioration, can be done?

The vaulting ambition of these would-be godlings! They and their progeny have turned the perfect plan to a phantasmagoric muddle.

✦ ✦ ✦

The word of God subtly deconstructs the old materials. Redactors agree—
let us borrow the ancient stories, altering, making them new.

So the final version is uniquely religious, touching the wellsprings of
death and life, justifying "the ways of God to man."

A hero is required; Noah steps forth. He introduces a theme to be drawn
on powerfully and repeatedly throughout biblical history. He is the first to
stand surrogate for the "remnant."

Which is to say, he is an icon of the faithful few; he and they will redeem
a near-hopeless plight. Through them, the entire tribe may come to collec-
tive good sense, may repent, even prosper.

Against odds, to be sure.

Presently, a just man, together with his family, will emerge from the deluge, to tread dry land once more. And their fidelity and obedience will per-
dure. The descendants, purified and chastened, will survive enslavement,
some in Egypt, others in Babylon, and will enter into the Promise.

✦ ✦ ✦

6:7   Need this be added? From the first dawn of consciousness, the "first
week" of dividing, of making things be and be themselves—from the start,
the Bible is resolutely ecological.

We are never to miss the point, underscored here by each of the two accounts. Enclosed in the vast vibrating hold of the *SS Noah*, stand-ins of all
living beings cohabit in a subtle, capacious, breathing unity. Safe, these
stowaways in a world gone to ruin. The sturdy beams and rafters hold firm,
as the ship bears its precious cargo on and on through the parlous nights
and days of Drastic Downpour.

✦ ✦ ✦

According to the Story of Origins, all things were created for sake of us
humans, all tend and bend in our direction, for necessity and delight.

The contrary too holds firm. Consequent on a pandemic, perverse will,
bent to evil and death, the creation can be destroyed.

The deluge is a symbol, harsh but healing. And it is offered our own generation as well.

✦   ✦   ✦

6:13   The divine pronunciamento is detailed, precise. The priests set it down; it bears an edge honed by fine minds, quite sure of themselves, portentous.

It is as though the Priestly Deity first took counsel, whether with himself or his acolytes (the priests themselves?) in some anteroom of the celestial realm. And only after reflection and referral with the anointed, did He (sic) speak.

High-minded and homiletic, as though to imply—take serious note of this tale. It concerns yourselves—you too have been plucked from utmost peril.

✦   ✦   ✦

The early Christians pondered the story long and deep. Then they proceeded to compose a midrash of their own—ark, church, baptism, salvation through the waters.

They had disobeyed as long ago as Noah's day, while God patiently waited until the ark was built. At that time a few persons, eight in all, escaped in the ark through the water.

> You are now saved by a baptismal bath which corresponds
> to this exactly. This baptism is no removal of physical
> stain, but the pledge to God of an irreproachable con-
> science through the resurrection of Jesus Christ. (1 Peter
> 3:21)

✦   ✦   ✦

6:17–18   God trumpets a manifesto of doom and caring, a wonderful juxtaposition. We note the concentration and clash of the salvation-destruction theme:

> I
> on
> my part
>
> am about . . .
> to destroy
> everywhere

all creatures. . .

in which
there dwells

the breath
of life. . . .

But
with you

I
will
establish

my
covenant. . . .

✦ ✦ ✦

Death is turned and turned about in mad winds. Barely, by a hair's breadth, the safe handful evades the edge of a maundering, towering wave.

But if that were all, this survival of a few—would we be won to the story, would it touch on ourselves? Who could resist inquiring (even at risk of a Jovian frown)—what of those others, the innocents who along with the guilty had no shipbuilder, no ark—and went under? What of them?

No hint of an answer. The God is hardly required, or inclined, to justify the decree—Stet! Let it stand.

✦ ✦ ✦

Thus early on, God marks the boundaries of a vast ethical territory. Compass in hand, like the god of William Blake, bearded, bending over creation, a towering Deity stands outside and above boundaries. This God sets taboos, and is not bound by them.

God will issue the Decalogue, and stand outside the Decalogue. Thus it is made clear, and from the start—the Divine is not to be thought answerable to questioning Jobs. He (sic) stands beyond any accounting sought by mere mortals.

Our story is of mercy, our story is merciless. So is its God.

And so shall matters stand, until the last cursive flourish.

✦ ✦ ✦

As to mercy. Even as the sky darkens and the locks that hold the waters are lifted, a rainbow is prefigured, a covenant announced.

The God of oppositions, contradictions, the God who keeps us off balance. The theme, the sequence continues. At every new stage of understanding (and of undergoing!), a covenant is sealed; here with Noah, later with Abraham (15:17) still later with the entire people (Exod 24:8).

✦   ✦   ✦

And in another momentous borrowing from Hebrew history, Jesus will seal a "new covenant, in my blood." His act is central to the dynamics of Incarnation. Scapegoating is done with; this God sheds no blood but His own, appoints as victim only Himself.

The law of the land, of the occupied, tormented land, the law that seizes and scapegoats, cannot abide the godly One, His unblaming, healing, reconciling behavior. He offers His own body and blood, His very life, standing resolute before the courts and executioners of this world.

A "new covenant, in My blood." The announcement is pivotal to right understanding and behavior. By strong implication and example, believers are forbidden to kill; in the breach, they are to lay down their lives.

The words, and the accompanying ritual, are taken close note of by three evangelists, and the apostle Paul (Matt 26:28, Mark 14:24, Luke 22:20, 1 Cor 11:25).

✦   ✦   ✦

In these early pages, we are never done with both ruin and repair. Even as tempers fray and ties grow frowsy, threads are woven anew. The God of deluge and rending of the web (and eventually the god of war and extermination polity)—imagine!—this one is also tender of heart and supple of mind.

Behold God's hands—they are like the hands of a pregnant woman, weaving a birth garment, dreaming of a child who comes through a dream, a hope, into being.

And another image; this is the God who quickens aged wombs, Hanna and Sarah and Elizabeth, and the womb of young Mary. No human brings such births to pass, no genetic. No human makes a first move. God moves.

✦   ✦   ✦

Yet another image, a negative one. This is not how things proceeded; it is not as though a mortal thought in his heart (as we are wont to think)—I will strike a bargain, I will set conditions to this friendship. "Conditions," to a friendship?

Implied in the covenant of Noah are no conditions, not one. At least for the present. In the future, conditions aplenty will be contrived. In Deuteronomy it is as though the deity presents a different face, as though second thoughts intervened. God "repented himself" of this stepping forward, this initiative.

As though love had gone too far? As though to God the thought occurred—These mortals coil and spring. They seize the advantage. Dare I permit this?

Goodness knows it; they wrecked the garden, lied and hid out and contrived a web of alibis. Brother slew brother, and frenzy mounted, staining creation with cruelties and bloodlust. And they repented nothing.

Dare I try again? I dare not. I will not.

✦ ✦ ✦

But in the present time of our story, the time of Noah—for some reason or no reason at all, a new start is decreed. The God dares.

> Noah
> walked
>
> with
> God. (6:9–10)

God makes a first move, goes ahead on the road, stands there waiting. Thus he creates a circumstance; we may respond and quicken and catch up, a saving pace.

It is as though before *ruah* stirred, we were stone dead, drowned in the deluge.

✦ ✦ ✦

The "ark" of Noah, that vast floating box, a zoo and its human keepers and kept, has been likened by the knowledgeable to the "ark" of covenant.

The second ark, too, made its way ponderously, through contrary weathers, places, occasions—and was wondrously preserved.

Each, the ship of Noah and the ark, a vessel of covenant, keeping the agreement (and the covenanters) safe and sound and on course, against awesome odds—ruinous nature and human malice.

✦ ✦ ✦

7:11 The Priestly account is meticulous as to date, year, month, day. Nature rises in revolt, chaos floods in. The dikes break, their bounds crum bling. This, though they had been set firm against the "waters above and beneath," the "abyss and high heavens."

✦   ✦   ✦

7   Spiraling time, not linear time. For the Yahvists (speaking here), there exist from the beginning "pure" and "impure" animals. The pure must be salvaged in greater number, if life is to be restored and the deluge overcome.

It is as though the distinction were a matter once for all settled in Genesis, cotemporal with creation itself. At the start, God so decreed, certain animals were fit for eating and sacrifice, others unfit.

For the priests, things are otherwise (6:19). The "clean, unclean" distinction is meaningless until the Law of Moses (Lev 11). Whatever, whenever. Pair by pair, even the fiercest among them for the moment obedient and docile, the endangered beasties stride, lumber, mince, dance, cavort, in pairs, willy-nilly into the ark.

✦   ✦   ✦

We are constantly offered such dual accounts, sometimes complementary, sometimes in sharp contrast. Thus in the creation account, God "speaks" all things into existence, or God "works" them.

An invitation to ponder two aspects of the creation? These perhaps; the Word is sovereign; so is the skill of the Craftsman.

✦   ✦   ✦

7:16   For good or ill, knowing nothing of outcome, the living too enter the ark in consort, Noah, his spouse, their offspring.

> . . . And
> Jawe
>
> closed
> the door
>
> on
> Noah.

✦   ✦   ✦

And what an artist is our storyteller! Simple, final, sublime; the door is shut, sealed against mischance. And this benefit and care worked by a godly hand.

The same door will swing open again, on an utterly new world.

✦ ✦ ✦

Vivid and detailed is the litany of loss; for "one hundred fifty days" the inundation mounts. No living being is spared. Any who "had the breath of life in nostril" perish.

As time is measured in Genesis, we are close upon the start of creation. And how shortly it becomes apparent; time is translated as catastrophe, whether in ethic or nature.

First the Fall, precipitous and headlong, then fratricide, and a spreading contagion of violence and duplicity.

Then, no wonder, the decree—*fit finis omnium,* "to everything, the end." The Deluge.

Except for the company sealed in the little vessel, battered and tossed about like a chip in wild waters, fair Genesis is swallowed in ruin. We were so close to beginnings—and we are perilously near the end:

> Jawe
> wiped
> out
>
> every
> living thing
> on earth. . . .
>
> Only Noah
> and those
> with him
>
> in
> the ark
>
> were
> left. (7:23)

O untamable God of wild weathers and darkness and bare survival, intractable and merciful at once!

✦ ✦ ✦

8:1   Mercy, at long last.

> Then God
> remembered
> Noah

and
all
the animals

that were
with him

in
the
ark. . . .

Amid the storm, as God gave full vent to fury, had God forgotten them? What meaning attaches to this sudden "remembering"? We take it for an interior sign of an outward grace, one with the reining in of the furies. Remembrance means the deluge of divine anger has subsided within. The Storm God abates. The memory of the holy One greens once more.

Another image; we shall see it again. The memory of the storm abates as well. Now memory is like a rainbow, overarching, many splendored, suffused with mercy. A new creation dawns.

Eventual, indeed inevitable. Noah, trust what will come.

✦ ✦ ✦

8:5 Ten months in the ark! and then,

. . . the mountain
peaks

began
to
appear.

Noah opens a window and dispatches a raven. Might the bird offer a clue as to the state of flora in a watery world? No luck; it simply "flew back and forth. . . ." At sea, and hardly a sea bird!

Another try; he launched a dove. It fluttered about, seeking a place to alight, found alas no relief, and returned at dusk.

How wonderfully vivid and tender:

. . . Putting
out
his
hand,

Noah
caught
the dove

and
drew it
back

inside
the
ark. (8:9)

Finally, another try—and success! The dove ventures afar and returns, a living sprig in its beak.

The entire world of life and hope is reduced to this.

No, it is not reduced—it is symbolized in this—hope, the future. *Multum in parvo*, "much in little," a sprig of green in the beak of a fragile bird! So frail a thing, and so apt. Like hope itself, living, vulnerable, snatched from the tide.

The dove, the sprig, shall we name these the "other side" of that great overriding Storm God? Of that One who looses chaos upon the world—and eventually, after death has had full sway, "remembers" and stems the fury?

To us humans, sorry recidivists though we be, a "crooked generation"— the sign is given. In the heart of this untamed, fierce Deity there dwells a dovelike compassion.

✦   ✦   ✦

We do well to linger over the scene—the receding waters, the sign of the dove. Alas, we, the lesser children of the God—have we seen the like, the sign?

The century just past has loosed an unremitting deluge across the world. Millions have perished; and the victims by no means to be accounted "corrupt, full of lawlessness."

Indeed, the anger of the God of Genesis cannot be justly invoked, as proving the guilt or criminality of those who perished in the flood.

But what of today, what of America? What of those who wreak death against multitudes—indeed, whose credential for high office is the implicit will to decree slaughter? Of these, let guilt and criminality with certainty be adduced—these and the anger of God.

Why must the wise and valiant, Romero, the Jesuits of San Salvador, whose only crime was their demand for just governance, their passion for justice—why must these die? These, together with the needy, the children, and the aged—why these, and in vast numbers? Why the bombing of Afghanistan, the horrors descending on Iraq?

For such crimes against the innocent, wherever the deluge, from Vietnam to Kosovo to East Timor to Salvador to Iraq—God have mercy!

And on September 11, 2001, the crimes come home, in New York, thousands die. And the bewilderment and fury and cries of vengeance and spawning of flags!

Very few ask a simple "why?" But in Tehran, endangered people hold aloft a banner before the world. Before ourselves. It reads, "Why are you Americans hated around the world?"

✦ ✦ ✦

Our culture is a deluge, a realm of chaos, of darkness and moral incoherence. It would have us isolated, competitive, bent on appetite and possessions and personal security, at all and any cost to others.

In such a deluge, are we to be found in the ark, safe and sound—or are we cast into the waters, fending for ourselves?

The church for its part (go slow church!) would assure us—I am the ark of salvation, abide in me. And the claim is verified in the lives of saints and martyrs (saints of our lifetime, those who have endured the waters and more, who have salvaged at least a few among the victims), the claim is authentic and can be trusted—abide in me.

Plight and opportunity; perhaps the image that best describes our condition is a double one. We are in both places, safe in the ark and plunged in the storm. (The ark too is both safe and plunged in the storm.) Barely afloat, we must do battle against the bitter wind and waters. And we are rescued, and recover and rest secure, within.

✦ ✦ ✦

A question, inevitably. Did noble Noah and his crew also "remember" those who died in the flood? Is there evidence of mediation and mercy and rescue, the drawing aboard of those who otherwise must perish?

We are left with the question; our story falls short of such comfort. Falls short, one thinks, of mercy, short of the prophetic word to come, as Isaiah and the Psalmist will praise our merciful God.

For the present, the era of deluge, we come on no hint of "universal salvation." Ours is a story of the renewal and rebirth of a remnant only, of survivors.

The nameless majority go under, a *massa damnata*. Or so the survivors judge them, together with the cosmic executioner, the God of dualities, as presented.

Thus a harsh lesson comes home. The God who walked companionable with humans in a garden of his devising, is also the God of Necessary Near Extinction. And the God of ever-renewed covenant. And of holy wars to come, wars of extermination.

And what part do we humans play in the awful drama of retribution? Large part indeed.

Instruction, confession, poems—tracts for the times.

✦ ✦ ✦

And as every Sunday school child comes to know, nothing of condign punishment works to the good of the punished. The deluge is absorbed in the soil of memory. Survivors crawl ashore as best they may. And life goes on, or something known as life.

Which is to say, the old game resumes. Once more the ancestors are caught up in the primordial rhythm of sin and punishment—a cycle the deluge was designed to expunge, once for all.

First, death by water, designed to cleanse the planet of sin and wickedness.

To no avail. Then let us essay another trial, an exile in Egypt.

Followed by exodus and secular kingship and glory, glory—Solomon and the raising of the great temple. Then, disaster once more. The proud city falls, the people are herded off to slavery in Babylon.

The wheel of fortune and misfortune turns. For each nadir, an apogee, and vice versa. From grandeur to rubble, from close friendship with God to condign punishment.

All to no avail, or small. A few keep nobility intact, even rise to heroism. And sin alas proliferates. The wicked and godly walk pari passu through the pages of the Book, the human *comedia*.

✦ ✦ ✦

Darkness, the dark freedom, our blessing and curse, remains—but deeply marred. The prophets know it; punishment from on high wins a spurt of conformity. But over time, harshness serves only to imprint more firmly a misbehavior-redress-misbehavior pattern.

Another image; it is as though a scourge fell again and again on the human frame, forty strokes, as many centuries. As though the world were a nightmarish "Penal Colony" of Kafka.

And the whip rises on the tormented body only a deeper stigma, a series

of strangely literate welts, furrows. More; the whip rises—signs, an alphabet
of revolt. The punishment is all but lethal—the cicatrices, the scars, all but
genetic. And nothing of this serves. To this day.

✦ ✦ ✦

Questions. What of the God who gives up on the likes of ourselves?

And once given up on, what possibility of godly longing, of longing for
the healing of our humanity—what remains of this for the likes of ourselves?

✦ ✦ ✦

> In Louisville, at the corner of Fourth and Walnut, in the
> center of the shopping district, I was suddenly over-
> whelmed with the realization that I loved all those people,
> that they were mine and I theirs, that we could not be alien
> to one another, even though we were total strangers. It was
> like waking from a dream of separateness, of spurious self-
> isolation in a special world, the world of renunciation and
> supposed holiness. . . .
>
> There is no way of telling people that they are all walking
> around shining like the sun. . . . There are no strangers! . . .
> The gate of heaven is everywhere. (Thomas Merton, *Conjec-
> tures of a Guilty Bystander*)

✦ ✦ ✦

And yet, and yet. The God who gives up and trashes the earth and rains
ruin down and down—this God also says to Noah, as though in an aside, a
whisper in an attentive ear:

> . . . But
> I
>
> will seal
> My alliance
>
> firmly
> with
> you. . . . (9:11)

So after all, God has not given up? A few survivors, teetering on the cusp
of vengeance—he holds them steady, in the palm of his hand. In view of a
new start.

✦ ✦ ✦

In Jesus, we have a God who in act, drama, tragedy, does not give up. On ourselves, on anyone. We are told it again and again, in metaphor, parable, instruction, example. Wide as the beginning of time and the week of creation, the net of salvation is cast. Wide as the horizon, high as heaven it spreads. Then it falls, gathering in its folds everyone—the aborted and miscarried, the desired and unwanted, the virtuous, the unguessably evil.

Its prey is all the living; vaster than the deluge's harvest of death. The net is drawn in, gently, firmly. It is the morning of eternity. And the Fisherman stands by the shore, task done, rejoicing. In denial of death's empery—and of the god of death—a full catch!

✦ ✦ ✦

PHILIP'S BATTERED NEW TESTAMENT, CARRIED INTO PRISON
REPEATEDLY

That book
livid with thumb prints and lashes
I see you carry it
into the cave of storms, past the storms.
I see you underscore
like the score of music
all that travail, that furious unexplained joy.

A book! the sheriffs
fan it out for contraband—
the apostles wail, the women
breathe deep as Cumaean sibyls,
Herod screams like a souped-up record.

They toss it back, harmless.

Now, seated on the cell bunk
you play the pages slowly, slowly—
a lifeline humming with the song
of the jeweled fish, all but taken.

(DB)

✦ ✦ ✦

Our God refuses to give up. Despite base schemes of affront and denial, despite the victimization by corrupt judges (their lockup, their executioners

at the ready), in face of the betrayal and corruption of the mighty, the firestorm of bombs and rockets and throttling sanctions against Iraqi children,
the firestorm over Kosovo, the annihilation of East Timor—our God refuses
to give up. We have Christ's word for it, His blood underscoring the word.
Even on us; refuses.

✦　　✦　　✦

8:15　The God who starts over, with a new welcome to a new earth! And
the blessing conferred on the fifth day of creation (1:22) is here repeated.

Feet planted on dry earth, family and four-footed friends released from
the ark, Noah proceeds to offer thanks to God. A sacrifice, the third recorded
after the ill-fated offerings of Cain and Abel.

Can we be known, can we know ourselves, apart from drama? The ritual
is a revelation, an epiphany. Subject to sin and death we are, to be sure. But
also purposing amendment, reconciliation, compassion, friendship with our
God.

And Noah for his part wins a significant response; into the divine presence, a sweet odor ascends. And God is moved, by dint of rather obscure reasoning, to a resolve:

> . . . Never
> again
>
> will I
> curse the earth
>
> because
> of humans,
>
> since
> the designs
> of their heart
>
> are wicked
> from infancy.
>
> Never
> again
>
> shall I strike down
> the living
> as

I
have
done. (8:21)

✦   ✦   ✦

Does the Deity admit to second thoughts, such as, "Man's evil is his own"
and "He shall pay for it, but solely in his own person."?

And more (in a Great Perhaps): "In dooming the innocent because of the
wicked in their midst, have I gone too far?"

✦   ✦   ✦

9   It is as though Leviticus and its champions were seizing the quill. Legislation is in high gear; we are deep in a Priestly tradition.

As things turn, the "new world" is not so new after all. The "law" is promulgated alas, in the world of Adam and Eve, the world of the Fall, the world
sin has brought into being (or into lesser being, or perhaps nonbeing). In
any case, a Fallen world. Noah's world.

Its look will be dire; tooth and claw, the beasts salvaged in the ark will
turn on one another—and it is implied, on humans as well. And shall humans turn on one another, tooth and claw? Beyond doubt.

Noah names the planet anew, but the dire fact remains. The ark has
beached in the Realm of Necessity. Henceforth spear and sword will be
forged and sharpened. Faces will be set in adamant, one against the other.

Behold the "new start"—an ambiguous matter at best. Antediluvian im-
pulses remain virulent, threaten to erupt and despoil.

Countering the regressive urges, the priests and the God of the priesthood
lay the law down, hard and clear.

Given the harsh weathers, "cold and heat . . . summer and winter," a
vegetarian regime will not suffice; humans hunt and kill, even as they are
hunted and killed. Thus a serious, even lethal prohibition is set in place; the
hunters may not partake of the blood of animals, only of its flesh.

✦   ✦   ✦

Which opens a topic to be constantly explored, and with an ambiguity
one can only call crushing. Not precisely the question of violence among
humans; here, killing is clearly forbidden.

The future unrolls, and another question arises; daunting, all but incin-
erating the text. The question of "divine" violence or (the same thing in effect) of divinely sanctioned violence. Of war upon war, legislated from on
high—exterminating wars, wars of conquest and eviction, wars of revolu-

tion, scorched-earth wars. Each, we are told, is waged on behalf of the "chosen." And each, no matter its blistering ferocity, will be declared from on high eminently just.

Thus socialized and sanctioned, imbedded in culture and religion, violence becomes the pervasive theme and atmosphere of the historical books. Through a bloody haze, we read of the smoke and fury of battle. Until the creation itself, all but shattered, is transformed to a battlefield. Until war making becomes the dominant fact and metaphor of the human condition. Until the warrior, together with his aides and abettors, sums up the scope and meaning of the Fallen human.

And what of the god of war? To right reason, this god loses a capital letter. The god's will becomes the prime credential of humans, bent on their conquests, in service to a god who sanctions atrocious crimes.

As the original vision deteriorates and violence looms large, a deity is perpetually at hand, the champion of this or that Homeric hero, nudging awful matters in yet more awful directions. What a book is in our hands, a bible like a field commander's handbook!

✦ ✦ ✦

Through the generations of patriarchs, on to the era of enslavement and exile, of exodus and judges and kings, of the rending in two of the kingdom of Solomon, we encounter again and again the violent god and his depredations, amid the glare and turmoil of "godly" wars.

Little clarity is proffered as to who this god is. A far greater clarity perhaps, on the issue of who the god is not. Until the prophets; and clarity explodes like an instant dawn.

At long last, who that fiery god was, is revealed in true God.

✦ ✦ ✦

9:5–6 In the light (or darkness) of what is to come, the legislation promulgated here is all but incomprehensible, absurd. Even wild animals, it is decreed, are to be held accountable, presumably for shedding of human blood. Humans too are held to stern account for bloodletting:

> . . . for
> in
> the image
> of God,
>
> has
> man

been
made.

✦ ✦ ✦

The "image" is, so to speak, two-edged. The Priestly insistence on a god of transcendence falls short. Matters develop, something momentous is implied. In the realm of human behavior (where such matters weigh heavy), the reality proclaimed after the Flood has been reversed.

Like Alice of the tale, we have stepped into a mirror; what it reveals is hardly a never-never land. We have reached the edge of existence, and tumbled in. Into the realm of the Fall, full force. Into the irrational. Into that which cannot be, and is.

Stark and strict, this is a fact of life behind the mirror. Logic is suspended.

Rather than God creating humans in a godly image, this transpired. Generation after generation, we humans created a god (sic) in our own image.

A close look at the "image of the god" proves painful, all but beyond bearing. Willed perennially into being, protected under an arc of weaponry and accruing wealth, is a scapegoating god, a very emperor of necessity. He (sic) will separate out, right hand and left, his subjects—the chosen and rejected, the expendable and the cherished.

Thus the image of a god is projected and paid sanguinary tribute, the god of a scapegoating tribe.

And the apogee of human striving, the imperium, will be the apogee of the god as well.

So we shall view the procession of rulers; darksome Saul begetting a trickster and killer, David. And David begetting Solomon—splendid, sordid. And the deity of these, hovering like a golden cloud of Danaë, is borne into the imperial city, a potentate ensconced in a splendid temple. To wax useful and complaisant under the canopy of imperial design.

So far have the chosen come—from humiliation in Egypt, from the desert years and the God of accompaniment.

And the wars go on, a continuum of night and fog, "all the days of Saul"—and onward. From wars of conquest to wars seeking world markets and expansion of borders.

Different strokes, wars alike. And each war, be it noted—just, holy, sanctioned on high. Thus the "accounting" here legislated, will be (to say the least), severely constrained by event. Behavior divine and human will give the lie to the law. The god who announces himself as a just judge, will notoriously act unjustly.

It must be stated, and clearly; by such behavior, he and his warriors and priestly acolytes will themselves be subject to judgment.

Let us grant the God that moment; in the shadow of the ark, he proclaims a law against murder. Grant him (sic) an incomprehensible, all but invincible ignorance of what is to come, in what crimes he will be complicit. How from the kings he will learn the ways of kings, from warriors the ways of warriors. How he will provoke his champions to worse and worse. How multitudes will pay, and dearly.

chapter four

"My covenant with you . . ."(9:8–14:17)

9:8 The door of the ark once shut, a fury of waters was unleashed (6: 18).

And yet, and yet—a promise was spoken. It will outlast the torrent. With due solemnity, the edict:

> . . . With
> you
> I
> will
> establish
>
> my
> covenant.

And now, as the waters recede, the promise is underscored once more:

> See,
> I
>
> am
> now
> establishing
>
> my
> covenant
>
> with you
> and
>
> your descendants
> after you
>
> and
> with

every
living
creature

that
was

with
you. . . . (9:12)

✦   ✦   ✦

Thus, and unconditionally, a covenant of *compleat ecologie* is set in place. And one is well advised to scan the text closely. It lays bare the heart of faith. In effect (the stipulation goes) the deepest meaning of existence is this bond and connection. You (plural—all living beings, humans, fauna, flora) are mine, I am yours.

Its sign will be one of overarching hope, a rainbow. The majestic spectrum in the sky signals fair weather after a storm. And more; no deluge, never again. From one horizon to another, a blaze of affirmation: "all things are good!" The arc includes in its vast embrace, the majestic creation entire.

✦   ✦   ✦

Thus a key reality of both testaments is signed and delivered. In the nature of things (more exactly the nature of humans, volatile and adversarial and fickle of mind as we are), the bond will require constant repair, renewal, refinement.

With Abraham and his descendants, circumcision will be a sign of inclusion in the circle of life (17). And under Moses, all Israel will be party to a pact of submission to the law (Exod 19:5); the sign of obedience will be observance of the Sabbath (Exod 31:16–17).

✦   ✦   ✦

And a shadow trails the bond. Up to, and far beyond the Mosaic era, the covenant bespeaks bloodletting and scapegoating. From circumcision, blood flows; in sacrifice, likewise. In war, the blood of enemies is let.

And each implies a stipulation, strangely awful, from on high; circumcision, sacrifice, and war are religious acts, necessary conditions of the flourishing of covenant itself. Cut the foreskin, raise the victim, wage war, thus prove yourselves mine.

What a God, what a people!

✦   ✦   ✦

Then, long ages after, something far different:

> This
> is
> the cup
>
> of
> My blood,
>
> sign
> of
>
> a new
> and lasting
> covenant
>
> in
> My blood. . . .
>
> Do
> this
>
> in
> memory
>
> of
> Me. (Luke 22:19–20)

✦ ✦ ✦

In Jesus we are granted a breakthrough, stupendous and modest at once. No more exaction of blood, no scapegoating, no enemies, no war. Instead, the giving of the Blood of Jesus, signified in the passing of the cup.

And be it noted closely; this, the turning away from bloodletting, is the sum and substance of discipleship as well. In His image:

> Excuse me for going on like this, but there is still something else. It is about eating and drinking together. . . .

> On January 1, 1994, the beginning of the year and month of Luke's eightieth birthday, we listened in the refectory to the cassette he was keeping to be used the day of his burial. It was Edith Piaf singing "No, I have no regrets." (Fr. Christophe Lebreton's diary. He and Brother Luc Dochier and five other monks were murdered in Algeria, May 21, 1996)

✦ ✦ ✦

I do not see in fact how I could rejoice if the people I love
were indiscriminately accused of my murder.

It would be too high a price to pay for what will perhaps be
called the "grace of martyrdom" to owe this to an Algerian,
whoever he may be, especially if he says he is acting in fidelity to what he believes to be Islam. . . .

And also you, my last minute friend, who will not have
known what you were doing; yes, I want to THANK YOU
and this ADIEU to be for you too, because in God's face I
see yours.

May we meet again as happy thieves in Paradise, if it
please God, the Father of us both. AMEN. (Fr. Christian de
Cherg, prior, martyred in Algeria)

✦ ✦ ✦

Is the gift, the "new" covenant, to be dismissed as no more than an idle
dream? Christ has died. Christ has also risen again, as we confess. Yet we
Christians darkened the centuries since Christ, laid waste the earth, passed
on the infection of war, a millennial bloodletting.

Christ died, Christ also rose again. The "also" is pivotal, ironic, redundant. Resurrection: grief or glory, which? Given the Christian record in the
world, which? In a painting since lost but amply documented, a supreme
artist gave the Event of events a bitter, perhaps crucial turn:

> This was the resurrection, not as an airborne triumph of
> clouds, shafts of sunlight, cherubs, ecstatic gazes and clean
> white-flowing linens and amazed earthlings below—how
> could it be, being Caravaggio's—but an emaciated lately
> dead man stepping blinking into the daylight like a pris-
> oner just freed from a concentration camp or like a survivor
> of the plague. . . .
>
> Visually too, utterly Caravaggio. The powerful composi-
> tion. The enveloping darkness. No glory. No majesty. The
> risen figure looming out of the canvas . . . stepping with his
> feet on the ground, not flying heavenward.

Most extraordinarily of all, what nobody imaginable would've dared except Caravaggio, the wretched build, the fearful, apprehensive look of the unexpectedly released prisoner, blinded by the sudden light, picking his way through the sleeping guards, wondering what was coming next, not yet believing his luck, furtive, suspicious, frightened and frightening to the viewer—what an image of the way Christ rose from the dead to heavenly glory. To an unbeliever four hundred years later, it sounded stunning. Seen as a wholly earthly event . . . acclaimed by those who recognized themselves in it—("people enjoy it . . . acclaimed for its newness . . . greatly admired . . .").

Caravaggio's name as the painter was forgotten, and . . . the painting itself disappeared altogether. It seemed an exemplary fate. (Peter Robb, *M: The Man Who Became Caravaggio*)

✦ ✦ ✦

Was this wild and wooly artist, this killer all but perpetually on the run—was he closer to the truth of things than the others, the artists of the Christ of ineluctable triumph, His foot planted firmly on the toppled stone, the banner, the dazzled lightsome form?

Could such images express in sum a longing—that we and our art (and our behavior) once for all have finished with a suffering, vulnerable Christ? That His glory frees us from the shame of His execution? More that His apotheosis guarantees here and now, our own? That the Resurrection as commonly portrayed is a kind of permissive cheap grace, leading straight to Constantine, the ambiguous "sign in the heavens," church and state in accord on perennial just war fantasies, vile and viable—to this shameful hour?

✦ ✦ ✦

The gift, the spurning of the gift.

The cup passed? It has passed us by.

Now, at the start of yet another tormented millennium, Americans are busily enacting a drama of regression. Whatever fragments of "covenant" remain intact, are scuttled—in Iraq, Kosovo, the collusion with mass murder in East Timor and elsewhere. In the galvanized assault on Afghanistan and Iraq, following the carnage of the twin towers and the Pentagon.

The "developed" nations more and more resemble a coven of inventive dwarfs. From the cave of Mars issues an endless stream of "omniweaponry," the product of those who in less demented times might be considered the "best minds."

> ... [T]he global context is significantly different from what it was a few years ago. Throughout the cold war, the nuclear arsenal was developed and maintained as the ultimate defense in an ideological conflict that pitted ... two historical forces against each other; capitalism in the west and communism in the east.
>
> Nuclear weapons and "Mutually Assured Destruction" were accepted as the inescapable context of that struggle.
>
> It is absolutely clear to us that the present US policy does not include a decisive commitment to progressive nuclear disarmament. The US today is committed to use nuclear weapons first, including preemptive nuclear attacks on nations that do not possess nuclear weapons. ...
>
> The "Stockpile Stewardship and Management Program" ... will create computer-simulated nuclear weapons tests that will allow the US to continue to test nuclear weapons. ...
>
> Instead of nuclear disarmament, we are witnessing the institutionalizing of nuclear deterrence. ... ("The Morality of Nuclear Deterrence," An Evaluation by Pax Christi Bishops, May 1998)

✦ ✦ ✦

And what of Noah's furred and feathered friends, early in the human story included in the pact of life—those,

> ... living
> creatures
>
> who were
> with you;
>
> all
> the birds,

and
the various

tame
and
wild
animals . . . ? (9:10)

In the covenant of death to which our millennium clings, these are expendable. So are the children, the aged and ill, the unborn.

And what of ourselves, who presumably have "come of age" in this century? What is our rightful place on the scale of human development, as the Bible would proffer a measure? Prehuman? Precovenantal? Post-Christian?

✦ ✦ ✦

The rainbow has long since dissolved in the heavens. In this world and time, we wonder. Does the promise hold, no deluge, ever again?

But what need of a deluge from on high? Humans have developed multiple ways of bringing down the creation. We read of it, hear of it, it is appallingly "normal."

A prolonged debate, secret, straight-faced, a discussion only the mad could muster, revolves around the research and deployment, and yes the use of nuclear weapons, and equally monstrous "conventional" weapons. That, and war in space.

Through technology, paradise was the promise. Or so we were assured, time and again. And the outcome is—hellfire. Hiroshima, Nagasaki. And a like inferno lit by "conventional" weapons, tipped with depleted uranium, in the Gulf, over Baghdad and Kosovo.

✦ ✦ ✦

9:20 A startlingly contrasting story of great Noah. Let it be taken at face value, obscure as its sources are.

Behold (but not too closely!) the heroic survivor of deluge, the party to a noble covenant. He is drunk and sprawled naked in his tent. Three sons stand near. One enters the tent and "takes in" his father, whatever the expression may mean. He notifies the other two. They enter backward, cover their father and withdraw.

They see nothing of his nakedness, purposing to see nothing. Noah awakens, is told of the episode, and proceeds to curse the son Cham, "father of Canaan," who "took him" in shame. And he blesses the two, Sem and Japhet, who took no advantage.

Mysterious, the curse, superstitious? In any case, belief held strong—blessings and curses are weighty with consequence, for the one on whom the spell had fallen, and for descendants as well.

✦ ✦ ✦

And here, one pauses over a clue, a clue and no more, ever so subtly inserted in the text. Eventually the clue will be revealed as immensely important. Important, one ventures, in view of a special need, the justifying of ancestors as time ripens.

In the Noah episode, we are in the second millennium of the common era. But the final form of the stories belongs to the era of David and Solomon. By then, the sun of imperial achievement stands at high noon.

The sun of imperial logic as well—at high noon. So splendid an outcome demands unshadowed origins. The genesis of the tribe must be presented in dazzling relief, its destiny mandated from on high, and from the start.

Thus we revert to the blessing of the two sons, and the curse laid on the third. The tribes of Sem and Japhet, foreign to Israel, were nonetheless integrated into the empire. A manifest blessing, as who could doubt? Whereas the Canaanites "of son Cham" were crushed. And no wonder; the ancestor of this "people of no promise" early on was relegated to the shadows.

Sic solvitur; or so it was (somewhat obscurely) written.

✦ ✦ ✦

10 We enter the Priestly account; it is all *son et lumiere,* diverse, celebrated with vigor.

Hear ye, hear ye! God has decreed it—peoples, tribes, races of every hue, issue as though from the splendid spectrum of the covenantal rainbow. Color, language, custom, religious rite, dance and song and poetry and handiwork—all are reflected in a mirror held to the face of God. And the God delights in us. In the circle unending of life, the divine venue flows in our direction, and back.

✦ ✦ ✦

These priest–scribes are also paragons of exactitude. Events, genealogies, must be set down in columns of time and place, as though time were a strong sounding, and we humans marched to an audible drumbeat.

Linear time! We read of tables of ancestors, neat summaries, varied genealogies, a conclusion:

> These are the groupings of Noah's sons, according to their
> origins and by their nations.

From these the other nations of the earth branched out,
after the flood. (10:32)

In a dry sacerdotal style, a hint is offered of something immensely hopeful concerning human beginnings. Sin has not been granted the last word, nor the first. Nor has death.

And what of God? Despite recrimination and fury, the Deity is hailed as the very seigneur of life. The Deity blesses the living.

Confused we are. The God seems a very Janus—God of the deluge ("so take warning"); God also of the calm, the receding waters, the intact survivors. God of the rainbow, the Promise.

The tradition, strong and forthright, does not stand unchallenged. The somber account of the tower of Babel will offer a "shadow" side of human beginnings. Still, one notes how cherished is the present tradition, and its implied urging—let our lives, our behavior, our structures be set in order, and chaos will never again lay hands on creation.

Is life to continue triumphing over death? If so, memory must be meticulously detailed, with naming of personages and places. Knowing from whom we issued, we shall mold a worthy future.

A properly biblical conclusion will be insisted on again and again. Humans are of common ancestry. The tribes, no matter their geographical or ethnic differences, are composed of brothers and sisters. And the bond that holds us close, links us in time as well; on the sons of Noah a blessing is conferred. Therefore, on all.

It will haunt us throughout the historical books, the question—how comes it that the Deity rather consistently contradicts himself? God stipulates, then cancels the stipulation; the tribes, no matter differences . . . are composed of brothers and sisters.

Then the contradiction—these "brothers and sisters" proceed with fervor to slaughter of one another. And their every war is launched in heaven as on earth.

God help us. We have the word of God for it.

But in our text the true God, according to this Word, is a scarce presence indeed.

And be it confessed in confusion of spirit; we Christians believe that Christ has walked our world. How speak then of the absence, the distancing of God, except this be wrought by malign human choice?

Is it profitable to speak thus early on in our story, of a hidden God, an unknown God, a God whose presence to the human tribe is—the absence of God?

We are slow learners indeed—if it can be claimed that we learn at all. In the millennial year, as these notes are set down, Americans persevere in our idolatries. And God is constrained to continue the game of "presence is absence."

We are reenacting the somber vision of Ezekiel, who saw an insulted Majesty abandon the idolatrous temple and vanish into self-imposed exile (Ezek 10:18–23.)

How was God to bear with the rancorous, banal tribe? How is God to bear with us? How could God be other than an exile, amid the shambles sin has made of sweet creation—the whelming malfeasance, wars, and nuclear bravado?

11   The priests are hopeful, the Yahvists are somber—a species of proto-Calvinists, one thinks. With an exception worth noting, these latter chroniclers prefer to tell stories rather than proclaim doctrine. Or to put the matter more exactly, they teach through storytelling.

God, to be sure, is portrayed in a like mode, as a storyteller, or a kind of director, intervening, fashioning outcomes. As here.

One is well-advised not to underestimate the skills on display. The storyteller is a marvelous verbal necromancer.

Are we to call it naive, this tall tale of the failed tower and the scatted tribe? Read close, and ponder long; the style is subtle and sophisticated.

Christian Scripture has taken careful note of the episode of "language as confusion compounded."

According to the account of apostolic times (Acts 2), the Spirit of Christ has turned the catastrophe around. The Topless Tower and the Babble of Tongues is a prelude. One day an unprecedented intervention will shake all creation.

Old assumptions, metaphors, images of stalemate and confusion; all are there in the text—and all, according to a noble midrash, are relieved. In wake of a spectacular epiphany, the stalemated speak up, the confused understand, the scattered and shamed are brought into unity.

First the Event:

> When the day of Pentecost had come, they were all together in one place. Suddenly there was a sound from heaven like the rush of a mighty wind, filling the house.
>
> And there appeared tongues as of fire, distributed and resting on each of them. All were filled with the holy Spirit.
>
> They left the house and began to speak in other tongues, as the Spirit gave them utterance. (Acts 2:1–4)

Then a manifesto makes sense of the Event, a "credo" communal, unassailable—and dangerous.

Dangerous indeed. The account of "Acts" proceeds. The manifesto, as shortly becomes clear, is hardly to be thought politically or religiously neutral, conventional, tribal, accepting of "things as they are."

The declaration brings crisis in its wake, it says loud and clear in face of established disorder, a NO. Offensive, politically dangerous, it strikes against received wisdom and common assumptions.

It presses for a hearing in "the world, the way it goes." It demands conversion of hearts and minds—and of public structures as well. Put it plain:

> ". . . Jesus of Nazareth . . . you crucified and killed, by the hands of lawless men. . . ."
>
> When the people heard this they were cut to the heart. "Brethren," they said, "What shall we do?"
>
> "Repent. . . . Save yourselves from this crooked generation." (Acts 2:23, 37, 38)

✦ ✦ ✦

And what if the world gives no heed, if hearing grows deaf and seeing blind and understanding blank? Let the consequences descend; as indeed they will.

The world knows it, so do the faithful; the language that bespeaks faith is hot with provocation. It rebukes and rebuts the principalities—the kings, presidents, shahs, tycoons, diplomats, generals, judges, prosecutors, war-

dens, executioners, the secretaries of war, the abortionists and "assisted sui-
ciders"—guardians and hucksters and provocateurs of "things as they are."
Which is to say, of the sovereignty and prevailing of the principality named
death.

The credo is uttered in the teeth of the powers of this world. Then the
powers seize on the words, as evidence of crime. By decree of the Roman superstate, the protagonists of the "Acts" are repeatedly arrested, tried, convicted. Eventually they are done away with. And their death, be it noted, is
in close accord with the "law of the land"; the murders are seamlessly legal.

✦   ✦   ✦

Thus the church was founded, thus it is founded anew; the faith and fate
of the apostles and martyrs of all generations are joined to that of their Master before them.

> Rain came early this year to Guatemala. On April 29
> (1998), two sharp drenching bursts marked the beginning
> and end of a funeral march for Bishop Juan Gerardi Coned-
> era. Among the 40,000 mourners, some murmured that
> God was weeping for another of the chosen.
>
> Like Salvador's Bishop Oscar Romero, Gerardi seems to
> have been targeted for speaking the truth to power. His
> body was found two days after his presentation of the Cath-
> olic Church's "Recovery of Historical Memory" report, his
> head caved in after repeated blows with a concrete block.
>
> An exhaustive three years study chronicling 36 years of
> civil war, the report catalogues . . . torture, unlawful deten-
> tion, and extra judicial execution . . . identifying more than
> 75,000 victims of the latter. . . . (Aziz Huk, *Peacework Maga-*
> *zine,* January 2001)

✦   ✦   ✦

> A suspect in the fatal shooting of an American nun in May
> was arrested after the police found him hiding in a house
> where he was recovering from bullet wounds from a sepa-
> rate assault. A government spokesman said there was evi-
> dence that the man, as yet unidentified, may have been
> involved in the shooting of Sister Barbara Ann Ford, a

member of the Sister of Charity of New York, in Guatemala City. She worked in Lemoa, west of Guatemala City, and assisted in excavations of civil-war-era mass graves. Authorities have said she died in a failed car-jacking. (*New York Times*, July 28, 2001)

✦ ✦ ✦

Once more, to the tower of confusion. The source of the imagery; a ziggurat of old, whose ruins litter the landscape of Babylon, symbol of an empire confounded.

Was the structure left unfinished, then abandoned? In any case, the temple–tower was immensely suggestive. Let us tell its story, "as though . . ."

"Though Babylon
scale
the heavens,

and make
her strong heights
inaccessible,

destroyers
from me

will
reach
her,"

says
God. . . . (Jer 51:53)

✦ ✦ ✦

The outcome is all but a classic Greek tragedy. Humans overreach themselves, play god. A challenge to Jawe, this affront, an essentially irreligious project.

Very well then. Provoked beyond bearing, God pounces on the tower like Blake's "tiger, tiger, burning bright." The builders are scattered like ninepins; the tower, a contrived affront, stands there unfinished. It is like the monstrous broken jaw of a behemoth set on end. In the abandoned city, a monument to—monumental folly.

"Fallen,
fallen

is Babylon the great!

She
has become

a dwelling
for demons. . . .
The kings
of earth

with her
committed
fornication,

and
the world's merchants
grew rich

from
her
wealth

and
wantonness." (Rev 18:2–3)

✦   ✦   ✦

Another mood steals over the Deity. The sin in the garden was not the end, the deluge was not the end; neither is the halted tower, or the city, stalemated where it looms.

✦   ✦   ✦

And we, the misapprehending tribes of earth, what of our nervy, sorry selves? Neither are we abandoned. No, though the text be sadly verified to this day, and we off-kilter spiritually, untrusting, envious, murderous toward one another—nevertheless. Though death has its day, and the day be long as an eon, God is not assimilated to our wicked will. God remains God; providential, caring, compassionate. So we believe, and believing mourn, and go on.

✦   ✦   ✦

11:29 Great and greater, the acts of God bear down on humans. In a nimbus of majesty, grand personages appear—though dimly, as though in a twilight or a first hint of dawn.

A dawn is to follow, surely, a dawn like the blare of a shofar. Great names are bruited about, grandeur enters the pages. While time lasts, these ancestors of our faith will be invoked—Abram, Sarai, names shortly to be altered by the most High.

New names are conferred—Abraham, Sara. Signs of choice, of grand tasks imposed, of vocations burdensome yet glorious beyond telling.

The chosen ones are tested—father Abraham, Isaac the innocent—in the darkest of nights they trust on. And what glory accrues!

✦ ✦ ✦

The lens of the author, focused on the sacred text, narrows. A page turns, simple and momentous, like the turn of a great hinge.

We are done with the story of origins.

And our hearts quicken. We shall soon know our own, and be known.

Our own story is underway! Resemblances strike like a bolt; likenesses of gesture, metaphor, praise, nuance of speech, body language. And above all and within all and crowning all, a common faith in God.

A grand recognition scene indeed—our ancestry, whence we come.

The first, Abram named Abraham, his life a long susurration of faithful trust. At the divine behest he ventures far from homeland, confident, trusting in a Promise whose fulfillment lies beyond human power, all but beyond imagining.

✦ ✦ ✦

Paul for his part will never have done with celebrating the faith of Abraham, the glory, the gift:

> What then shall we say of Abraham, our ancestor according to the flesh? Certainly if Abraham was justified by his deeds, he has ground for boasting.
>
> But not in God's view. For what does scripture say? "Abraham believed God, and it was credited to him as justice." (Rom 4:1–3)

✦ ✦ ✦

Consider the case of Abraham. "He believed in God, and it was credited to him as justice." This means that those who believe are sons (and daughters) of Abraham.

> Because scripture saw in advance that God's way of justifying the gentiles would be through faith, it foretold this good news to Abraham, "All nations shall be blessed in you."

Thus it is that all who believe are blessed along with Abraham, the man of faith. (Gal 3:8–9)

✦   ✦   ✦

12:1   It begins with a command, a response, and a journey undertaken. The patriarch is summoned. A paradigm of faith itself; the beckoning, the initiative of Another.

Into the unknown Abram goes, a sterile wife at his side, far from "land, kinfolk, father's house." He is to leave these behind—familiar faces, a beloved landscape, the shape of things that shape the heart—the endearing shape of life itself.

The vessel is broken. Life is taking new form. Faith is taking shape in the world.

A hand lies on a shoulder, a finger points. The going forth will touch the unborn. Ourselves.

> It is sometimes necessary for sons to leave the family hearth; it may well be necessary at least for intellectuals to leave their country as it is for children to leave their homes, not to get away from them, but to recreate them. (W. H. Auden, on Henry James)

✦   ✦   ✦

We are staggered at the simplicity of it; the command, the response. The trust, the sublime mutuality. And the pain.

In a catalogue of cruel exactions, each item, each loss is set down, dwelt on, dear and familiar as it is:

"Go
forth

from
the land

of
your
kinsfolk

and

your
father's
house. . . ."

Where will it end, where will the caravan of faith come to a halt? What awaits, what land, family, descendants?

Of these nothing, or near nothing, a vague reference point, a "somewhere" beyond all visible horizons.

A Someone has seen it first:

"A
land

I

will show
you."

✦   ✦   ✦

There will be more of these demands, sorrows, exactions; in scope of sacrifice, they will grow outrageous.

Each episode stands like a stepping-stone carved in a mountainside, leading up and up, to—what shall we call it? A summit of absurdity, cruelty, obedience—a mountain, and a kind of Aztec altar (22).

Who could have imagined this nightmare, its exactions? On an intolerable peak the dearest of lives is to be exacted.

What to make of the fierce bloodlust—a deity gone mad? It is like a Toltec chant, the god demands a human victim:

"Take
your
son
Isaac,

your
only one,

whom
you love,

and go
to the land
of Moriah.

There
you

shall
offer
him

as
a
holocaust. . . ." (22:2)

"Your only son, whom you love . . ." Open the wound, wide. Let no point
of affection, flesh, bone, be untouched by the blade. What finesse, what skillful cruelty, so to mock the heart's affection, to play its theme on a parent's
heartstrings!

We will never understand. A hand from a cloud reaches into the heart of
love, tears the heart from breast, raises it in sacrifice.

And many will never accept this excruciating paternity on high, making
sport of human bonds. Making of a loving parent, a filicide.

✦ ✦ ✦

What then of Abraham? Shall we speak of a trust grown mature, match-
ing the One who demands all? Or has the father, acquiescing in sacrificial
crime, like his god–berserker gone quite mad?

It is never done with, the drama, the tragedy, the impassioned debate.

This "ancestor of our faith" takes center stage again and again, his tears
falling as the harsh drama unfolds.

Of the father and son on the road to the mount of sacrifice, more later.

✦ ✦ ✦

The drama continues, to this day. We see it or hear of it, with what fear
and trembling. Faith precisely as crisis, testing:

> "Our inner fire, our enthusiasm, our souls, also Eros—all
> must be merged with the one great light, with the heart of
> God, with Jesus Christ must gain new life, and be newly
> born in Him. . . .

> Everything to do with desire, possessions, the will for power,
> selfish demands, vanishes in this blazing sun. The old
> world disappears . . . the new is born with its sacrificial, all-
> embracing, generous love of God and joy of God.

Such an attitude is altogether alien to this world. . . .

In the moment of greatest tension, when the majority feared for their economic future, Eberhart's message was, "Work for the joy of it. Trust, and base your livelihood on trust. . . ."

Humankind must turn around. What good are all its religious practices, what good are all its church services, what point is there in all its devout singing, if God's will is not done and hands are covered with blood?

What does people's faith mean if injustice is done to the poor as casually as one drinks a glass of water? What good is it to profess the divine if not even a little finger is lifted when countless children and poor people die . . . ?" (Markus Baum, *Against the Wind: Eberhard Arnold and the Bruderhof*)

✦ ✦ ✦

13:5–6 How laconically it is put, this grievous matter of "taking possession of the land"! Ethnic cleansing? It will stain page after page of the Bible, century after century.

The stage is carefully set.

Almost as an aside, as though in parentheses:

"The Canaanites were then in the land." (13:7)

✦ ✦ ✦

13:18 Abraham arrives at Hebron. First the place is declared sacred:

The holy place
of Sichem,

near
the
divining
tree.

He builds an altar there, in acknowledgement of—the Promise.

The Promise is spoken, and twice recorded (15:7, 18). A fateful moment, heavy with consequence for (and against!) generations unborn:

"To
your
descendants

I
will give

this
land."

✦ ✦ ✦

"As though in parentheses"; as though the writer shrank from dwelling on the fact, a boiling brew of contention-to-come.

An appalling implication is reduced to a footnote. This is plain fact; inhabitants dwell there, the land is long settled.

And what of those Canaanites, how does the God regard them? How are the chosen to regard them?

Thus. The inhabitants stand beyond the pale. They are to be exterminated (one account), or, at the least, assimilated.

The chosen arrive, bearing their irrefutable credential—a divine promise. Contention is inevitable. The text hurries on.

And we take note of an ancient tactic, as old as human pride, as ancient as greed. We have noted it before. Somewhat like this—sanctify the beginnings of a people, bestow on early events a divine sanction. Incorporate these in the Holy Book. Presto! they are transfigured. They bespeak the will of the God.

Thus the later social and political (and religious) structures gain an aura of transcendent truth, placed as they are beyond doubt or debate.

✦ ✦ ✦

Doubt, debate? These become forms of heresy; purportedly they betray the word of the God. Is "possession of the land" a grievous point of contention between two claimants? The two are forbidden to coexist; at least according to the present version (happily there exists a less-draconian account). The "Word" forbids it. And that Word—let it be clung to with all one's might—includes superior military might.

✦ ✦ ✦

The keepers of the Word are in the right, the adversaries in the wrong. Their claim, whatever its nature, antiquity, sponsoring god, is canceled. Worthless, superseded.

✦ ✦ ✦

The game is complex. Defense of the integrity of the Word in one hand, raging self-interest in the other. A territory is first sacralized, then militarized.

And what of the text? Boundaries are staked off, warnings posted—Keep Off. And shortly the land is drenched in blood.

✦ ✦ ✦

What then of this Word from on high? Two contrasting versions, as above. According to one tradition, the land is given over to newcomers, the Canaanites are thrust into oblivion. Another tradition softens the blow. Canaanites are absorbed. The Hebrews defeat the baals and assert the sovereignty of Jawism.

Bewildering at first glance. Why are both traditions, seemingly contradictory, set down? Is the duality a literary device, urging that we pause, and ponder? Did something of both occur, assimilation and slaughter? In the popular mind, in that time of upheaval, were contrary instructions issued from on high; yes, intermarry; no, do away with them?

✦ ✦ ✦

Is the God merciful? Surely the chosen have tasted mercy upon mercy. Or is God merciless, and would have us so, a baleful twist on that early encomium, the first humans created as "images of God"?

Pause, ponder. A (possibly fruitful) stalemate; we are nowhere near understanding this God and his (sic) peculiar, off-putting interventions.

✦ ✦ ✦

Presented as myth or fact, we have here the seeds of a series of holy wars. And a mighty puzzle concerning the integrity of the Word of God.

In resolving the puzzle, or even shedding a measure of light upon it, the Bible of Jerusalem is of little help. The note on verse 6 is laconic and laced with religiosity: "Gift of the Holy Land [sic]. Abraham pays tribute to the lordship of Yahve by building an altar."

Such comment carries a tincture of bad faith; no mention of the bloodshed or cultural contempt entailed in "the gift"!

✦ ✦ ✦

Equally dense is the question of a befitting reverence for the Word of God. And all the more puzzling, when that Word is modified, circumscribed, nuanced, even contradicted, by a later Word.

As in, let us suggest, a defining moment in biblical history; the end of tribal religion announced by Isaiah (Isa 2, and passim), his inclusion of "the nations" in the orbit of divine favor.

✦ ✦ ✦

Another aspect of the problem is suggested by the mystic Adrienne von Speyr:

> If a person reads scripture simply in order to get to know the text as such, the meaning of the words and the sequence and context of events, one will be content with the written word.
>
> But if a person meditates on the same passages in a spirit of adoration, laying hold of them not only with reason but with a concretely lived faith, in thorough determination to seek God . . , God will often initiate such a one more deeply into the reality behind the words.
>
> Contemplation is not merely a psychological process, it is not the soul's monologue with itself. It is prayer, dialogue with God, in course of which the Word acts in sovereign freedom.
>
> In contemplation, God is always veiling and unveiling . . . there is both day and night. Some things are brightly illuminated; others are in darkness. . . . God wishes them to remain wrapped in mystery.
>
> But at this stage it is no longer merely a question of human knowledge and ignorance; it is a question of sharing in a specific manner, in the way God sees things. . . . (*Three Women and The Lord*, Ignatius Press, 1986)

✦ ✦ ✦

"The way God sees things." Who but a high mystic is to attain that "way?" And further, does God see things differently at different times? Or is the question rather—do we humans sometimes intrude in the text, substituting ambition and appetite for an uncontaminated word?

Surely, Scripture is affected by the social or individual self-understanding that, at the time of writing, comes to bear.

People of this time, this place! Genesis, with its vast sweep of history and Shakespearian press and tumult, its multitudinous flood of characters, its grins and grimaces, is relatively untouched by later refinements of spirit, by holiness or prophecy.

✦ ✦ ✦

Genesis tells of beginnings as such, and this in a double aspect. First, a vast sweep; the mighty act of creation, how all things came to be. Then the beam narrows, focusing first on one people, then on one personage; Joseph, sold in Egypt as a slave, settling there, prospering together with his clan.

✦ ✦ ✦

This time, this place! The saga of latter Genesis and Exodus bears the coloration of a later, vast achievement, wrung from exile, slavery, and desert heats. The text is Davidic–Solomonic, which is to say, a triumphant paean, a trumpet blast of grandeur and glory.

And why not—one almost thinks; how not? The achievement stops the breath; law and covenant are codified, grandiose economic and military powers are concentrated in Jerusalem.

How mightily the ragtag arrivistes of Exodus have reversed their ill fortune! Secure and glorious, the empire is in full flower.

Those who prevail are close guardians of social memory, of images and versions of events. Appointed historians own, shape, color to imperial taste and ideology, the genesis, the story of stories, from Abraham forward to the great (and not so great) kings.

✦ ✦ ✦

In regard to a later, believing community, a strict requirement arises. Must there not exist a moral focus, against which these pages, their welter of confusion and ambition and betrayal and wars of extermination, are to be assessed? To be judged and, where required, found wanting?

Otherwise, if everything stands on equal ground, if the story of Solomon and David, morally baffling, by turns banal and bloodridden—if this is not scrutinized by an unbeholden eye—of what spiritual weight, offering what instruction, is the history?

What can it mean that church and synagogue alike agree in naming the tale, so often unsavory and demeaning of the human (and of the God!)— name the text "holy?"

The point, it would seem, is—judgment.

One after another, the kings claim respectful attention. These makers and breakers hold center stage, forge history. They wage wars, accumulate riches, secure the throne, and die.

Their pride of place is vast, foolish, and ultimately (and sometimes shortly) bootless. And as time passes, they are persistently declared so—bootless. For prophets also arise; their moral grandeur makes of the kings mere foils, against which holiness—holy God, holy humans—shines the brighter.

The prophetic eye is close and relentless. The misdemeanings, murders, betrayals, and charlatanry of the high and mighty—name these aright, call them to accounts! Their crimes are a coarse grist for the mills of Isaiah, Jeremiah, and their like. Denounce the great ones, defend the "widow and orphan, the stranger at the gate"!

Through these clairvoyants, the Hebrew Scripture honors its vocation, which is, as Paul insists, for "our instruction." And we are enlightened and encouraged in the task of faithful following.

✦   ✦   ✦

Through the era 700–500 C.E., the pronouncements of the prophets, their oracles, visions, moral guidance, must be accounted an apogee of God's self-revelation. What bears comparison with Isaiah's suffering servant, or Ezekiel's dry bones, animated wonderfully by the Spirit, or Ezekiel's great chariot, its Occupant and attendant seraphs?

In Genesis we are grateful for moral grandeur when it appears—sparsely to be sure. We read and ponder; we summon an "alas." Most of the book, the great "tide" omitted, languishes in Shakespearian "shallows and miseries."

✦   ✦   ✦

12:10 No sooner are matters of divine preference clarified than a strange deviation occurs on the part of the one favored.

The road Abraham must tread is so long, the night so bleak! Famine lies on the land of promise. And as would seem, with no consultation of his celestial patron, Abram takes a wrong turn. Into a dark landscape he goes, a place of deception and moral fog, Egypt. The move will come to no good.

An outsider, he labors to render himself invisible. Shortly he adopts what might be thought Egyptian ways. Thus he reasons; his wife is beautiful, she may be in danger among the heathen; so may he. What if Sarai is claimed and seized by another, and he conveniently done away with?

All of which speculation implies that the wife's honor is one matter, his own survival another—the latter manifestly of greater import.

So we are treated to an early instance of the famous "lesser evil." Abram must at all cost be vigilant, survive. The woman lies in the orbit of his power; if required, she must alas, be sacrificed for sake of a "greater good."

So it was done.

Our contemporary casuists draw a line here, so faint as to be almost invisible. The Bible of Jerusalem offers a tortuous, verbose comment:

> Placed here, the story aims to show how the promises (of former verses) are compromised; and this by the patriarch himself. He abandons the Holy Land [sic] and hands over the woman from whom the chosen race [sic] is to be born. Still, for the first time, the plan of God is vindicated. . . .

Reservations, excuses, show that the redactors of Genesis hardly approve the entire conduct of Abraham. He shocks us more than they; but the story dates from a time when lying is not invariably reproved, when the life of a husband is valued above the honor of a wife.

Humanity, guided by God, comes only gradually to knowledge of moral law.

✦　✦　✦

13　The pendulum swings. Abraham's nephew Lot chooses the easy life and sinful atmosphere of the area of Sodom.

A more attractive Abraham asserts himself. And is rewarded on the spot.

Uncle and nephew alike have grown rich (by implication through the largesse of the Pharaoh?). And thereupon did a dispute arise? The Yahvists judge so, and so report. But the priest–scribe takes a rather mellow pacific tack; no, it was simply that the local water supply could not support large flocks.

In any case, uncle and nephew separate. And Abraham is magnanimous; Lot may first choose his direction and go where he will.

Lot's eye lights up; and no wonder. The irrigated plain of the Jordan stretches away and away. Watery air, airy water? The horizon dissolves like a veritable

> . . . garden
> of Jawe,

like
the land

of
Egypt. (13:10)

For Lot, that way and no other is his; let us part!
An ominous note shadows his choice. Disaster impends:

"Jawe had not yet destroyed Sodom and Gemorrha. . . ."

And again, a judgment impending:

"The people of Sodom were wicked sinners against Jawe."
(13:13)

The interjections read like a decree of death. For multitudes, the worst is
in prospect.

But for Abraham? The cornucopia is full; it tips upon him an unguent of
healing, and blessing upon blessing. Let him turn what way he will, far as
the eye can embrace, the land is his. Land and descendants superabun-
dantly, redundantly promised. Guerdons of prosperity, and more—of immortality.

14:1–17   These verses invite questioning and a troubled spirit.

What deep necessity, plunged like a stake in the human heart—in the
heart of our history—governs the inclusion (one almost wrote, the intrusion)
of the Four Great Kings?

What social or military urging, what motive, what voice in the blood
ignored the three great traditions of the Book of Beginnings, and appended
this episode? It is as though an aspect of the patriarchs' story, heretofore
ignored or deemed unimportant, suddenly loomed as crucial. Crucial to a
later quest for self-understanding.

This people, grown great in the world, must know from whom they
spring, what qualities make for noble ancestry—what promise, like a seed
in good earth rising in hundredfolds, urges celebration of the preeminence
of Jerusalem.

The city existed in the mind before it stood—peerless, supreme, the grand set piece of Solomon. Include it then, foreshadow it from the beginning! A story of wisdom, wealth, largesse of spirit—or perhaps mere cleverness, the trickster twist?

✦ ✦ ✦

Up to this episode, the portrait of the ancestor is incomplete. Granted, the face befits, it bears the hard-won nobility of a late Rembrandt self-portrait. The look pierces the soul, we are rendered thoughtful and grateful at once.

We note too the ancestral hand. It rises in a gesture of command, now "halt," again "go forward." Or perhaps conferring a benediction.

Nonetheless the portrait is incomplete.

Is the right hand lifted? But it is empty.

It must not be so, it must bear a sword. Only then will we know the great ancestor as our own, and be known by him—his progeny, armed and ready.

The episode bespeaks the warrior breed, Abram. Invincible!

The text enlarges the odds; let the kings stand greatly against him. And let the predicament be of small moment to a great patriarch and patriot. His chances are large, and grow larger by the moment. They rest in a seigniorial glance, a piercing intelligence. He outwits and circumvents the great kings.

Then the world gains a clue, and the scribes of imperial Jerusalem gain assurance. The niche is filled, the portrait complete. Through the encounter, Abraham grows to a surpassing eminence. A military eminence, to be sure.

✦ ✦ ✦

But is that all, or does that suffice? It does not. Christ has issued a new law; insofar as we humans grow violent, we are rendered redundant in face of a divine hope.

And the first so characterized are not the victims. They are the warriors, those who entrust all to a sword.

Passé, the warrior and kings. Nothing to offer our beleaguered modern selves.

chapter five

"A priest of the Most High God . . ."
(14:17–21:22)

14 The favor, choice, grace of gracious God—these surpass any and every bloodline. These also rebuke and judge; tribal wars attacking the freedom of the Gift (and the Giver) are condemned out of hand.

Jesus for His part will launch a stinging critique against those who claim Abraham for ancestor. In a momentous, stormy exchange, a whirlwind of cross-purpose. The lineage of His adversaries is merely carnal, Jesus insists, an accident of birth (John 8:39); nothing of special status before God is implied.

He is blunt, provocative; their claim is without value or merit. A bloodline, a biological reality implies nothing holy. Abraham, undoubtedly a great ancestor, may produce for progeny saints or rascals.

The tirade mounts in fury. Claims of excellent ancestry, boastful assertions, reliance upon the great progenitors for self-justification—these raise a massive obstacle against welcoming the truth of life.

Those who so boast come to a wicked impasse; they trace their bloodline to great Abraham—and they refuse "the works of Abraham." Which is to say, they make little or nothing of the repeated submission of Abraham to the demands of faith, the heartbreaking intrusions of the Divine, the cruel testings under the divine hand.

What do His adversaries make of this—the son of Abraham, Isaac "whom you love," is ordered sacrificed? Nothing in sum, do these eminences show of the spirit of Abraham, nothing of his trust in the Promise.

Jesus presses on. The incredible attitude of His adversaries; they revel in works of death. Malice possesses them. One greater than Abraham stands in their midst, and they seek to kill Him.

They work to a secret, vile purpose; encompassing His ruin.

The indignation of Jesus rises in a torrent; the truth for which he stands surrogate and witness, is being covertly violated. In these opponents, blood rules supreme; the spirit is quenched.

In them, a vaunted bloodline yields—to bloodlust. He knows their dark secret. They seek His life.

✦ ✦ ✦

Hell knows no fury like an Iago unmasked. Jesus unmasks their designs. Now they must stand in the light; in that light called judgment. His tongue is a whiplash. They are liars, murderers, demonics. *Eccolo*, the vaunted ancestry has wrought this—a degenerate progeny, at opposite poles from great Abraham. Blood and bone, they are immune against the truth. Sons not of Abraham, truth told, but of ha-satan.

Let them be astonished, shaken, enraged, as he rips in tatters the fabric of pretension and concealment. Do they claim Abraham? Very well, He will seize upon the claim for His own, an epiphany, a blaze struck before their eyes.

Can they bear it? Can they come to faith? Will they receive His stupendous utterance as a call to repentance, to a better mind, to renouncing designs taking form in darkness?

A greater than Abraham stands before them, The Eternal:

> "In
> truth
> I
>
> tell
> you,
>
> before
> Abraham
> was,
>
> I
> AM." (John 8:58)

They cannot bear it. The alternatives tighten. No other outcome; He must die.

✦ ✦ ✦

With chapter 14 of Genesis, we see the cult of ancestry mightily shored up. Abram emerges as a doughty warrior, a veritable David in face of a Goliath.

Must he battle a clutch of kings and their armies? Fear not; these are a massed array of—nothings, shadow warriors before a surpassing might, his own.

Against seemingly insurmountable odds, Abram wins through. The kings fall to a tactical error, all but fatal. They seize nephew Lot and his goods and chattels.

The news is brought to Abram; his leonine heart quickens. With a mere 318 followers, he falls upon the kings in the night, defeats them roundly, and rescues family and dependants.

✦　✦　✦

14:18–20 A crucial encounter follows. It must be accounted a watershed of sacred history, as well as a fruitful source of midrash, both Christian and Jewish.

This befalls. Returning from his triumph, Abram meets with a priest–king, possibly (though improbably) a native of Jerusalem. The eminence is graced with a nearly unpronounceable name, Melchisedech.

It is as though the heartbeat of time slowed, to appraise, to pay tribute to this moment, its mere mention. Here and now, redoubtable and mysterious, the King of Peace enters history.

In many shadowy, rich ways and metaphors he lingers, his memory a perfume on the page. It is as though he never departs. His coming in mortal flesh, his departure, start multitudinous resonances in Scripture and tradition.

Neither progeny nor ancestry are recorded of this vaunted, haunted king. Was he ruler of Jerusalem, the city-to-be of David and Solomon? That is very nearly all we are told of his identity—and at that, speculation.

Long before the time of the Levites, a king and priest "of the most High" appears. Attend closely, the text urges. Something unprecedented will shortly be underway. With Abram in attendance, Melchisedech offers unheard of elements of sacrifice—bread and wine.

It is as though generation after generation, the dead and the unborn, in tomb and womb are startled.

Or as though the text were a verdant tree, alive with singing birds. The tree is shaken; images take wing and fly:

Melchisedech, image of the Messiah;

God
has
sworn

and will not
repent;

You
are
priest

forever,

according
to

the

orderof
Melchisidech. (Ps 110:4)

✦   ✦   ✦

What of this personage, rupturing time and place, majestic, elegant, all
but speechless in the text, announcing through the gifts he holds aloft, sacred things to come?

He bestows on Abram the ancestor, a serendipitous blessing.

✦   ✦   ✦

Christians too have seized on the event, and its apotheosis through the
psalmist. In a magnificent burst of rhetoric, Paul makes much of the small
evidence at hand:

Without
father,
mother,
ancestry,

without
beginning of days
or end of life,

like the Son
of God

he remains
a priest forever. . . .

See
the greatness
of this man,

to whom
Abraham the patriarch

gave
one tenth

of
his
booty. (Heb 7:3–4)

✦ ✦ ✦

Deep waters indeed. To enrich his allegory, Paul seizes on every detail. Abraham hands over a portion of his spoils to a foreign priest. So doing, the patriarch he pays tribute to a superior, a

"king
of
justice,

king
of
peace" (Heb 7:2)

And the mysterious outsider blesses,

. . . the one
who had received

God's
Promises. . . . (Heb 7:6)

✦ ✦ ✦

To Paul, a conclusion is inescapable:

Now it is indisputable that a lesser person is blessed by a greater. (Heb 7:7)

✦ ✦ ✦

14:19–20 Melchisedech is a gentile; astonishingly, his blessing includes the essence of Jewish faith. How comes it that he utters a purely Jewish formula, as though it were native to his soul?

"Blessed
be Abram

by God
most high,

the creator

of
heaven

and
earth. . . ."

And more, Melchisedech is prescient. Ironically, "king of peace," he
knows of the recent victory:

". . . who
delivered

your foes

into
your
hands."

The points are far from subtle, and dovetail nicely with the vast promises
soon to descend on Abram. Heaven and earth conjoin; what mightier fortress than our God?

Thus too, the blessing befits the national ethos, the mix of imperial ego
and divine favor that surround like an aureole of gold, the head—now hel-
meted, now crowned—of Solomon.

And yet more; the primeval blessing is a pledge of things to come, of
blessings still in the offing.

✦   ✦   ✦

We tread softly; our text is set down in an era of "blessings"—mixed
blessings indeed, one thinks.

From Melchisedech, on to David and Solomon. If such as the latter are
to be accounted "blessed," the favor has taken a peculiar twist—if not an
ominous, threatening one. For the deity of Melchisedech is god of creation—
and of battle.

Not only does the priest–king appear in the text, as though from nowhere. The warrior–god also appears; like his surrogate, for the first time.

✦ ✦ ✦

We have a notable development here. The god of Melchisedech is to all evidence, the god of Abram. The episode is a recognition scene; implicit is a close congruence of mind—and of act. The priest blesses, the patriarch-turned-warrior is blessed. He bows and welcomes the blessing.

Each sees in his acknowledged god the same guise—creator–warrior.

✦ ✦ ✦

In a brief episode, a major theme of the Hebrew Bible opens. It will run like a full artery throughout the historical books—as well as though Christian history. An artery, swollen with blood. And torn open. This; violence is sanctioned and sacralized.

The long and short of biblical history: conflicts here declared blessed, will shortly be named explicitly as Holy Wars. Including wars of extermination. The warrior god will favor his (sic) own kind—the "godly" warriors, the chosen from among the "chosen." These will offer sacrifice; then proceed, firm of conscience, to slaughter.

✦ ✦ ✦

More and more, the evidence and its implications mount, concerning the meeting of the two notables.

The pen of Paul takes wing, and soars. A small omission becomes a matter of capital moment. Thus, the death of Melchisedech goes unmentioned. It must follow that he is immortal:

> Mortals
> subject
>
> to
> death
>
> receive
> tithes,
>
> but scripture
> testifies
>
> that
> this man
>
> lives
> on. (Heb 7:8)

✦ ✦ ✦

Thus the evidence mounts up and up, a very Olympus on Etna. Melchisedech must be a type of Christ, priest eternal, king of peace, whose priesthood springs from no mortal, but from God.

Paul's text is a midrash, striking, very Jewish, a word-for-word delving into hidden meanings. Even the silence of the great king is accounted eloquent. Melchisedech speaks not a word. And Paul scores a key point, in favor of claims centering on Jesus.

✦ ✦ ✦

15 That faith of Abram; it is like an incandescent wire, bearing a current of warmth and light throughout Scripture.

Paul again, lingering lovingly over the theme. To him, it is a grand and central portal; through the faith of the great ancestor, gentiles stream into the sanctuary:

> Abram
> believed
> in Jawe,
>
> and
> it was credited
> to him
>
> as
> justice.
>
> He believed;
> what
> God promised
>
> would
> be bestowed,
>
> for
> God
>
> is
> faithful. (Rom 4:20–21)

✦ ✦ ✦

The content of the promise is a matter of evidence, a matter of the senses—eyes can see, ears hear, hands weigh. Descendants are visible, we hear the voices of children, we hold them close, beloved, our hearts ache at their absence.

So is the earth visible, tactile beneath our feet. We walk it, whether as "undocumented," "illegal"—or as those in possession; as slaves indentured, or as free agents. Thus the bittersweet fictions of time and place, fictions made facts; facts, as is said, of life. Often rather, facts of death.

In such ways too, a given culture lays claim to the text, declares itself singled out, chosen. And *eccolo!* the promise has come true.

15:2–3 Faith that comes easily, departs just as easily. But the faith that is tested, stands firm.

Here the testing takes the form of delay; the promise is tardy in coming true. And for the first time, Abram addresses God directly. His voice is plaintive:

> "See,
>
> you
> have
> given me
>
> no
> offspring. . . ."

And the response includes no hint of reproof on the part of this often-touchy god. Nothing of disdain or anger; quite the opposite, the plaint is taken in good part. It is as though the god were yielding (for once) before this man. As though the deity were honoring (for once) a purely human timing.

(And how we, too, long to see a benefit bestowed, a promise kept; or at least some part of it, some evidence or immanence, a halt to violence and rancor, as the world's sole empire goes its unimpeded, awful way. And bearing us along, like flotsam in a stormy channel. Alas, alas for the children of Afghanistan and Iraq!)

Our awful, unimpeded way? The phrase was set down prior to the catastrophe of September 2001.

The phrase must be altered. That day dawned, business hummed along as usual in "the capital of the world."

Then the skies vomited a firestorm. "The topless towers of Ilium" collapsed in an hour. Thousands died.

✦ ✦ ✦

The Deity speaks: Here then, Abram, your evidence.

The scene is homely, unwontedly genial. The holy duo have evidently been conversing face to face, indoors. In a lovely gesture, God led him outside and said:

> "Raise
> your eyes
>
> and
> count
> the stars,
>
> if indeed
> you can
> count them.
>
> Such
> will be
>
> your
> posterity." (15:5)

✦ ✦ ✦

What to say?

Ordinarily, time is neutral or painful—or now and again honeyed with fragrant presences. As here.

The future is written in the stars, a showering cascade of light and life.

✦ ✦ ✦

The poet Hopkins knew a like moment, and seized its forelock; he also leads us outside, and says; "raise your eyes . . ."

Look at the stars! look, look up at the skies!

O look at all the fire-folk sitting in the air!

Peculiar, wonderfully turned. He sees each star as though a kind of vehicle, a chariot perhaps, wheeling through the heavens, steered by a holy chauffeur. Innumerable, the stars become a metaphor for a celestial populace, the communion of saints.

And hardly undifferentiated, a very hierarchy of holiness:

> . . . This piece-bright paling shuts the spouse
> Christ home, Christ and his mother and all his hallows.

✦ ✦ ✦

15:9 Between Abram and the deity, an altogether strange commerce follows. Dusk descends, then darkness. The atmosphere grows thick, ominous. The patriarch prepares beasts and birds for sacrifice, knifing each animal in two parts.

O dark night of Scripture! It calls to mind the night of Macbeth. (Or the last night of Saul [1 Sam 28].) Half-mad, surreptitious, a warrior doomed, he stands at the door of the woman of Endor. His disguise is pierced by her gaze. What does he ask? His fate?

(He shall be told it straight; he will die on the morrow).

✦ ✦ ✦

It is the night of Abram. He falls into a stasis of awe and dread, an uneasy somnolence ridden with nightmare. Then he is startled awake; birds of prey descend and harry the meats of the altar. He must beat them back.

The ravenous birds are omens, portents of things to come. A voice tells him so. Has he sought progeny? Very well then, through the cawing and shrieking, hear their story, a welter of affliction, terror, exile, enslavement, four hundred years of it, a harrowing of hell.

Nonetheless, believe, believe! At length will come deliverance.

As for himself, an honorable old age is granted.

✦ ✦ ✦

Awesome proceedings, attested elsewhere. The rite is consummated with a symbolic act of divine approval.

In the dead of night,

> . . . a
> smoking
> brazier
>
> and
>
> a
> flaming
> torch. . . . (16:17)

pass between the meats. Abram does not pass; the initiative is not his. Solitary, unutterably majestic the Flame walks, the Presence, the Guarantor of covenant.

The protocol goes thus; parties to the agreement walk between the

halved carcasses. If the covenant be violated, the party at fault is liable to
the fate of the sacrificed animals—death.

Thus God speaks to Jeremiah:

> The men
> who
>
> violated
> my
> covenant . . .
>
> I will make
> like the calf
>
> which
> they
> cut in two,
>
> [as]
> between
> the two parts
>
> they
> passed.
>
> The princes . . .
> the courtiers,
>
> the priests
> and the common people,
>
> who passed
> between
> the parts
> of the calf,
>
> I
> will
> hand
> over,
> all of them,
> to their enemies. . . .
>
> Their corpses
> shall be food

for
birds

of
the
air. . . . (Jer 34:18–20)

✦   ✦   ✦

15:18   Out of the darkness, a Voice speaks to Abram:

To
your descendants

I
give

this
land,

from
the Torrent
of Egypt

to
the great
River. . . .

✦   ✦   ✦

Descendants—and what a blessing in any age—were earlier promised,
against vast odds of age and barrenness.

✦   ✦   ✦

And what of the land? From the patriarch's time to our own, it has
known for the most part strife and bloodletting.

The "promised" land, the "holy" land? Who dares say so, and on what
basis? The land is soaked in blood. And bellicose humans are degraded, together with their religion, their sense of one another.

No end of strife, no end. Holy wars, wars of extermination create again
and again such societies as were mourned by Isaiah. Societies like his own:

". . . full
of chariots,

full
of silver,

full
of
idols. . . ." (Isa 2:7–8)

✦   ✦   ✦

16   Are Abram and Sarai to have that child, a promised one, at last? It appears they shall—and it appears they shall not.

Well, at length let matters be mended. Since the rightful wife cannot conceive, why not a substitute mother, conceiving a substitute child? (And shall we not have other instances of the sweet cheat, in stories of Rachel and Leah?)

The arrangement falls well within custom, if only it suits all parties.

It would seem to suit—for awhile. The tradeoff is consummated.

But then, but then (how unsparing is our author!) in the mixed household, conflicts rear up. The servant girl, pregnant by Abram, grows insolent before her mistress. And Sarai complains to her liege lord.

The great man, it will be recalled, is a skilled oiler of troubled waters—when, that is, the waters threaten his freehold or composure of mind. Thus in Egypt, he judged it expedient that Sarai "front" for him, in favor of his own well-being.

So here, other undoubted male concerns occupy him and his (undoubtedly male) god. Our scribe, what subtlety and skill and unrelenting! Another woman, a lesser to be sure, together with her child and Abraham's, must be offered on the altar of ego.

Has he fathered a child who embodies the crucial promise? Is he not responsible for the child's well-being, and its mother's as well?

Such (minor) matters are waved aside with the sweep of a patriarchal hand. The great man is manifestly superior to minor flurries in the female dovecote. Let the untender mercies of his spouse deal with the two.

We cannot but note the offhandedness, the contempt toward both women. Neither name, Sarai or Hagar, passes his lips. Each, in degree, is declared expendable:

"Your maid
is

in
your power.

Do
to her

whatever
you
please." (16:6)

✦ ✦ ✦

The gods resemble humans, it is said. The opposite holds true as well. And we find much to ponder. Is Abram grandly permissive, or does he indulge a degrading show of power? In a few verses this complex patriarch stands revealed, flawed.

First, a sturdy, unbowed faith, a daring contention with his God. Then—unfaith. He grows self-absorbed, short of mindfulness, devoid of compassion.

The "father of our faith," as Paul extols him?

Let us add, sotto voce—the father of our unfaith as well.

✦ ✦ ✦

How cunning our author, and how prescient. He dwells at length on the myth, then he pricks the myth. The ancestor is deemed ideal, a Platonic icon. Then his seams are shaken before our eyes.

Shaken. And as the myth is shaken, questions arise. Does not someone nobler than a mere icon stand there? Yes. Enthroned in a near pantheon of high praise, Abram is brought down, takes human proportions. He is heroic, and he is petty and self-serving. He is faithful, and he betrays. He loves greatly, then lo, he grudges and withholds love.

A hero in sum, his faith stretched on the rack of the exigent divine. A sinner as well, on a scale both grand and petty.

✦ ✦ ✦

As to Hagar, what a fate is appointed her! Pregnant, ill-treated by a jealous mistress, she is denied recourse to her lord and master.

She flees the unbearable scene, into the wilderness.

There she is lost—and found. She pauses near an oasis. And all unexpectedly, compassion descends to her; she is granted an epiphany. Be it known—the God of Abraham is also the God of Hagar.

The God seeks her out. Whence has she come? Where is she bound? Strange questions, reminiscent of the first summons to Abram, also a story of "comings and goings." We recall the momentous original:

"Go
forth
from
the land

of
your kinsfolk

and
from

your father's
house

to
a land

I
will

show
you. . . ." (12:1)

✦   ✦   ✦

We long to make sense of this God, to corral him (sic) in our categories,
our logic. Impossible. He (sic) will favor whom he chooses, will reject whom
he rejects. . . .

In an anguished spate of questions, Job entered a like contest and quest.
Equally impossible.

And here, inexplicably and at long last, at the thin edge of survival, the
servant Hagar is favored. Abram, her lord and master, had disdained her,
leaving her nameless—"your maid."

Here God names her, fondly, one thinks: "Hagar, Sarai's maid."

The first query of "the Lord's messenger,"

". . . where have
you

come
from . . . ?"

is easily answered. The second,

". . . and
where

are
you
going?"

is beyond knowing. Her mind falters. Where might she and her child find refuge? She knows only this—in the camp of Abram her situation was beyond bearing.

✦ ✦ ✦

She is like Mary of the Christian testament, mysteriously pregnant. With one crucial difference; Hagar is without a protector, a Joseph.

Still, we marvel at her strength. Alone and cast out, she says her "no," loud and clear. She will risk her life and the life of her unborn in the wilderness, rather than tolerate derision and indignity.

Strength strikes against strength; Sarai against Hagar. And for the moment, in shocking contrast to the two women, Abram fades, a pale specimen indeed.

✦ ✦ ✦

16:10 It is difficult to decode the sequence here. What is Hagar's place in the grand design, what place for her son Ishmael? And what of the promise of multiple descendants, to one in so dire a predicament?

A dark promise, a promise that implies a threat? Ishmael will be:

". . . a wild ass

of
a man,

his
hand

against
everyone,

everyone's
hand

against
him. . . ."

For her, the God's design is ambiguous, neither grand nor great. Hagar will mother a multitude of—whom?—of Ishmaels. Nothing better, nothing of nobility or honor. Her descendants and his, like a herd of wild asses, witless and angry, all teeth and hooves, galloping hither and yon, contentious and untamable.

Wonderment. Is the divine word with regard to her son a matter of decree, "this he must be . . . ," or of simple prophecy, "this he shall be . . ."? Is the deity molding the unborn to his will, or is the God simply a bystander, with a third eye open on the future?

We are left in the dark. So, as goes without saying, is Hagar.

✦ ✦ ✦

The instruction of the God is sharp, and cuts to the bone. No relief is offered her distress, no miracle. No ravens will bring nourishment in the desert. Only this—she must return home, she must bear with her martinet–mistress.

Moreover, this is made clear—Ishmael is not the promised son. To the contrary, he and his descendants will stand over against the promised one and his descendants. Thus the blessing in the wilderness is profoundly ambiguous; progeny yes, promise no.

✦ ✦ ✦

For her portion, Hagar remains a classic outsider, a bare survivor. Instead of an honored place in the story, the God appoints her the role of a servant. Let her turn the scroll and read. It tells the story of others than she.

She and her son are mere serviceable hands, turning, turning, shadowing the pages. Thus her grudged place in the ancestral story.

There she stands, servant, chattel, to be used and misused by her betters. Her fruitfulness, her son, her part in the genetic to–fro, these are useful to be sure—to others. But beside the main point.

Let her strength be manifest, but let it spend itself in tears, dwelling as she does in a corner of life. All said, the future is shaped without her. She does not signify; Sarai does.

Even at a third or fourth remove, this is hard to bear, this icy turn of what shall be. Others than Hagar are in possession. They own the text, it validates them, honors them, alive as it is, aglow with vision and promise.

They, so to speak, dwell in the great house, vastly in possession.

Hagar is appointed a different place—a shadow, a destiny, hardly a vocation.

Vision yes, promise no. She dwells among the servants, those who inhabit shacks and outhouses, who labor in the fields. Who are owned. Who at whim, the text and the God of the text all but disown.

✦ ✦ ✦

What is Hagar to us? The text neither instructs nor advises.

Perhaps we too are meant to disown her and her kind. Or perhaps we see another intention at work.

Are we to discover something of ourselves in Hagar, this woman without cause or merit—something in her abused life, her harassment and ejection from the circle of favor?

Whatever the case, we come to love Hagar and her coltish son, this "undocumented" duo thrust about the world by a crusty, unpredictable deity and his ever-so-obeisant cohorts.

✦ ✦ ✦

This God. He sets logic on its head, shakes out its seams. Beyond accountability, beyond the heart's scope, we see him (sic) veering about in winds of his own making.

For the moment, in the Deity's mind looms this lorn woman in the wilderness, and her child. The God would be, at least in measure, accountable, even providential.

Thus the God chooses and rejects—and seldom if ever gives his hand away. We too, are we invited to choose and reject?

✦ ✦ ✦

The God named her: "Hagar, servant of Sarai." And turn and turn about, the woman names the God. This is extraordinary, that the woman so placed, so implacably misplaced, should "name" God.

She is in wonderment, one thinks, at her own audacity. Or perhaps at her surviving this astounding moment, a mortal sighting of the God. In any case, the meaning of the Hebrew is uncertain:

> "Have I
> seen
> the one
>
> who
> has
>
> seen
> me?"

or perhaps (in the Tanakh):

> "Do I
> go on

seeing,
after
seeing
him?"

As to the name she confers, the text leaves us unsure. Perhaps,

"the one
who
sees
me."

✦ ✦ ✦

We are astonished, halted, in wonderment. There is an inkling—and more—a sublime efflorescence of power here, even as she stands powerless. She, her plight, her infant, have moved the heart of the God, have induced a strange unveiling. She has seen the deific—a reality for the most part (and from most humans) jealously concealed. This she saw—the God has a heart.

That "naming." And Hagar wins an oblique acknowledgment of her plight, her chances. Does the command to return to a scene of torment seem arbitrary, cruel? Give it a best face—providential.

This at the least. Sought out by the God, she and her unborn will not die in the wilderness.

✦ ✦ ✦

17 For the moment, the mood from on high is benign. All concerned (Abraham newly named, Sara likewise, Hagar and her son Ishmael) are heaped with benefits. Each, in accord with foreknowledge and rank, is to be a founder of "many," a progenitor.

Covenant is announced, and its sign cut in the flesh. (In the flesh of males only, to be sure. The supernal preference could hardly be made clearer, or the assumptions of the nascent tribe with regard to the gender leanings of its God.)

The asides and innuendos and hints offered by the text! We read as we run, are instructed and rendered thoughtful.

✦ ✦ ✦

17:7 Abram falls to ground before the unnamed, who deigns to name him anew. And he arises, Abraham.

Let us pause. Prostrate, the patriarch hears the promise—a son will be born to him. The author of the tale omnisciently records the wonderment of the father—to-be. How is this to come about, that a man of a hundred years and his spouse, a woman of ninety years—these will bear a son?

Face to ground, Abraham laughs. Sara will laugh too, as will Ishmael; a veritable congress of risibilities echoes the name of the unborn child, Isaac; "God smiles!"

(One is led to reflect; how comes it that laughter rings out from Jewish faith, but hardly from Christian? Of no paragon of our testament is so much as a smile recorded. Can one imagine Paul lost in a great guffaw, or Jesus easing with a smile the rigors of His Sermon on the Mount?)

(Did the founders of the tribe Jewish-Christian lose their sense of humor along the rocky road?)

✦ ✦ ✦

Abraham prostrates, and he laughs. A son, a promised one! The prospect is issued without qualification, from most exalted quarters. It must be respected.

And the prospect is plain ridiculous. How human, this Abraham!

And the deity, it would seem, bears with the smiles, hastens to underscore and clarify. Ishmael is not the scion of the chosen; no, there will come another. And no delay.

The birth may be a year or more distant, no matter. On the moment of annunciation, prior to conception the child is named; Isaac. Laugh away; the birth is certain.

✦ ✦ ✦

18   And we come to the exalted event of Mambre, immortalized in our Bible (and in the icon of the sublime St. Andrew Rublev).

Is it angels who appear, or perhaps a triune Divinity, or a Divine One accompanied by two angels? The text is at no great pains to enlighten us; here as elsewhere, noble events are shrouded and revealed, veiled and half unveiled.

In the best tales, the best parts are veiled. The mystic Adrienne von Speyr underscores the point:

> . . . It is extraordinarily important for God that He not simply show us everything, but that He open and close, reveal things and veil them again. . . .
>
> It is not a case of making good or bad "guesses" as to how things may have been; it is not a case of guessing at all, but

a kind of shared experience within a given perspective. . . .
We can follow the tracks for a short space, and we know the
destination; the path in between is up to us. . . .

Psychology always acts as if the soul can be exhaustively
understood, as if there is no hiding place from the objectiv-
ity of its laws. But the nearer a soul is to God and the more
it shares a common life with God, the more God covers it
with a veil, letting us seen only what He wishes us to see.
. . . (*Three Women and the Lord*)

✦   ✦   ✦

It would seem that Yahve is addressed in verse 3, that he speaks beginning with verse 10, and is explicitly named in verses 1 and 13.

Tres videt, unum adoravit, wrote St. Hilary. "Abraham saw Three, and
bowed to One."

Probably, we are told, the primitive story spoke only of "three men," and
left matters there, at the door of the tent, the door of the mind—ambiguous,
and fruitful as well.

Certain is this, neither God nor angels commonly sit at table, fortifying
their spirits "in the heat of noon" with a sumptuous feast, the menu recorded
in mouthwatering detail.

✦   ✦   ✦

Courtesies accomplished, serious matters are at hand. A promise, always
a promise, and a reward as well. From good news to better; a year hence, the
One (or the Three) will return, and Sara will be found pregnant.

She, where is she? Eavesdropping. Perhaps behind a tent flap, she hears
the stupendous promise, and laughs. And her laughter is known to the All-
Knowing. Confronted in good humor, she dissimulates. An exchange, short
and sweet, "I did not laugh!" (For she feared greatly; as who would not?) The
Reader of hearts insists, "But you did!"

The point is made, leave it at that.

✦   ✦   ✦

18:16   The drama quickens; it is a portent alas, of a worsening future.
The actors assemble for a walk, "the men"; and "Abraham was walking with
them."

". . . downward, toward Sodom." It is as though the universal evil that
brought on the deluge were now concentrated in one place, a nonpareil Sin
City.

Reports of urban wickedness reach even unto high heaven. The God is constrained to investigate, firsthand. Our text is firm on the point; justice demands that the judge visit the scene of socialized crime. Mere reports, hearsay, will not do.

Well and good. And it befits that Abraham be made privy to the divine intent.

✦   ✦   ✦

Then, an interruption; the coil tightens. The celestial visitors walk on ahead. And Yahve is led to reflect grandly, in the manner of a potentate whose autarky admits of both proffer and withholding. (And surely not to be missed, with what uncanny skill our author reads the mind of the Reader of minds.)

Yahve:

"Shall

I

hide
my intent

from
Abraham,

who
is to become

a nation
great
and powerful,

through
whom

all nations
of earth

will
be
blessed?" (18:17)

A splendid resume, befitting both his majesty and the noble subordinate. Only wait, Abraham too is gifted with a lofty spirit, and daring. He will question the divine disposition.

It is a first, momentous indication; Abraham has come of age. A seigneur of the faith, a paragon held in high regard by the word of God, a towering spirit honored by Muslim, Jew, and Christian—here he acts on his own—"one who raises questions"; such questions as a lesser spirit would prudently let pass.

✦　✦　✦

We note in the author (as well in Abraham, speaking for the social conscience of the time) a quite vivid sense of justice. Part of the announcement of Yahve, his stated intent, rankles. It demands a second look. Let me, Abraham, proceed to it.

An assumption is at work here, both promising and dangerous. This Abraham is no passive integer on a chessboard. He is God's friend. Which is to say, on occasion God's opponent. Abraham is responsible.

✦　✦　✦

Let us alter the chess image. Abraham stands over the board, a player who judges, weighs, then moves. And in this, be it noted, his behavior is godly. From time to time (as here), Abraham considers the God as other than partner in the grand design. And the deity in no wise reproves the altogether new role of each player.

✦　✦　✦

18:22 Extraordinary. The two angelic "men" have gone ahead to investigate the wicked cities. The text, laconic, understated, prepares us. Abraham is "face to face with Yahve."

Is this the God to see Whom is to die? Rarely so detailed are bodily gestures. A human stands vis-à-vis the Divine. Abraham dares greatly; he "draws nearer to the Lord."

And the merchant of mercy undertakes a holy bargaining. Thus, let us push hard, let us see what number of hypothetical just ones would cancel the threatened judgment against Sodom.

Abraham grows passionate; it is as though he were judging the judge:

> ". . . Shall
> the judge
>
> of all
> the earth
>
> not
> render
> justice?"

He is a wonderfully canny, plausible, nervy bargainer. If fifty just ones can be found, will the number suffice, will tenderness rise like a leaven and the cities be spared?

Is Abraham himself dubious of fifty being found? How then forty-five? Abraham presses hard. And Yahve yields and yields before the importunity of this life-and-death pleader. Forty, thirty, twenty—ten just?

No longer a chess game. The numbers go down and down, a game of pins and a skilled bowler.

End of episode. We are not told. But the implication is shortly made clear. Ten are not found. The judgment stands—devastation.

✦ ✦ ✦

19 Meantime, the two angelic ones arrive in Sodom and are met at the gate by Lot, who offers them hospitality. They enter his house and are amply entertained.

Then late at night, ugliness erupts. The men of Sodom—all males of the city, young and old, it is stressed—clot at the door. Their demand: deliver your guests to us.

Wickedness up close. Do the angels require more evidence than this, the lascivious outcry of spoliators ringing on the air?

Lot is at wits' end. Are his guests to be seized from under his roof and raped—these two angelic men or human angels?

Bravely he stands in the portal and makes a proffer. A monstrous substitution; let them have his own daughters.

Women; and the angels indoors are so to speak, male. Male and more; they are guests. The bonds are doubly woven, and irrefragable. Hands off the men, let the women pay!

✦ ✦ ✦

The scene is like an old icon. At a foreshortened portal, Lot pleads with the noisome intruders. All in vain.

Then, a salutary interruption. Help nears, through hands that must be accounted more than human. Fourfold, the hands reach out from within the house, pull Lot to safety, slam the door. And the besotted hedonites are momentarily struck blind.

Then the angels seize the moment. All is up with Sodom. A command rings out. Flee the city, it is doomed!

And forebear looking back! They obey, this little band of survivors.

The sky of dawn is a crimson glare of retribution. The scene is reminiscent of the fall of Troy and the escape of hero Aeneas, bearing his aged father from the burning city.

Thus the excesses of the Canaanites are reproved in fire.

✦   ✦   ✦

(Thus too, coals of a fiery text burn on, purportedly offering comfort to those who would make of the episode a condemnation of homosexuals.)

(But enough said.)

✦   ✦   ✦

Among the refugees, not everyone escapes. One turns and looks back. She is unnamed: "Lot's wife."

The woman is transformed on the spot, to a pillar of salt. An anonymous woman becomes on the instant—what? A column of marmoreal, solidified bitterness?

From a woman—to a warning, it is implied. A stele is raised in punishment. Backward looks inhibit, stall, impede the pilgrimage.

How cruel.

> Wisdom
> delivered
> the just man
>
> from among
> the wicked
>
> who
> were being
> destroyed,
>
> when he fled
> as fire descended
> upon the five cities—
>
> where,
> in testimony
> to wickedness,
>
> there yet remain
> these;
>
> a
> smoking desert,

plants
bearing fruit

that never
ripens,

and
the tomb

of a
disbelieving soul,

a
standing
pillar

of
salt. (Wis 10:6–7)

✦   ✦   ✦

What to make of the ending—the saline column, the bizarre fate of the hero's spouse? How, one asks in dismay, could she not look back, not grieve for the loss of her home—she who for all we know, was also just, equal in virtue to her husband?

She is turned to salt, an ambiguous metamorphosis.

Let us not prematurely despair. The Bible is as ambiguous about salt as about women. Salt and women; there are virtues, compensations, completions, moments, years, lifetimes—of the one as of the other—that bring a hardly bearable world to its senses, that make sense of a world long gone in madness, that relieve savorless food on the tongue, in the nostrils.

Our (at times) awful Bible reminds us of the virtues of the tangy element, which among nomads and settlers alike, preserved foods. Which sealed friendship with a symbolic sprinkling:

. . . It is
a covenant
of salt

forever
before God,

unto
you

and
your seed
with
you. (Num 18:19)

✦   ✦   ✦

And, in the Christian testament, believers are urged to speak with persuasive eloquence:

Let
your speech

always be
gracious,

seasoned
with salt,

so that
you may know

how
you ought

to
answer
everyone. (Col 4:6)

✦   ✦   ✦

Matthew's gospel identifies disciples themselves as—salt; their preaching
and example add savor to a doughy mass.

Or a warning too, their preaching and behavior may be at odds:

"You
are the salt
of the earth;

but
if the salt
has lost savor,

how shall saltness
be restored?

It is no longer
good for anything

except
to be thrown out

and
trodden
underfoot." (Matt 5:13)

Thus the image of "woman-turned-to-salt" turns and turns about in the ear, on the tongue, in mind and heart—and mostly to her praise and credit.

> Blessed are they who are "worth their salt,"
> who are pillars of strength and integrity,
> who shore up our world.
>
> Blessed are the "salt of the earth,"
> who carry on,
> who follow through,
> who go the extra mile.
>
> Blessed are the "pillars of salt,"
> who take a stand,
> who are signs of life amid desolation,
> who "look back" in order to understand.
>
> Bless are they who "pass the salt"
> of human tears and sweat,
> who are bonded with the despairing,
> who shoulder the oppression in our midst.
>
> And blessed are You who season with salt,
> God of all occasions,
> who lend our insipid days
> new hope, new perspective.
>
> Blessed are You;
> throw salt on our doubts and our demons.
>
> May the covenant of salty friendship
> endure.
>
> (Elizabeth McAlister)

✦   ✦   ✦

19:30–38 The Moabites and Ammonites enter the text. In the books of Samuel, we shall encounter those fierce, perennial enemies of the Israelites. Here, short and ugly shrift is made of their beginnings. Enough said of an incestuous clan, is the heavy implication.

✦ ✦ ✦

20 This chapter is a curious retelling of the story of Abraham and Sara in Egypt. The coloration, we are told, is Eloist.

Why the tale twice-told? According to this version the king, unlike the pharaoh, forgoes abuse of Sara. Further, the deception of Abraham is reduced to a simple "mental reservation."

Moreover, the deity, a vigilant overseer of morality, intervenes only in a dream. He parts the curtain, and enters the sleep of king Abimelech.

The God's opening salvo is a priggishly moralistic charge, and a threat:

"You are going to die because of the woman you have seized, for she is married." (20:3)

The king protests. Is it the God's intention to kill the innocent? He has done no wrong, in no wise has he harmed the woman. Besides, was he not told by both Sara and Abraham that they were sister and brother!

Now the God must step back from his thunderations. Why, he booms, he knew all along that the king acted in good conscience! And more, it was himself, the God, who kept the king from overstepping, from bedding with Sara. So there!

The king comes awake, much shaken. As who would not be? He confronts Abraham. Why have you so deceived me?

The "prophet" (so named by his God—hardly by us) also resembles the deity. Abraham savors a sour delight in his moral superiority:

"I knew there was no fear of God in this place, that they
would kill me because of my wife." (20:11)

Quite a judgment against the king—who despite heavy provocation, holds himself equable. Simply, he dismisses the duet, giving them rich gifts and free rein in his realm.

✦ ✦ ✦

In the episode the high drama of the "Yahviste" style is reduced, alas, to drab.

It seems helpful to recall once more; we are scanning a text composed far later than the event. Set down by Jerusalem priests, those paragons and protectors of imperial rectitude. Their God must indubitably be shown as godly. Which is to imply—and this early on, and startlingly, in the imperial Decalogue—sexual morality is accorded pride of place.

Dare we add, the morality of war is accorded no pride of place?

Another curious caveat. In this tradition, let us admit of no anthropomorphisms, nothing of that companionable, all-but-corporeal deity, walking with, eating with, conversing face-to-face with mortals!

Here the transcendent makes itself known; but the deity is a mere apparition, a wisp of his formerly robust self, a murmur within a dream.

Not to miss the irony; the God and his "prophet" are shown as less human, so to speak, than Abimelech. And this, even while the deity and his obeisant favorite proclaim a moral superiority beyond the scope of a mere foreigner, king though he be.

✦ ✦ ✦

21 Literally, God "visited" Sara. A near-sexual image?

The child is born, and named Isaac—"that God may smile," or "may God favor." Indeed the whole of creation smiles. And Sara speaks,

"God
gave me

cause
for laughter;

all
who learn
of this

will smile
also"

(or perhaps,)

"all
will
mock
me." (21:6)

No uncertainty surrounds the joy of the aged mother, her youth wonderfully renewed. She breaks in spontaneous song:

"Who

could imagine,
who declare—

'Abraham,
your Sara

will yet
suckle!'

Lo,
old man

though
he be—

a son,
a son

I
hold

to
his
gaze!" (21:7)

✦　✦　✦

21:8　Alas, every paradisaical moment passes. In the patriarchal tent, conturbations again combust. Sara is now a mother; her gaze rests with a feline intensity on the newborn infant. Her son, a miracle!

And shall the child of another cast a shadow over this perfect hour?

Isaac is weaned; a feast is set, the guests are met. And Sara's cup of joy brims—almost. "That woman" has crept back from the wilderness, along with her child Ishmael. Must Sara bear with the presence of these interlopers? The prospect is intolerable.

The prior episode still rankles; Sara, childless and barren, and Hagar the abundant, daring to mock her.

Sara had thought herself rid of the trespasser, once for all. But no, there she stands wreathed in smiles—and her little bastard at play with darling Isaac. In the eyes of guests, are the two children to be thought equals?

We have heard of the expulsion; here, cruel details are added. To her lord and master, Sara issues an abrupt command—Rid us of them!

And the God intervenes. Ignoring Sara, speaking as though male-to-male, he whispers advice in the patriarchal ear. His words are sage, worldly, male, compromising; do as your tigerish spouse asks. In effect, the bloodline must be kept pure, Isaachian.

Meantime, no worry, I know that Ishmael is of your loins; his descendants shall prosper also. Send the mother and child away.

✦ ✦ ✦

One ponders it, this deity turned merciless, his panderings. In what can the presence of a servant and her little son offend great Abraham, as well as the greater one above, and their male mutualities and interests?

Thus the second telling. Abraham is nothing if not obedient—even when obedience mimes divine cruelties. He prepares a cache of bread and water and dismisses the mother and child.

In a desert place they languish, near to perishing. The child cries aloud in hunger and thirst. And the God hears, as befits (the name Ishmael—"God hears"). The deity as it were, repents himself. From heaven he provides well water.

And more—he issues a promise, a minor one indeed. These two lesser beings, along with the greater, Abraham and Sara, will be progenitors of a "great people."

✦ ✦ ✦

A difficult story, this. And twice-told, underscored for our attention, as the two hapless beings wander in a desert place.

And a question. Has Abraham, in starting the great motor of history, also conjured a god in his own image? In what does the scenario of the God differ from the ego and urge of the patriarch?

First an instruction. Cast Hagar forth, but let her and her son not perish. Let them almost perish. Then an intervention—of sorts. Let it be known beyond doubt or recourse, that the woman and her son remain outsiders. Let the son grow up in the wilderness; let him marry one like himself, like his mother—a lesser being, an Egyptian.

✦ ✦ ✦

Our brows furrow as to the deific intention, contriving as he does a parlous circumstance, an "almost," an "all but." Thusly, the deity draws a boundary in dust. Some shall stand inside, others be elbowed out, classic outsiders.

The mirror image again. Cruelty creates cruel contrasts; these hapless castaways—and the chosen few, secure and warm in the yurt of Abraham. And with which of these are we invited to stand?

✦   ✦   ✦

Paul, for his part, allegorizes the story, creating as is his wont a notable midrash (Gal 4:29–30).

Abraham, the two women, the two sons, each emerge as a figure of "something to come." The women are images of covenant—Hagar, figure of enslavement, Sara of the "Jerusalem from on high."

And, for our part, we Christians are "sprung," in the manner of Isaac, from "the Promise."

✦   ✦   ✦

Then in a nice (not to say novel) turn, Paul announces that Ishmael was the "persecutor" of Isaac and that this clash continued between their descendants.

Can this be so? Perhaps, one speculates, Sara's soul was prophetic? Did she see in the child of Hagar a possible rival, and so command the expulsion of both mother and son?

For his Christian community, Paul goes further:

". . . we are not children of a slave, but of a free woman." (Gal 4:31)

✦   ✦   ✦

But wait. The freedom of Sara seems a mere juridical matter, a specious jugglery. One wonders if she could be called free—of envy, of destructive anger, of proclivities tending to a preemptive strike against a rival.

No wonder if we Christians, with due respect to Paul, lean in sympathy toward the young mother and her child, castaways both.

Despite human and divine machinations, they live in accord with the Promise. What dignity, how noble a calling! And the vocation would seem verified, then as now, by some Jews, and some Christians, alike.

✦   ✦   ✦

21:22 King Abimelech approaches Abraham; accompanying him is his chief of armies. The encounter seems designed for a show of force, an intimidation. Hidden in a proposal; let there be a pact of peace between the local ruler and Abraham, newly arrived.

(Isaac, a tradition holds, will conclude a like treaty with the same king [Gen 26]).

Abraham plants a sacred tree, as Isaac will raise an altar. And Abraham invokes the "God of eternity," a title not found elsewhere.

chapter six

"Take your son, your only son, whom you love so much . . ."
(22:2–28:8)

22 So we come to an episode many would say epitomizes the heart (others, the heartlessness) of our book—the sacrifice of Isaac.

A unanimous opinion at least in this; the story is the most problematic in all of Genesis—if not in the entire Hebrew Bible. Over the saga of the son and father, so nearly tragic, so beyond conventional right reason, oceans of ink have been expended—in praise and fulmination both.

A brew of complexities! A test initiated by a relentless god, a blood-ridden illustration of faith, faith enduring, faith both implying and impelling a mortal crisis. Also a paean to the spirit of Abraham, his grandeur vindicated on the Mount of Testing.

Through the awesome event, Abraham takes honored place in the history of faith—at least according to some. The author of the letter to the Hebrews extols his,

> . . . confident
> trust
>
> in what
> we hope for, . . .
>
> conviction
> about
> things
>
> we
> do
>
> not
> see. (Heb 11:1)

✦   ✦   ✦

A historical reflection might prove useful here. It is speculated that the story arose, as such tales do, in a given context. Here, in a place of worship in Israel. Abraham implies much, speaking to his servants at the foot of the mountain of near-sacrifice:

> Both
> of you
>
> stay here
> with the donkey,
>
> while
> the boy
> and I
>
> go
> over yonder.
>
> We
> will worship
>
> and
> then
>
> come
> back
>
> to
> you. (22:5)

(Heartbreaking. "Or at least one of us will return.") The text implies that Abraham was confronting boldly, Canaanite practices of infanticide. In Jawism the firstborn belonged to God, beyond doubt. But the infants were not to be "sacrificed;" they were "offered," then "bought back."

✦   ✦   ✦

So Christians are told of an event, in some respects similar.

The parents of Jesus brought the Infant to the temple (Luke 2:23–24), there making "the offering of the poor" in accord with the law (Exod 13:13).

And this was no empty ritual, but a consecration of parent and child alike, to godly ways. (And to such ways, as we gratefully record, both mother and son adhered, in face even of juridical obloquy and death.)

Notably, the consecration was dramatized and verified in the "Magnificat" of the mother (Luke 1:46–55) and later, in the Sermon on the Mount, the manifesto of the Son (Luke 6:17–38).

✦ ✦ ✦

To our story, and its protagonists: God, Abraham, and Isaac. The son, as the God has often assured the parents, is the crux of the future. He is innocent and precious, beloved beyond words.

And Isaac must perish, the crux be broken in pieces.

Rarely in the Bible or in life, do paradox, irony, sheer contradiction clash so closely. It is as though the God donned the iron guise of a Canaanite deity, designing for himself a capricious, ineluctable role.

And this, as is implied, in order to unmask the idols once for all, to reveal a different god, a God of tenderness and providence.

✦ ✦ ✦

The drama includes two acts. First the command, whose dire effect is the unraveling of the Promise, embodied in Isaac. No. Sacrifice your son!

And the reversal, which on the moment restores the Promise—No, restrain your hand!

✦ ✦ ✦

22:2

> "Take
> your son,
>
> your
> only son,
>
> the
> apple
>
> of
> your
> eye,
>
> Isaac. . . ."

A literary tour de force. We cannot but recall the terms of Abram's vocation; at the start, what is to be relinquished, let go:

> "Go
> forth

from the land

of
your kinsfolk

and
from

your
father's
house. . . ." (12:1)

Here too, it is as though the God were at pains to underscore the enor-
mity of the demand, saying: I know the cost. I know you, I know the child, I
know the bond that joins you, father to son.

And I command; sever the lifeline.

✦   ✦   ✦

To see my small son
running ahead, pausing above a flower,
plucking some trifle of hedgerow
wearying, sighing, seeking my hand
unable in all his being
to give death credence,
his heart agile
to prove youth upon a ditch or stile—

to see this you must know
my heart like a kettledrum commanded
alarms and marches, shook old age
like treason from its majesty.

My heart now
drums—
I am nearer I am death

Who is child, who old? my tears
or his song?
I am sift of dust
in that Hand unmercifully blown

Love Me! his thunder never cried
Love me
my child never—

until this dawn
and under
under
this knife

(DB)

✦ ✦ ✦

The command sets Abraham's world tumbling about his head.
Early on, he was summoned to start life anew:

". . . Come

into
a land

which

I

will
show
you." (12:1)

Where, where? To a land-without-a-name, a land whose name is darkly
withheld. "I will show you." And that is all.

Now this further sacrifice, against nature, against the heart's dearest impulse. The child of the Promise is to be slain. And the future is placed in
question. No, worse; is canceled.

The past was erased at the time of summons. And now—is the future
itself denied? What meaning remains in that moment, reduced to a sweet
cheat—the present?

The new summons seals the lips, awakens awe and renders words redundant. A summons and response; faith that is pure folly, faith a stumbling
block to—faith.

Foolishness, Paul would have it; the cross. A faith that surrenders all.

✦ ✦ ✦

And what of the God? (This is the God of Abraham; the Capital Letter
stands before us in the text), a Deity of whom we make what best (or worst)
we may.

Some confess obeisance before a mystery; others, in fury, deny fealty to
a monster. To the objectors, the story unmasks one god among others, no

better, no worse than the derided, defeated idols. Blood ridden. This god eats children.

✦ ✦ ✦

In all this, we seek and are silent. What costly grace the story conveys, what near damnation of body and spirit, what light and darkness. What way it opens in the world, and what it brutally closes, what surrender of heart it prompts and what distraction of mind, what horrified flight from Moriah, mountain of calamity, mountain of the merciless One.

And mount of mercy as well. On and on, the names; mount of the mercy that need not have been—that should not have been.

✦ ✦ ✦

Caravaggio, that wayward genius, has caught the moment in his stupendous painting, "The Sacrifice of Isaac":

> The boy victim was literally overshadowed, resting almost nude on his elbow with his wrists still tied, his face reddened by the fire and swollen with weeping, his father's knife still held against him—but the worst moment had passed. . . .

> The boy's terror here was still present in his puffy sob racked face. Abraham's knife was still in place and his left hand holding Isaac's head, ready to cut the boy's throat, but the grip had slackened. The angel had caught Abraham's attention and taken Isaac out of his self absorbed misery, he was the focus of the triangle of figures isolated in the dark, the same age as Isaac. . . .

> Light fell on the angel's face and the skull and neck of Abraham interrogating him. This Abraham was the first of a long line of formidable strong featured bald pated, grey bearded patriarchs that'd run through Caravaggio's work, obsessed with the play of light on skin over bone and the ineradicable dignity of age. . . . (Peter Robb, *M: The Man Who Became Caravaggio*)

✦ ✦ ✦

Is the story to be taken seriously, as the "word of God concerning God and ourselves"? How could it slip past us easily, with no entailment, no anger welling in us, no frustration? How could not ambiguity arise in us, not affright us? How could this God, after creation and murder multiplied and flood, not prove once more a scandal?

Scandal. By what right is such a testing decreed, so inhuman a prodding of the father, so terrible a fate laid on the child, as the two climb up and up, the mountain of no return?

✦ ✦ ✦

22:7–8 They ascend together, father and son. De we dare follow, in fear and trembling, as did Kierkegaard and so many others?

Are the father and son companionable? They are not; the brow of the father is clouded with foreboding, he turns aside and weeps. The little son is doomed. Will Abraham return from this bizarre errand of "adoration," the bereft surrogate of a killer god?

And what of the boy? The story pays him small heed. We search the text for a word or a plaint. Nothing of this. Only a masterful, heartrending dialogue. The boy questions, innocent, ignorant:

> "Father."
> "Yes, my son."
> "Here are the fire and wood. But where is the sheep for the holocaust?"
> "God himself will supply the sheep for the holocaust."

Then Isaac is bound and placed atop a heap of wood.

✦ ✦ ✦

And what of memory, we ask? In time, would the child's terror be obliterated, the memory of such a father—of such a god? Or is child Isaac permanently scarred? Has the event on the mountain diminished him to a passive bystander of a life only half his own? Why does he so yield before the protagonists, those he sprang from and fathered, Abraham and Jacob?

For lesser abominations, fathers are roundly hated by sons; for less, a god is cursed for a lifetime.

✦ ✦ ✦

22:12 And what of the last ditch commutation of sentence, the relief from torment?

Relief? A hand from a cloud restrains the weapon:

"Do
not

raise
your hand

against
the child.

Do
him

no
ill. . . ."

We are stopped short. The God is as he is. After the ordeal, only this, laconic:

"I
know
now

that
you

fear
God. . . ."

✦   ✦   ✦

Useful might be this tack; the story of Abraham and Isaac and the
God—as analogy. We venture a close look upon the world today, its horrors,
its pursuit of death, its mordant despair, its wars and armed camps and
death rows and abortion dumps. Its multitudes of refugees, fleeing the firestorm of war, in Afghanistan and Congo and elsewhere.

And we summon those friends who refuse the hellish brew held to our
lips. We ponder the cost of such resistance as the Plowshares resisters have
paid, since 1980. Successive groups have poured their blood on bombs and
naval destroyers and air force bombers. Inevitably they are summoned to
trial in hostile courtrooms, are silenced, denied expert witnesses, relevant
testimony of international law, conscience, biblical faith, are heavily
charged, criminalized and speedily convicted and punished.

And the media remains torpid, mum, as does the public and the church.
At best, one hears a grudging condescending tone of "yes but. . . ." At best,

wagging of heads, the old canard dusted off—"We agree with their aims, but as to their means. . . ."

And one summons more terrible analogies—the death of the innocents in the Bush-Reagan era. Under Clinton, no relief; sanctions against Iraq and Cuba, the bombings in Kosovo, the complicity with slaughter in East Timor.

And the massive catastrophe of September 2001. The immediate, bellicose response—an all-out war against a shadowy, skilled enemy.

And through it all, the scandal, the wound unhealed, the God who allows such outrages to continue, to go unredressed. The scandalous God. The One we call on, invoke, hope in. Hope against hope.

In our lifetime, one ventures on a different ending than that of the Mount of Testing. Ours is a harsh lesson; the nonintervention of God. No last-minute substitution, no hand restraining the knife. In instances beyond count, no mitigation. No ram in place of a doomed child.

We ponder, half scandalized, half put to silence. Our gospel says it plain; for sake of God's own Son, there occurred no intervention:

> "Father,
> if
> it pleases You,
>
> take away
> this chalice
>
> from
> before Me.
>
> Only
> as Your
> will is,
>
> not
> as
>
> Mine
> is." (Luke 22:42)

Jesus, gifted (or cursed) with an eerie foreboding, calmly shifts the terms of the dilemma. Shifts our attention. To this—God so acts (or so refuses to act)—out of love. Love even of us, of our fractured, demented world, unworthy as we are of so condign a gesture:

"For
God

so loved
the world,

that
God
gave

God's
only
Son. . . ." (John 3:16)

The words point to Himself, the new Isaac. He appoints Himself as substitute, the One who gives life on behalf of the many—even on behalf of those who obsessively destroy.

And to what purpose, this noble self-donation?

". . . That
whoever

believes
in Me

may
not die,

but
may have
eternal
life."

A belief that is an outcry—"Down dog death!" Death, the death of the heart, the putrefaction we name racism, sexism, war making—these are not our destiny, not the curse that prevails.

To be sure, such forms of death are wrought of bizarre choices, pursued despite good sense and sound tradition, despite the example of saints and martyrs, despite sacrament and Gospel.

But Someone has paid up, has lived and died differently—neither victim nor executioner. Such a One has turned life around. To this degree, at least; wrong choices can be abrogated, wrongs repented. The clutch is weakened, if not broken.

An act of sublime altruism is also a proffer. He stands before us, beckoning. The response we name faith:

"God

so
loved
the
world. . . ."

By virtue of a gift, it lies in our power to become—human at last. In our power, if not in our will.

This is the gift too of the many Plowshares, including those jailed in December 1999, the Depleted Uranium Four. Let their names be recorded in honor here, a worthy commentary on our Scripture. Elizabeth Walz, Susan Crane, Stephen Kelly, S.J., Philip Berrigan. Their lives, their faith, form a palimpsest traced on the original. Rather than obliterating the Word, they heighten it.

All gratitude to them, who pay up, and dearly.

✦　✦　✦

Many rabbinic stories are spun about the famous text of the Testing. One of the most engaging:

> The Holy restrained the hand of Abraham, and appointed a ram in place of the child. But the ram, whose horns had been tangled in a thornbush, broke away and fled, entering a nearby cave. Abraham pursued the beast.
>
> The cave stretched back and back, endless. For mile upon mile, day after day, month upon month, the patriarch pursued the ram. And at long last, after many years, Abraham stood at the earth's center. Was it the last day, did he come on the ram? (Abraham Cohen, *Everyman's Talmud*)

The ram, and more—a wonder. There, in a great chamber, the heart of creation, he came on the tomb of the first man and woman, Adam and Eve.

✦　✦　✦

22:15 A second vision; probably it is granted on the mountain where "God provides." Here the Voice is all reassurance. Obedience has won the day, Isaac is safe and sound. Through him, posterity is assured:

". . . Because
you

have not
refused

your son,
your only son, . . .

through
your posterity

all nations
of earth

will find blessing,

because
you

have
obeyed

Me."

✦   ✦   ✦

On one event, one choice, all depends. Or so it is written. Abraham's behavior on the mountain is like an unwobbling pivot; he chooses aright, life
holds steady. By analogy, creation, which awaited his decision, is safe.

Until that plenary submission, rhythms, tides, seasons stood stock still,
breathless. Now the rhythms resume. Earth turns in its course, night follows
day, season follows season.

All of which suggests something concerning this God of Abraham, God
of creation, God of the mountain named "God provides." The drama on the
mountain is pivotal—to the God as well as to humans.

✦   ✦   ✦

The story is a matrix, for us Christians as well. It grows and grows; it
grows on us, it becomes a helpful illustration of a truth-to-come. Eventually,
through Christ the scene is altered. The drama of the Day of Testing is elevated above the mountain, to high heaven.

There, a new aspect of the Holy emerges from the Shekinah. We are done
with testing, with ambiguity and cruelty and a hallucinatory god. Instead,
we are party to a *commercium mirabile*, a wondrous exchange. We are shown
the God of love.

This God is a giver of gifts; no, of the Gift:

"God

so loved
the world

as
to give

an
only
Son." (John 3:16)

✦ ✦ ✦

23 Sara dies; her death occasions a transaction of moment. By way of a gravesite, Abraham secures a crucial foothold in Canaan.

The story is delightfully told. (And we sense in the hand that wields the quill, a subtle slant toward Priestly self-interest.)

In reconstructing a remote past, every detail of ancestry must dovetail nicely. No loose ends for these scribes, functionaries of empire, their names cunningly interwoven in the grand cope of Aaron!

It makes good sense; Abraham must show a delicately balanced understanding of where he stands vis-à-vis the Canaanites. He is a "resident alien," a foreigner. Let him prudently acknowledge his status; he has no right to ownership of land.

Still, let mercy be heard from. Look, the residents urge, an old man comes among us. His spouse has just breathed her last. He rises from mourning and approaches us for a favor; all said, a small favor. He seeks nothing for himself, only a gravesite for his beloved. Who would grudge him so slight a gift?

His hosts make a heartfelt proffer. Without charge, let him possess the cave he seeks, together with an adjoining field.

But wait, he is canny, this ancestor—canny as his descendants would have him be! Abraham reasons; what is freely given can as freely be taken back. Let these gracious friends be pleased then to accept a fair price for the property.

Agreed. The transaction is sealed and signed before witnesses. Abraham has gained a juridical, perpetual title.

The conclusion of the episode reads like the document itself:

"Thus the field . . . together with its cave and all the trees
within its limits, was conveyed to Abraham by purchase in
the presence of all the Hittites at the city gates." (23:20)

Signed, sealed, delivered, the first fruits of the Promise!

✦   ✦   ✦

24   The death of Abraham approaches (or it does not; according to the
next chapter, he takes yet another wife, and begets numerously with her!).

In any case, a weighty matter hangs in midair—son Isaac as yet has
taken no wife. The situation must be remedied, and forthwith. So we have a
first "type scene" in our Bible—the search for an ancestral bride.

Conventions will be observed; a messenger or the swain himself lingers
at a well, a maiden arrives, gifts are exchanged, hospitality is offered. Finally, a bargain is struck. All very formal, ceremonial.

✦   ✦   ✦

Abraham summons a servant, and closely instructs him. He must depart
for Mesopotamia, procuring a bride from among Abraham's own clan.

A crucial moment. The integrity of the errand is guaranteed by a solemn
oath; the "senior servant" is made to swear,

". . . by
the God

of heaven

and
the God

of
earth. . . ." (24:3)

A new title, and significant.

✦   ✦   ✦

The outstanding effect of Abraham's mission was to proclaim God's sovereignty over earth as well as heaven. Until
our father Abraham came, the Holy One, blessed be He,
was, as it were, only king over heaven. As it is said, "The
Lord, the God of heaven, took me from my father's house."

But since the time that our father Abraham entered the world, he made Him King over the earth also; as it is said, "I make thee swear by the Lord, the God of heaven and the God of earth. . . ."

[W]hile avoiding the suggestion that He could be located in any spot, the rabbis invented certain terms to express the divine Presence without giving support to a belief in His corporeality.

The most frequent of these terms is "Shekinah," which literally means "dwelling." It denotes the manifestation of God upon the stage of the world, although He abides in the far-away heaven.

In the same way that the sun in the sky illumines with its rays every corner of the earth, so the "Shechinah," the effulgence of God, may make its presence felt everywhere. (Abraham Cohen, *Everyman's Talmud*)

And a veritable desert idyll unfolds, charming, innocent, a story woven by genius full-blown.

The behavior of the God, we note, is unwontedly discreet. No direct "descents" from on high; only a promise of companionable providence, as the servant undertakes the quest.

Who shall be a suitable bride? How is she discovered, under what "sign"? Lovingly, the story dwells on such details. The impression is of an overflowing generosity of spirit; it is as though in the servant's footsteps a trail of wild flowers spring in full bloom. Follow then, follow the fragrance, the blossoms like stars underfoot!

The servant pauses at a well, and a beautiful young woman offers him a draught of water. And more, water for the camels. Her nuanced goodness is elevated; it becomes a grace, a "sign." She is the one.

The servant offers gifts, the maiden invites him to pass the night with her family. He accepts, she returns home in a flurry, to prepare the niceties of hospitality.

Her brother Laban dwells with her. His eye is sharp. He takes note as she enters. Did she not set off on her errand unadorned? Now—jewelry! The brother's ears prick up. Up and out he hastens, to greet the stranger, source of the glitter that has fallen to his sister!

We shall see more than once, the vein of self-interest and greed running deep in this fellow.

Laban hurries to the well, fervently urging the (affluent) stranger to his hearth.

✦ ✦ ✦

We are favored with yet another charming oral tradition. It requires, in the way of stories passed mouth to ear, much repetition. The words are like delicate morsels in the mouth, to be savored again and again.

So the servant, banqueted, and as guest fittingly ensconced, must tell once more his tale. All of it, every detail—his master, his master's wealth, his master's wife and son, the quest for a bride!

(Omitting as of no point to the occasion, the saga of the raised knife, and the childhood trauma of Isaac bound on an altar. . . .)

The sweet cheat of the fiction postulates a new audience, unfamiliar with the tale. Tell the tale once more, every jot and tittle! And conclude with a momentous proffer. Will the maid consent to accompany the servant to his master's home?

In short order, amid excitement, blushing and paling, the maid utters a word, a gesture of consent. She will go with him, will become party, possibly, to a marital union.

So it is done.

And ever so shortly (our story making of time a game of skilled concentration), she and Isaac meet. A glance, and each is dissolved in the other.

We savor the moment, the tenderness, the glances. And we may be pardoned for thinking; if ever a mortal merited fortune's smile, it is this youth. In his tender years, heaven and earth conspired to pummel him so grievously!

✦ ✦ ✦

25:1 Like son, like father. Abraham, blessed in Isaac, is blessed once again, and yet again. First, a virtuous daughter-in-law, and in succession, a sestet of newborns!

Abraham dies at age one hundred seventy-five years, full of days, honors, and descendants, an exemplary being indeed. He is elevated to an icon of beatitude: "to his bosom" virtuous descendants will be gathered.

He is buried amid universal travail, in the field bought from the Canaanites, where also was laid the body of Sara.

✦ ✦ ✦

25:19 And we take up the stories of Esau and Jacob, episodes hilarious and violent by turn, deliciously unpredictable—in sum, Yahvist in origin.

We shall never, in the entire scope of the Bible, see their like.

To start then. Rebecca, alas, is sterile. But the God intervenes. And lo! she swells like a tent in desert wind, abundant with twins.

Unborn, the two commence jostling one another. For pride of place, primogeniture? Beset with internal commotion, the mother sighs despairingly,

> ". . . If this
> be so,
>
> why
> go on
> living?" (25:22)

Pious woman, she consults with the God. Did he not in the first instance fulfill her hope to overflowing?

The deity is equal to the plea, and composes a poem on the spot, a kind of koan instinct with prophecy. Mother Rebecca will puzzle and meditate long and hard, and come perhaps to a bitter enlightenment:

> "Two
> nations
>
> lie heavy
> in you
>
> Two peoples
> break
> like a pod;
>
> One
> lords it
> over,
>
> the
> older

serves

the

younger." (25:23)

Cold comfort indeed! The implication is clear—purpose, resolve, conflict take form in the secret womb of resolve—dual purpose to be sure. The unborn twins are brothers in name only; they are destined for tragedy, for playing out once more, just short of murder, the awful drama of Cain and Abel.

✦ ✦ ✦

25:24 The future is present, the two come to birth. Esau the hairy is born first. So he inherits the birthright—for which he will care not a farthing.

And Jacob enters the world, clutching the heel of his brother. Last but hardly least born, blond, bright as a burnished coin, he will gamble everything—and win.

Give him time, he will pounce, this supplanter of his somewhat dense brother.

Each flourishes. And from the start, one senses that slight affection reigns in the breast of either. Esau becomes a great, burly ranger of the hills, a hunter. Jacob, a domestic spirit, dwells at peace in the tents.

✦ ✦ ✦

On a certain day two temperaments, warm and hot, come to a boil. Jacob, domestic as usual, prepares a stew, apparently for his own delectation. His brother enters, redolent of the hunt, ravenous. Abrupt as a desert storm, he demands a portion.

Jacob's eyes gleam; the main chance, the quid pro quo! On the moment, a challenge. Swear, give it over—the birthright—and a portion of meat is yours!

Great beast of a man, Esau falls to eating. Carelessly, between mouthfuls, he swears the treasure away.

Wily Jacob, supplanter indeed. And a saying is born—to let go a precious thing "for a mess of pottage."

✦ ✦ ✦

26 Contrasts. In his tender years, Isaac was bound like a lamb above a nest of wood, awaiting the death stroke. He comes to manhood, marries, begets. He is passive, self-absorbed, lingering at the edge of events, acted upon by forces too large for coping.

Of him we learn little, of his father and sons, a great deal. Perhaps more than we bargained for.

The present episode is all but unique. In childhood, Isaac was literally victimized. Now for an hour, he stands directly before us, at center stage, an adult. Our heart goes out to him—and this perhaps the more, since the text grants him small interest—this child so sorely used by unanswerable powers, a patriarch and his God.

Against awful odds, Isaac has come of age. But who is he?

The traditions present his life as a kind of replica of his father's.

Was he in no sense an original? Perhaps we overpsychologize. Still we are led to question—did the episode on the mountain all but break his spirit? Was not a decree issued against him, that he be removed from the earth, through an incomprehensible rite of blood?

To be sentenced to death, with no more voice or choice than a sheep or goat; what comes of this maltreatment? On such matters our text is brutally silent. It is as though the memory of grown Isaac were a tabula rasa, blocked for survival's sake.

Is his habitual mood a kind of functional despair? The surmise is left to us, the temperament of this ruminating shadow-man.

Now and again the God deigns to speak to Isaac, only to register a kind of blank-eyed praise of—his father. As though the blessings, posterity and land, were being transmitted through an automaton named Isaac. As though his existence merited neither large pause nor small praise. As though, as though. He might be a tool of the trade, useful if picked up and wielded, in view of a good to be granted—to others.

The voice from on high, its commendations or reproaches, the grand design whispered in ear, denoting dignity and affinity—these speed past him like a precise arrow. It is aimed, it whizzes by. The irony is masterful. He counts for little or nothing, he is merely useful.

The deific message to Isaac is a kind of Deuteronomic incantation of praise, praise of—others. The law, the law, Abraham, Abraham!

The juncture is forged, it closes with a clang—all praise to Abraham, who obeyed! But what the fealty of the father cost the son is hardly worth mention:

". . . blessing . . .

this
because

Abraham
obeyed
me,

keeping
my
mandate,

my
commandmennts,

my
ordinances

and
my
instructions." (26:4–5)

For the rest, we have a duplication of the wife-sister theme, first played
in the story of his parents. The beauty of Rebecca becomes a point of contention between the ruler's harem and her husband, etc. etc.

✦ ✦ ✦

26:12   And we note the first mention in the era, of the tilling of soil.
Isaac settles into farming. The farmer grows rich; his hosts (here named Phi-
listines by anachronism) grow jealous. King Abimelech summarily evicts the
interloper.

Isaac departs, but the peace is precarious. A lengthy dispute over water
rights breaks out; wells are dug and destroyed, claims and counterclaims
rage. Isaac perseveres; finally, free of challenge, he digs a viable well.

And that night, an epiphany cracks the heavens. The incantation, the
identity of the deity together with the liturgy of praise, are aimed as usual.
Beyond; at the noble dead.

Does Isaac have ears? Let them be full vessels, for praise of others. But of
quality of his own, not a word.

How does Isaac receive the paean? Is he the most altruistic of sons? (How
great was my father!) Is he secretly furious? (What outrage this God, this
father worked against me!) Has he gone dead within? (Why give a farthing?)

"... I
am

the
God

of
your father
Abraham. . . .

I
will
bless
you . . .

for
sake

of
my
servant
Abraham." (26:24)

Like a pallium or a cloak of Elias the credential is bestowed. But this
night-ridden life is cold, and the covering thin. As in a former episode, the
ancestor is very nearly all, a blaze of integrity and purpose, honored perennially.

The dead are warmed, the living left in the cold. Isaac? Let him be content, the promise is his, affectless. No favorite he. He is like a jar of clay,
sealed. Within lies the precious scroll, radiant with magnificent Promise.

He, his life, his place in the grand scheme? A vessel, no more. Precious,
precious beyond words, the scroll, the Promise.

If required, the vessel can be broken. It was nearly "required." As he
learned so long ago.

✦ ✦ ✦

Each in turn, father and son, entered Canaan and put down roots there
(Isaac literally). Each grew wealthy, encountered difficulties from those in
prior possession, each was skilled in works of mitigation. Such ideal ancestry, such oil on troubled waters!

Thus the rhythms, bracing and surprising. A generational blessing is
nicely intercalated between episodes of rumbling conflict; the dispute over
well water, the confrontation with Abimelech.

The king arrives on the scene, again with his commander in chief; beyond doubt in a show of force. But the language is unexpectedly pacific,
even more astonishing, pious.

"We have heard that Yahve is with you. . . ." (26:28)

The ploy is evident, though nicely concealed. To wit, if their god is more powerful than ours, it behooves us to move smartly and conclude a pact. Otherwise, who knows what disaster may rend the heavens?

✦ ✦ ✦

The final version of our tale, the one before us, gives pause. Why this doubling of episode, folding two into one narrative? Might it be a way of underscoring its import?

The point is undoubtedly complex; one aspect we have seen before. The story is aimed at sacralizing the ancestors, casting about them an aura of virtue. Also it aims to legitimate the Hebrew claim to Canaan, resting the claim not only on human fortune, but on divine choice. Thus we have two approving theophanies, as well as two pacts with local rulers.

Talk about a vigorous designing of worshipful ancestry!

✦ ✦ ✦

And yet, and yet. A massive history will contest the idealized one. The books of Judges and Samuel and Kings and Maccabees are bloated in bloodshed. Holy wars, just wars, wars of extermination, literally above debate or denial or second thoughts—wars, sanctioned by the God, wrested the promised land from the inhabitants.

Thus goes one claim. Every war so undertaken could be, and in fact was blessed; a holy war:

> Even wars undertaken for no other purpose than loot, or for
> no purpose at all other than the initiation of a fresh cohort
> of warriors, achieve a mythic status when fought in the
> name of the true cross, the ark of the covenant, a relic of
> the prophet, or the honor of the fatherland. (Barbara Ehren-
> reich, *Blood Rites: Origins and History of the Passions of War*)

✦ ✦ ✦

If not a holy war, still, waged by the chosen, it would at the least, be irrefutably just.

> The deeper we delve in search of these "causes," the more of
> them we discover, and each single cause or series of causes
> appears to be equally valid in itself, and equally false by its

insignificance, compared to the magnitude of the event. (Leo Tolstoy, quoted in *Blood Rites*)

✦ ✦ ✦

We humans constantly commit barbaric injury, for God and country, recognising our barbarism only from the distance of time or geography.

Furthermore, we construct and believe wildly improbable accounts of our past, attributing wisdom, power and agency to our beleagured ancestors. (Sandra Schaffer, in *The Nonviolent Activist*)

✦ ✦ ✦

26:35 One succinct verse records the shame wrought by a renegade brother on the sensibilities of Isaac and Rebecca. (Abraham, we recall, had a like concern for the purity of the bloodline.)

The Promise, above all, the Promise must be kept intact and tribal. It has taken a life of its own; at the least hint of incursive outsiders, it bristles and vibrates like an anemone.

Who endangers the Promise? Esau. He dares take foreign brides. Toil and trouble.

✦ ✦ ✦

27 We are plunged in a wonderfully artful story of deception, of collusive maternal sangfroid and sleight of hand. The theme is a puzzle—who is who? Or, will the real Jacob step forward? Pure Pirandello.

Not unexpectedly, over centuries the episode has set eminent heads whirling, eminent tongues crafting with capricious care their casuistries.

Jacob, that darling of derring-do, at whatever cost to good sense or the roaring obvious, must be rescued.

Thus, St. Jerome refers to the ruse of his favorite as a "praiseworthy lie." Thomas Aquinas excuses Jacob outright; within his rights he mimes his brother; since, for a mess of savory stew, he had already won the birthright.

St. Augustine however demurred, on purportedly deeper grounds. He jettisoned the literal sense of the story. Let us spiritualize a most unspiritual tale, contrive a holy analogy; Augustine sees in the disguised Jacob—Jesus loaded with the sins of our race (!).

The learned bishop goes further; in Jacob supplanting Esau, we have a figure of gentiles preferred over Jews (!!). Then a nice pirouette. He avers that in the episode there is "no mendacity, only mystery": *non mendacium sed mysterium.*

Thus grand Augustine, skating on thin ice, rapidly melting.

✦   ✦   ✦

In any case, to our story. Aged and dim of eye, Isaac summons his favorite—Esau. Let the hunter take to the hills, procuring game for a stew; his father would renew his strength, in view of a final blessing.

That stew again, a portentous entree!

Mother Rebecca, much like her renowned ancestor, bends an ear to the tent flap. She hears the instruction of her aged spouse, takes resolve and hurries to her beloved Jacob. Quick! Procure two choice kids from the flock! (She knows of course, the recipe for Isaac's favorite meal.)

In a trice she prepares it. Then she clothes son Jacob in the finest of Esau's garments and spreads the pelts of kids over arms and neck. So accoutered, he bears the savory dish to his father. Who reaches out tremulously to touch, and exclaims wonderingly and famously:

> ". . . The
> voice
>
> is
> of Jacob,
>
> but
> the
> hands
>
> are
> of
> Esau." (27:22)

The deception, the disguise works well. The blessing is bestowed. And a strange blessing it is:

> "Yes,
>
> the odor
> of my son
>
> is
> the fragrance
> of a field

fertile,
blessed by God.

May God
give you

dew of heaven,
fatness of field,

grain,
wine abounding!

Let
the gentiles
serve you,

the nations
pay homage!

Master
of
your brothers,

lord
of

your mother's sons—
cursed
be

who
curses you,

blessed
who
blesses!" (27:27–29)

✦ ✦ ✦

The inconsistencies are quite wonderful. The odor of a hunter strangely evokes the odor of a plowed field. And Jacob, a shepherd, is blessed as though he were a farmer.

And what matter? The warp in time is large; centuries yawn between the era of the story and the final editing.

✦ ✦ ✦

This record of beginnings reaches us tardily, manipulated to the satisfaction of scribe and king, magniloquent and glorious. A saga of the Davidic era—a capital clue—purportedly offers true beginnings.

But, but. David, then Solomon sits the throne. Blessings on blessings have come to pass. The Israelites have risen from a settler enclave to a massive superstate, an empire, prosperous and self-confident. World markets enrich a world power.

And as it goes without saying, the God stands with the chosen, from the beginning, and—for a time—irrevocably with David and Solomon.

✦   ✦   ✦

The blessing uttered by aged Isaac has only the slightest connection with the actual beginnings of a half-nomadic tribe—or with its herds. Or (as later books will testify) with its assault by fire and pillage against Canaan. None of this.

As for the blessing, who could doubt its bestowal? Is it not manifest in magnificent Solomon, in the temple and its god, the palace, the oceanic and land trade, the, the . . . the preeminence and gorgeous panoply of empire?

✦   ✦   ✦

Something magical, bold, ominous, a child's tale told by the Grimms, something even of grand Guignol, hovers about the scene of the bizarre banquet and blessing.

The words of dying Isaac are primal and final at once. They need only be uttered; they turn the vocal moment to adamant, an event-to-come. No revocation is possible, no transfer, no admission of mistake.

Or it is as though the words were incised in stone and placed apart in the Holy to await the Day.

✦   ✦   ✦

27:30–41 Then the finale; the chagrin and distemper of Esau and his father, as the hunter returns, prepares a stew, and enters the room of Isaac.

Jacob and his mother have vanished, their faces wreathed in knowing smiles.

Esau bellows like a bull under a hammer blow. Birthright and blessing, his brother has stolen both! Is there nothing left for myself?

The aged father withdraws in spirit, steeped in silence. And the rugged man of the wilderness, red as the sunset of hope, weeps like a lorn child.

Then, only this from Isaac, the lees of a blessing whose wine is stolen and spent:

"Ah,

far
from fertile earth—

your dwelling.

far
from the dew
of heaven!

You
shall live

by
the sword

and serve
your brother.

But
when

you
grow restive

you
shall throw off

his
yoke."

✦   ✦   ✦

Cold comfort, no blessing at all. Shall we name it a reversal of blessing, the cold obverse—a near curse?

Only a faint gleam of hope shows at the end; the descendants of Esau, the Edomites, one day will cast off their bondage to the descendants of Jacob.

Intolerable, this residue of a benefit stolen. Revenge rears up. The text is vivid and candid. Esau will have his hour of redress.

✦   ✦   ✦

Soon the clan must mourn the passing of father Isaac. Esau will observe the amenities attendant on a venerable death—all the while, with murder coiled in his mind.

Fraternal love, family bonds, immaculate ancestry? Our Bible forgets ideology for a while. It is inexorable; its stories sear our eyes with malice, envy, fratricide, fire, and sword.

Once more, the ominous emotions of brothers command the tale. Fealties weaken, appetite and ambition reign. *Eccolo*, the behavior of a preeminent family, the ancestors of all. The family of the Fall. And we have, at least in intent, another Cain-Abel episode of blood.

✦   ✦   ✦

Jesus will speak differently, of vocation; its invocation is "follow Me."

". . . I give you my word.

There is no one who has given up home, brothers or sisters, mother or father, children or property, for me and for the gospel, who will not receive in this present age a hundred times as many homes, brothers and sisters, mothers, children and property—and persecution besides—and in the age to come, everlasting life." (Mark 10:29–30)

There we have it, nicely spelled out, the blessing of the disciple, a blessing mightily surpassing all that Jacob could summon in favor of his sons. The earth itself, all creation, its myriad beauties and solaces, is the bequest of Christ. Creator and redeemer, He gives what is eminently His to give.

The circle of familial love is expanded; freed from the bondage of the bloodline, a new community is born, purified, and strengthened. Human variety gloried in color, gender, race, grow endearing, are embraced and celebrated.

More, many doors stand open to the disciples' need. The community gladly offers hospitality; nothing grudged, nothing lacking.

Then all unexpected, a kind of afterthought, as though the cost of discipleship were taken for granted—"and persecution besides." A dark foreboding of Christ, solidarity with His disciples in bitter outcome? In the world of the Fall, how could the truth be otherwise dealt with—and the truth tellers as well?

✦   ✦   ✦

In any case, the murderous mood of Esau is reversed and renounced. Whatever morality governs the cheated brother and sends his hand to the sword, no such vengefulness is allowed the disciple of Christ.

Quite the opposite; fidelity places the disciple squarely before the untender mercies of the Cains and Esaus of this world, their courtrooms, jails, death rows, exiles, torture chambers, gulags.

As we have witnessed in our lifetime, as many dear ones have suffered. As the mood of the nations, including our own, comes closely to resemble that of berserker Esau. In this year, 2001, of the twin towers of New York, fallen to rubble. And in an unutterably bitter hour, the lives lost.

✦ ✦ ✦

Let it be noted; the disciples too are tempted. A culture of death seeks a blessing upon its works.

Shall a blessing be granted? Something far different; an exorcism, the truth:

> American "exceptionalism" is a heresy. America is not a city set on a hill. It is not a chosen nation. It is not a new Israel destined to play a special role in God's scheme of redemption. It is not the primary agent of divine activity in the world. It is not the primary society in which American Christians are to discover their personal and communal identity. It has no hope of becoming the community of righteousness.
>
> The transfer of churchly attributes to the body politic has ceased to be quaint and touching. From the genocide of Native Americans to the incineration of Hiroshima and Nagasaki to the open veins of Central America, the myth of our exceptional virtue, backed by the blasphemy of our national divine election, has served again and again to make us tolerate the intolerable, accept the unacceptable and justify the unjustifiable.
>
> American "exceptionalism" is an ecclesiological heresy. America is not the church and cannot be described in terms appropriate to the Church. Let us begin by quietly removing the American flag from our sanctuaries where it does not belong, and from the sanctuaries of our hearts. (George Hunsinger, "Toward a New Confessing Church")

✦ ✦ ✦

27:42   And what of Rebecca, that matriarchal schemer? Witting or unwitting, she has played the wrecker. Now she must cope with the kindled hatred. The family is split. The blessing, gone awry, has turned to a curse.

Abruptly she summons her favorite. Until his brother's fury is spent, Jacob must flee the scene.

✦   ✦   ✦

27:46–28:1–8   There follows an emendation of the above. And we observe the priests, laboring to cleanse the text of embarrassing episodes. How solemn and stiff, one thinks, are these scribes, how easily scandalized!

Mitigate, modify, amend! It could not be borne that the above machinations be set down, that the central line of ancestry be portrayed as a veritable house of Atreus!

Thus the struggle of our texts, torn between a protective coloration of event and the truth of life—painful as the latter is, and brutish. (Yet on reflection, how strangely helpful is that truth!)

The priests would cleanse the text, but the chronicler is our friend; he would have the priests seen plain, omitting and correcting.

Thus we learn, through text and subtext.

✦   ✦   ✦

The priest–scribes assign a far different motive for the sudden dislocation of the family. In this version, Rebecca is obsessed with blood purity, thus her manipulations are greatly, if clumsily improved as to motive. She urges; son Jacob must depart and seek a bride among their clan—lest like his brother, he fall to a liaison with a foreign woman.

And more, to the same end; according to the priests, infamous Esau also comes to a better mind. While his brother is packed off to his mother's family, let Esau likewise go. Let him seek a spouse from his father's clan.

Thus the uneasy marriage (so to speak) of minds. The original rambunctious tale is left intact, together with the discomfited postscript of the Davidic priests. The two accounts rest side-by-side, wonderful and strange.

We make of them what we will. Perhaps we choose. Perhaps even smile.

chapter seven

"A stairway, from Earth to Heaven . . ."
(28:10–36:8)

28:10

> When I look back I see
> I've spent my life seeing;
> Under that flat stone—what?
> why that star off kilter?
> Turn turn I intoned, and
> out of the stone there stood
> What-Not in a white garment.
>
> Jacob's ladder descended,
> the angels holding steady—
> I mounted, and I
> saw What
>
> (DB)

✦ ✦ ✦

From the conflicted to the sublime we come. In the image at hand, two traditions join, the Eloist and the Yahvist, like two rivers converging to form a greater. Each is a complex system, ecological by analogy. Each weaves in and out of a changing landscape of time.

Now the current grows urgent, a rapids, stirring, surfacing a sediment of imperial ideology. Dare one suggest that the waters reek of self-interest, plain and plenary?

✦ ✦ ✦

We have first a vision of the sacred ladder, then an epiphany of Jawe.
Throughout the ages, the vision and its image have proven arresting,

185

fruitful. The famous ladder of Jacob! Then comes the vision, renewing the promise made to Abraham—not to worry, land and progeny are yours.

✦ ✦ ✦

No matter that the expression "ladder" is etymologically troubling. The experts speak of "steps," as of a Babylonian ziggurat, or the tower of Babel "with its top in the sky" (11:4). Others prefer that we mount a "ramp" or "stairway."

Little matter. Saints, artists, mystics, Jesus himself, have seen—a ladder with rungs, and angels stepping daintily skyward and earthward. Up, down, the unworldly beings venture, busy with intercessions, perhaps whispering messages in terrestrial ears asleep.

Philo and the church fathers summon an image of Providence; angels shore up the world and mediate in heaven.

Others see the incarnate God Himself, a Bridge between heaven and earth.

✦ ✦ ✦

Jacob sleeps, his head resting on "stones from that place" (Bethel, a day's journey north of Jerusalem). And he dreams of angels, as the Elohist tradition would have him dream. And he hears a Voice—an event proper to Yahvists. Thus the epiphany honors two traditions, each set firm in heavenly-earthly commerce.

A dream, a voice; surely sleep has offered the exile an environment more sacred, more spiritually populated than the day's awakening!

Then, a momentous theophany—Jawe appears, "standing" not atop the ladder, but "beside Jacob." The deity repeats the ancient Promise. Let Jacob be reassured, he stands within the grand orbit of divine choice.

✦ ✦ ✦

I keep my eyes peeled, alert to Your nod—but
There's a balky horse in my head,
a backward jackass braying.
Only bit and bridle
will bend this two-way will Your way.
Come then, unmuddle me, master me!
Loud, clear, tell me the way to go.

(DB, *Uncommon Prayer: A Book of Psalms*)

✦ ✦ ✦

28:17   Jacob is awake, and charged with awe:

"How
wondrous

is
this place,

it
is

the
house

of
God

and
the
gate

of
heaven!"

✦   ✦   ✦

He takes in hand the rock that had served him for pillow (!), heaves it upright, a stele, and pours oil upon it.

✦   ✦   ✦

As for that celestial-terrestrial ladder. We have the word of Jesus, guaranteeing those "much greater things" promised a new disciple, Nathaniel. The "greater" incomparably surpass the "lesser thing," when the Master saw his recalcitrant apostle-to-be, "under the fig tree."
Greater?

"I

solemnly assure
you,

you
shall see
the sky opened

and
the angels
of God

ascending
and
descending

on
the
Human
One." (John 1:51)

Does Christ himself hold the ladder steady? Or does the image suggest
rather the Human One as the ground on which the ladder rests, the cosmic
Christ, the One "through Whom, with Whom, in Whom" the "wondrous exchange" between heaven and earth continues?

In any case, as His end approaches, Jesus identifies Himself, with assurance and lucidity:

"I
am

the way,
the truth

and
the life.

No one
comes

to
the Father

but through Me.

If
you really

knew
Me,

you would know
my Father also. . . .

Whoever
has

seen
Me,

has
seen
the
Father." (John 14:6–7)

Thus He takes to himself the sublime activity of the "angels of the lad-der." He is—way, truth, life, the One and Only. Intimacy with the Father and advocating on our behalf; behold the dynamics of Incarnation.

✦ ✦ ✦

The vision of the angelic ladder fades with the dawn, the Voice is heard no more. And Jacob is heavy with second thoughts. Were the dream and the Voice true, or were they figments of desire?

It was prudent to lay a test upon these events, in form of a vow.

A vow, but with stipulations appended. If, if, if! If I be kept safe on the road, if food and clothing be provided. Then this God of my ancestors, of Abraham and Isaac, will be my God.

A man of quid pro quo, of fierce independence and no dead tribal as-sumptions invoked—as though a merely inherited deity would do.

Still one must admit, in despite of the vision and voice, the faith of Jacob is partial, still in formation. He lacks unconditional trust; his vow is hardly to be compared with the faith of Job: "even though He kill me, yet will I trust in Him."

✦ ✦ ✦

At last, it is as though the grand future were close at hand. Lo, in the event at Bethel we have the solemn start of a tradition. A simple stone will one day become a cornerstone, and more—it will be elevated to "the house of God," a stupendous sanctuary. Pilgrimages will be undertaken, pilgrims (the first of whom must be accounted Jacob himself) will set out from afar.

Grand Bethel! The tradition goes back and back, to the beginning. Abra-ham we are told, built an altar there (Gen 12:8, Gen 13:3). In years to come,

Bethel will be a center of assembly for all Israel, a glory reflecting ancient cultic renown (Judg 20:18). Samuel will hold court there (1 Sam 7:16).

Bethel will also be a formidable center of prophetic activity (1 Kings 13), a setting too of political conflict. There in time, forbidden worship will be assailed by a "man of God," challenging the incursion of Jeroboam in the sanctuary.

Toil and trouble! The holy place will reflect the religious turmoil of the era of Hosea (Hos 4:15, Hos 5:8, Hos 10:5) and Amos (Amos 3:14, Amos 4:4, Amos 5:5), both of whom railed against the images set up in the sanctuary.

Bethel, in sum, famous and infamous both. Of the place yet another terrifying episode is recounted. Prophet Amos will be ejected from the "royal sanctuary" by the high priest Amaziah (Amos 7:10). And the holy countryman will in no wise be set back by the insult. He will pronounce a terrible sentence against the false shepherd; will wash hands of the place and return to his country tasks.

✦   ✦   ✦

The sanctuary will even survive the building of the grand temple of Jerusalem by Solomon (1 Kings 12:29).

But worse and worse befalls; Jeroboam contrives a calf of gold and sets it up in the holy place. His intent, it would seem, was political, a show of power against the centralizing edicts issued from Jerusalem. In effect, the image is designed to draw worshippers from the surrounding areas to their own temple, abandoning the pilgrimage to the royal city.

So the image of the calf could not be accounted idolatrous in the strict sense. Still, a danger lurked. The image could not but recall similar forms, the idol of the desert years, the gods of Egypt. Thus the door might well be opened to idolatrous assimilation.

✦   ✦   ✦

Finally, a doomsday arrived. Under the reform of Josiah (2 Kings 23:15), the notorious sanctuary was stigmatized as a setting for idolatry. It must be pulled down, the walls toppled, reduced to a rubble.

But to prophetic eyes, evil would outlast the foundations. Jeremiah harped on the shame of Israel, stemming from the idols of Bethel.

✦   ✦   ✦

29 Meantime Jacob's journey continues, into "the land of the sons of the East." There a lovely pastoral scene opens, an echo (rather deliberate, one thinks) of the courting and marriage of father Isaac.

We have visited the setting before, a noble stereotype, a romantic interlude—a well, that precious resource to shepherd and flock.

Shortly, if all proceeds according to form, a beautiful maiden will arrive. First though, suspense—a band of shepherds approaches. Jacob introduces himself. Yes, they know Laban, and lo! a happy chance, here comes his daughter Rachel, leading her father's flock to water!

This time, it is not the maiden who offers help; it is Jacob himself. "Who shall roll away the stone?"—the stone which covered the well's mouth—"for it was very great."

We are attuned to the drill, and its implication. Jacob, that behemoth of a man, somewhat wooly-pated, expends years of his life coping with near impossible tasks, burdens, reverses.

Are they to have water for flocks and shepherds? Many shoulders must bend to the hundredweight and heave it aside.

Not to fear, in those days there were giants upon the earth. A simple moment, and crucial; the formidable obstacle, and the alternative as brute strength is invoked and strides forward.

Jacob gathers force, breathes deep and heaves the great inert weight, up and aside. It is as though the rock were of papier-mâché.

The maiden's eyes, we may well imagine, widen to saucers.

Masterfully, the story conveys nuances of character. Jacob is a concentrate of headlong vitality. Five actions tumble one upon the other. He "saw Rachel . . . rolled the stone away . . . watered the sheep . . . kissed Rachel . . . and burst into tears." A watery episode in sum; white water, a rapids all of churning love.

And climactic, charmingly Dickensian; on the instant, strangers become lovers. Jacob, that great child, is dissolved in tears. And Rachel, beribboned and blushing, hastens prettily away over hill and dale, to inform papa of the arrival of a dear relative.

Laban hurries to the well; a redundance of embraces all around, and Jacob is led home in triumph. There he unburdens himself of his tale of woe. Relations with brother Esau have grown incendiary, the paternal domicile is fraught with danger, he has been forced to make himself scarce.

Laban listens, agape. He fairly rolls his eyes, scandalized. That such things go on! And against you forsooth, my own flesh and blood!

So Jacob abides with his new found relatives an entire month.

And a suspicion arises. The prolonged hospitality is neither spontaneous nor gratuitous; a ploy rather of alert Laban, eye fastened to the main chance.

He loses no time in arranging a vis-à-vis with his nephew. Tactic; an oily assumption, followed by a loaded question.

Somewhat along these lines:

"Why, your being my relative hardly obliges you to work for me without pay. Perish the thought! What then would you think a fair salary?"

"Salary? I seek the hand of your daughter Rachel."

Not, be it noted, sister Leah, "she of the sloe eyes." But Rachel too has her points—she is "well formed and beautiful."

And Jacob enters his uncle's service, a shepherd without pay, for seven years.

Long years? They pass like a few days, we are told, servant Jacob being wound about in a silken thrall of love.

The end of indenturehood nearing, he approaches his uncle—"Now, my bride!" So a banquet is laid, fitly to celebrate. And afterward a virgin, closely veiled, is led to the marriage bed.

And lo, in cruel morning light, the bedded bride is revealed—Leah, not Rachel!

All in a lather of frustration and foiled desire, Jacob hastens to his adroit uncle. How can you do this to me?

The tongue of father Laban fairly drips with oil of vindication. Are you not aware that Rachel is the younger sister? It is not our custom (implied: you, a new arrival, can scarcely know our ways . . .) to give the younger in marriage in advance of the older!

Shall it be clear now, that Laban has benefited from the tale of Jacob and his deception against Esau? For every tit a tat. Brother defrauded brother, as Jacob has admitted; why then should not uncle similarly deal the cards to nephew?

Laban's eyes narrow, this merchant of megrims. He will strike a second bargain. First, (another) seven years tending the flocks, after which Rachel will be yours.

Meantime, in excess of beneficence, Leah is also yours.

Women, to put the matter simply, are bargain chips in a male game. And this is quite taken for granted.

In any case, the God of fecundities stirs the pot, biologically speaking. A ménage forms thusly; one male, serving maids, wives—Jacob–Leah–Rachel–Bilha–Zilpa—surely one must add all those eponymous maternity figures!

And our heads spin, as a very blizzard of male offspring tumbles into the world; six sons by Leah, two by Rachel, two by each of the servants. Twelve in sum, that magical number signifying the tribes to come. And lo, as the Davidic scribes would have us know, Jacob is neatly installed as progenitor, the ancestry of the tribes is legitimated—and more, it is nicely spoken for!

✦ ✦ ✦

30:25–43 Does the last word here, and the last laugh as well, belong to Laban the wily? After all, he has weaned from poor Jacob an outrageous fourteen years of indentured servanthood.

But wait, another tit for tat. Wily uncle is about to be bested by wilier nephew. A new contract is discussed. Jacob asks no money. Only let him choose from among the goats and sheep, a number to augment his own flocks.

The episode is anciently borrowed, we are told. Possibly it arose among a seminomadic people, skilled in animal husbandry, but credulous as to the effect of visual objects on breeding animals. Thus Jacob's stipulation—give me only those of unusual coloration.

All of which is set down in circumlocutory style. (The story is insolubly obscure.)

In any case Laban agrees to the terms. And immediately he takes steps to insure that Jacob be allowed no wage, even in kind. Craftily he removes from the flocks all sheep and goats bearing unusual stripes or colors. These he secretly gives over to his own sons, then hustles offstage, "three days' journey from Jacob."

Jacob is not at all set back. Breeding time, and he insures (who knows how?) that the most vigorous sheep and goats bear offspring of unusual coloration. According to the contract, these belong to him.

Thus he prospers, in servants, camels, and asses; and now in the quality and number of his flocks. Clever Jacob!

✦ ✦ ✦

31 Reflection offers light on literary form. The preceding chapter could be taken as no more than a series of ruminations from the pen of an attentive pagan, a story grounded in simple greed and conflict of interest.

A pagan tale, no god talk? Such will never do. Corrections are called for. A deus ex machina must be engineered. The text is an imperial composition, and empires are scrupulous as to a nice religious overlay.

Hence a palimpsest is laid on, a series of unexpected, rather intrusive pieties. Jacob summons his wives, to tell in some detail how he was defrauded. He ends with the proposal that they shake the Labanese dust from their sandals.

Has integrity vanished from the episode? It would seem so. But this will never do. Let us lay on, with a broad brush, a thick layer of pieties.

In support of his reconnaissance, Jacob is led to invoke the deity no less than five times. And in a dream—a sharp turn, for who but the dreamer is to know the dream?—the God assures and reassures him grandly. To wit; the God has witnessed the cheating of Laban and the unfailing uprightness of Jacob.

More, the ineffable visitant is announced as the God of Bethel, where, as the vision recalls, Jacob dutifully raised a stele in the divine honor.

One thinks; this wily forebear doth protest too much. Though, as would seem, not too much for godly ears.

Nonetheless, a crucial question hangs on the air. Will the wives stand firm, taking the part of Jacob? Will they dare go counter to their father, and depart with their spouse?

They will, with a vengeance. The women are at one. They have endured enough, and more than enough, of this crafty parent. Why, in his eyes they rank no higher than strangers; he has sold them for gain, and stolen their dowries. Twice, echoing their pious husband, the women invoke the God who, unwittingly it seems, has "given riches to our parent"—riches which in justice "belong to us and our children."

The consequence? Jacob is free to do "as God wills."

✦　✦　✦

The part played by the deity in these events is extremely puzzling. He intervenes—or he does not, apparently at whim—with a bias in favor of Jacob and his interests.

Still, what of the fourteen years of demeaning service, what of the wives and servants enlisted in the prospering of the bloodline? And what to make of a complicated rigmarole, to all appearances aimed at a coherent, persuasive, impeccably virtuous account of the ancestry of the famous twelve tribes?

Our heads spin. Under the rubric of "Word of God," we are exposed to the unseemly scheming of the chief protagonist and his mother, followed by the even more unseemly greed of uncle Laban. And then the countermoves of artfully dodging Jacob.

Perhaps the Word of God would have us know this—the Bible, when required, is fiercely anticultural. Let the priests cleanse and conceal as best they may. The Word goes counter. Truth told (and the truth shall be told, pace the priests)—much in our ancestry is fetid and sinful.

Thus the Word would have us beware the idolatries proposed, whether in the time of David or of Christ—or of today. Would have us reject a culture of myth and fantasy, greed and violence, together with its weighty assumption of virtuous ancestry.

We have seen it before, this clutching at an immaculate and impregnable heritage, whether in favor of religion or of bloodline.

And we all but hear a door slammed shut. A Truthteller stands there. He scorns the ironclad, self-justifying claim:

> They
> retorted,
>
> "Our father
> is Abraham."
>
> Jesus
> told them,
>
> "if
> you
> were Abraham's children,
>
> you
> would be following
> Abraham's example.
>
> The fact is,
> you are trying
> to kill me,
> a man
> who has told you
> the truth
>
> which I
> have heard
> from God.
>
> Abraham
> did
>
> nothing
> like
> that. . . ." (John 8:39–40)

✦   ✦   ✦

The door slams indeed. The percussion is all but final.

Perhaps a more apt image would be—a trap door springs, and a hanged body falls. The claim, unexorcised, deadly, leads to murder.

Someone must die:

> "I
> realize
>
> you
> are
> of Abraham's stock.
>
> Nonetheless
> you are trying
> to kill me
>
> because
> my Word
>
> finds no
> hearing
>
> among
> you." (John 8:37)

✦ ✦ ✦

31:17–21   The priests of our text will have their day, and their say. It is humorous—though a smile, slightly derisive, would win only a frown from set faces.

These scribes of empire value good order—a precise accounting of material goods. The original verse is simpler, expressing the relative indifference of a nomadic people toward riches. Thus,

> "Jacob proceeded to put his wives and children on camels, to go to . . ."

But no, this will hardly do for the imperialists; they must interject,

> ". . . together with all his livestock and all the property . . ."

And Rachel improves the occasion, whether in rancor or for gain, we are not told. Perhaps a bit of both? She strips her father's house of its domestic idols. She too has been cheated, and is red with resentment.

Shall we suggest here, an early example of "occult compensation"? Delicious. (And we shall hear more of these images, and their larceny from the paternal roof.)

Laban meantime learns of the flight, and resolves to pursue the refugees.

But wait. The God, swift on the scent of danger to his own, works another epiphany (this seems extraordinary, and probably was thought so by the scribes). This time the deity appears to—Laban.

The message is ominous, fraught with warning:

"... Keep close watch of your behavior; you are under observation."
(31:24)

Not at all (or only slightly) daunted by the ominous visitation, Laban speeds on toward the Jacobean entourage.

How describe the demeanor of this chameleon? He is candor incarnate; he wears the innocent phiz of a magisterial hypocrite. Turn and turn about, he is straightfaced, indignant, wounded, unctuous, aggressive.

How, he blurts, how could you, Jacob? How so mistreat me, sundering the double bond of father—in-law and uncle? He, Laban, has been hoodwinked, his daughters seized like a booty of war. He waxes lyrical, this Pecksniff:

"Why, had you let me know, I would have sent you off with
a merry song, to the sound of tambourines and harps!"
(31:27)

Despite the divine warning, he cannot forbear a hinted threat:

"It is in my power to do ill to all of you. . . ."

As though his narrowed eye ranged over them, Jacob, the daughters, his hands twitching with frustrated fury; if only a sword were mine, or a club. . . .

How many changes the charlatan rings! Now his tone waxes pious:

"... but last night the God of your fathers said to me, "Take care not to threaten any harm against Jacob. . . ." (31:29)

And again, as though with a sigh of resignation, giving in:

"Granted, you had to leave because you were desperately
homesick for you father's house. BUT (and on the moment,
his fury explodes) WHY DID YOU STEAL MY GODS?"

Passing strange; gods and the God. Idols scattered about his home. And then a night's warning, from another deity. And the mix quite taken for granted.

✦   ✦   ✦

Stolen your gods? Jacob, for his part, is bewildered at the charge. He blinks, he swears aloud:

"Search our effects for what is yours; the thief, once revealed, shall die!" (31:32)

How wonderfully inventive is our author!

Suspense thickens. The search is thorough—the tent of Jacob, tent of Leah, tent of the servants—no images.

Finally to the tent of Rachel. We omniscient bystanders know it—she is the thief.

What to do? She has hidden her dangerous loot in a camel cushion. As father enters glowering, on the pillow (and the images) she gracefully lowers her elegance.

Courtesy would urge that she rise. But no, she sits there. Sweetly, with delicate indirection, she hints at her condition, "a woman's period is upon me" (31:35).

A wily Rebecca *rediviva*, this Rachel! Laban rummages about and of course finds nothing.

✦   ✦   ✦

In the to–fro of winner take all, both nephew and uncle revel in bad faith, each huffing the louder his litany of unimpeachable integrity and wounded innocence.

Thus Jacob. The injured tone of an auto-panegyric is remarkable, in view of his massive thinning of the flocks of Laban.

Not a word of that. No. Grievances multiply; has he not slaved without respect or recompense, enduring in the fields fierce weathers by night and by day? And for all that, was he not bilked repeatedly of a just wage? . . . etc., etc.

Of course, the God must be invoked. And confidently. The deity has long since taken sides; witness the dream of Laban, here taken for a "judgment"—and rightly.

The histrionics are amazing. We are meant to laugh, or at least to smile. Hypocrisy, that vice of the would-be virtuous, is lathered on like a marinade, sweet and sour, loud and loutish, the dominant mode of two scoundrels.

The gap between behavior and rhetoric has seldom yawned more wonderfully wide, more penny-dreadful ominous—a long look at the soul (the soullessness rather) of the ancestors.

How skillful the author, this surgeon of motive and appetite probing "the distempered part." In Laban and Jacob and Rebecca and Rachel, in their preening and posing, scheming and web weaving, he shows us, self-revealed (and as often self-deceived)—our beginnings, ourselves.

Self-deceived in their (our) God as well? Thus early on, the deity takes his (sic) appointed role—advocate of shady causes, a projection of appetite and aggrandizement.

We shall see much of this god—and worse. Patriarchs yield the stage to imperialists, the god keeps pace (and peace) with the ambitions of a line of very Macbeths—Saul, David, Solomon, and their like.

Mirror images? The god, together with his acolytes, can hardly be accounted transcendent, or compassionate, or a healer of human ills.

For that God we must wait long and long. Until prophets arise to confront the tyrants and their idols.

✦   ✦   ✦

May one not generalize here, suggest that the "projected god" is a contrivance of us humans at every stage of history?

The patriarchs summon such a deity. So on a far grander scale, do the sponsors and founders of empire.

At the start, as in the patriarchal period of Genesis, small-bore crime rears its head—deception, cheating, self-justification, and greed. These are approved, even impelled from above. To favorites, visions are granted; to their opponents, warnings. Cruelties abound, as scapegoating humans follow the lead of a like-minded god.

The message: there must perforce be an enemy, someone must pay up.

✦   ✦   ✦

In this scheme of things the innocent are fair game. If they survive maltreatment, like Isaac they tend to repeat the low behavior they have endured. Thus wounds multiply, deceptions are refined, with an ever-renewed distemper.

Clotting and plotting, humans in pursuit of preeminence and domination, declare efforts toward community or equality—redundant, null, and void. Trust of experience yields to questionable experiment, mystery to magic.

The human rainbow, diaphanous and sumptuous at the start, fades to a twilit grey, then dissolves. Everyone is diminished, attenuated.

Either of two roles defines, even as it degrades humankind—victim or victimizer. Stuck there.

✦　✦　✦

The predicament of the tribe has been proclaimed in the Fall, dramatized in fratricide, punished in deluge.

Long after, the era of empire opens. Then, whether in silken fashion or brutal (or a mix of both), the Fall, the predicament, is institutionalized, hooped in iron. What appeared in the patriarchs—as a malaise of individuals, regrettable, sometimes humorous, even loveable—has become a "system," an "order of the day"—of every day, every year. Standing armies, brutal taxation, war, world commerce, overbearing temple and palace.

Does the litany strike a note of recognition? A horrid, demeaning "system" is imbedded in institutions, in conscience, in appetite—the engine of war, greed, pride of place—the empire. This our day.

✦　✦　✦

Dare one venture that, given time and opportunity, a kind of pharaoh sits the throne of the "holy city"? Bondage for the many, and no relief; forced labor, standing armies, tax collectors, courts and prisons, a tightly maintained class system of wealth and want.

✦　✦　✦

And what of religion? A high and mighty priesthood arises, another social claimant to reverence and wealth. The hierophants are listed in the king's scroll, half contemptuously one thinks. The king owns them. The lists acknowledge their status and the wages due; the priests are bureaucrats and clients, nothing more. In sum, religion as anodyne, priests as hirelings.

And wars—let us not omit to mention these shows of brawn, the health and wealth, all said, of the superstate. Wars aimed at possession of the land, wars of aggression, trade wars, wars for control of world markets.

The diplomacy becomes hectic. Historic enemies are stroked and welcomed as overnight allies; pacts of mutual interest with oppressive regimes proliferate.

Israel, in sum, joins the great bloodletters, Assyria and Babylon. Israeli diplomats range far and wide, even "go down to Egypt," as Isaiah rages, in quest of imperial amity.

Egypt the oppressor has come home; the enemy is us.

✦ ✦ ✦

And what to say of the god of the Kingdom of Saul, of David and his son Solomon? The projection is momentous, awesome. This deity is installed in a splendid temple in the capital of empire, is paid court in magnificent liturgies—a deity at beck and call of an earthly king, to be sure.

Religion, in fact, has become a function and tool of empire. Wars, world commerce, religion; on this tripod, the imperial throne is set in place and holds steady. For awhile.

✦ ✦ ✦

Not forever. After Solomon, ill times beget worse. Royal blood thins out. A succession of mini-kings, puny in person and enterprise, testify to the breakup of the grand Solomonic scheme. The people languish, rulers connive and are conspired against, kill and are killed.

Still, the awful era bears in its warrior's loins a noble seed, a progeny of spiritual genius, the prophets. This will be their gift—they announce for all time, a "new" God.

In that Name, that Authority, they speak in season and out, on behalf of the "poor, the widow and orphan, the stranger at the gate."

✦ ✦ ✦

It is this God of the prophets whom Jesus will both reveal and embody:

"I
and
the Father
are
One." (John 10:30)

And it must be affirmed, once for all; the God of Jesus abominates the tawdry, bloody apparatus of empire, the savage system of domination and enslavement.

No more of this! Let the realm of God flourish—on earth. Let the tyrants be toppled, the poor fed, the rich sent empty away.

✦ ✦ ✦

31:43 Back to Laban, bested for once.

Time to call a halt. Jacob has had enough of this bootless meddler.

But wait; one more try. Without further ado, Laban blathers his ownership of "everything in sight."

The claim aims to create a last-ditch crisis. But it proves no more than a show of braggadocio. Shrewd as Laban is, he knows it, and resolves quickly to curb his losses.

Why not then a pact of mutual toleration? Let geographical boundaries be set (a crucial factor, as both parties know, in preserving peace between keepers of flocks).

Laban, as might be expected, also invokes the eye of Jawe upon any violations. How persistent, verbose, shallow, "religious" is this specimen!

Jacob, for his part, has nothing to lose by the agreement—wives, children, servants, vast possessions, are safe and sound.

The worst is contained, the best may yet be. Let Jacob, let Laban, part. In peace, or a semblance of peace.

✦ ✦ ✦

32:2 Almost in passing, a beautiful verse meets our eyes. Jacob keeps encountering angels, from the famous ladder of his dream, until now. And later he will wrestle nightlong with a being both valiant and mysterious.

It is as though the author were underscoring the recurrent conflict between character and vocation. Jacob is earthbound—to possessions, self-will, family, to deception and cheating. At the same time, he is bound elsewhere, higher. Heaven will not let him be, disallows the sway of his worst instincts. Heaven continually urges upon him the dynamics of grace, of a better self.

✦ ✦ ✦

A crisis looms, perhaps the most vertiginous of his life. After twenty years, Jacob must come face to face with Esau, the brother whom he has maltreated. At long last, realization dawns on darkness. Jacob must put aside bravado and cunning, must approach his brother with open heart and hand.

To Esau he sends a series of princely gifts. The encounter is near, let the wronged brother meet a delegation loaded with favors. Wave upon wave of benefits arrive, designed to soften the hardiest resolve.

At long last can the two meet, in brotherly embrace?

✦ ✦ ✦

To his God, the supplanter offers a prayer. Pondering it, one is impelled to think—at long last, the rapscallion heart of Jacob is purified. The wording is simple, the tone tender, filial. God has impelled his return to native soil.

And more; the deity has repeated the promise uttered in favor of his father and grandfather; Jacob will be gifted with land and descendants.

The irony is tightened to the breaking point. A fierce obstacle stands in the path of the Promise, a threat all the darker for being unknown; his brother.

Esau draws nearer. Will he erupt in fury, will his face be wreathed in a smile of reconciliation?

Jacob prays. Save me, unworthy as I am, from the hand of my brother.

✦ ✦ ✦

32:22–32 The morrow will see the outcome. He arises in the night, his soul grown prophetic; he must pass the hours of testing alone.

And a mysterious being appears, hostile and invasive. Without prelude, a terrible conflict is underway. Jacob wrestles with the mysterious one. Sleepless, tormented—and now this demon or angel of darkness! He is wounded, and even the name of his adversary is withheld from him.

This mighty visitant concedes nothing!

But at length, toward dawn, Jacob wins the blessing.

✦ ✦ ✦

32:29 We are told no more than this. Only the blessing.

The night god? Now dudgeonous, now benign, perennially beyond our grasp.

But we are reminded of another, even more ominous assault upon a hero. Returning to Egypt, young Moses was attacked by the God, blindly, without known motive (Exod 4:24–26).

Was the hero seen as a rival who must be removed? Thus the god, thus the humans. Thus the god of the humans, and an obscure decree; a rival beyond bearing must be removed. By whatever means.

✦ ✦ ✦

And now, this supernal nightlong wrestling match. What is at stake, for the assailant, for Jacob?

As to the "Name," this is none of his affair, and will not be revealed. The blessing is another matter. It is no cheap grace, to be bestowed on a moral fainéant. No, the blessing has a price attached, and must be striven after.

No wile will win it. Duplicities are done with. Jacob is stripped naked of old ways, ways that have served him well in contests with those worse than himself. (Ways that, truth told, have served him ill.)

✦ ✦ ✦

The trickster is summoned to a better existence; grace will not have him stuck in place. He is like a stubbornly rooted tree, bearing a poisoned fruit; he must be pruned and pruned, and a new fruit grafted on his limbs. This is the decree of a merciless mercy.

He wins the blessing. And is left wounded, a reminder in bone and marrow—of the encounter, of that night when "all was changed, changed utterly," when "a terrible beauty was born."

✦   ✦   ✦

We have a sequence that bears pondering—the prayer, the dark night of the spirit, the struggle. And in the morning, far different, chastened, dare one say reborn—Jacob encounters his brother.

Has Esau also prayed for deliverance, has he undergone a struggle similar to his brother's?

Of this not a word. This is not his story.

✦   ✦   ✦

Still, something momentous can be inferred. The memory, the deception, the larceny of birthright—all have faded from memory. The heart of Esau too is softened.

With warmth and tears, the man of the sword greets his brother. Courtesies are observed; Esau is introduced to the women and children of the entourage.

What relief! The prayer of Jacob, the agon of spirit and body, these have won the day, the grace. Have won against odds—sour, destructive, obsessive memories.

Cain need not be the awful type, the icon of fratricide. At long last brothers reconcile, are brothers in truth.

Go, and do likewise.

✦   ✦   ✦

Jacob has embraced his brother, and been embraced. Still, for all the sea change, old wiles cling and inhibit. The two have yet to build trust. Esau urges that Jacob and himself, together with their entourage, proceed homeward together. Jacob demurs. In his heart a "Yes" speaks. Also a "But" . . . , a "Go Slow" . . .

Guile and self-interest return in a subtle tide. After the simplicity of the prayer, we must hear a time of amplified speechifying.

More is less; what contrast, what a loss! It is as though an overblown rhetorician spoke not to, but at his brother.

To wit, Jacob speaks. No, we cannot walk together, the children are frail, the ewes lambing. You go ahead then, we will follow at a more moderate pace.

Esau departs. When he is out of sight, Jacob abruptly turns about and goes the opposite way.

Our hope is halted in its tracks. The text is merciless. Mistrust, cunning, fear, tricks of the trade once more abound.

33:18–20 Jacob settles for awhile at Shechem in Canaan. The territory is rich in history. There, Joseph was buried after his sojourn in Egypt.

There too, like father Abraham, he purchases a field, his portion of the promise.

And there, Christ will sojourn awhile at the "well of Jacob" (John 4:6). And thence will arrive a Samaritan woman to draw water. She will earn His sublime discourse on the "water that fails not."

34 We have various efforts—as in the above transaction, and in the similar story of Abraham's purchase of a field—efforts to convey an expedient message. To wit; the Canaanite annexation in the age of patriarchs was—peaceable.

Still now and again, it is as though this or that page were found intolerable, were torn from the scroll, and another summarily substituted. As here; an episode of extreme violence.

The story opens innocently enough. A maiden Dinah, daughter of Jacob and Leah, ventures forth "to visit the women of her area."

(One is reminded of a scene from the film *The Virgin Spring*.) Along the way, Dinah is abducted and raped by one Shechem. Unexpectedly, the author seems sympathetic to the rapist. We are assured that he loves the girl, and seeks her hand in marriage.

Together with his father Hamor, Shechem approaches Jacob and his sons. The latter are seething with fury, that such an infamy be committed "in Israel" (surely a *lapsus linguae*, since the entity does not yet exist).

Hamor seeks a general pact with the Jacobites. Let us intermarry; thus you will put down roots here. And Shechem the son seeks only to win his beloved. Assign him if you will, a fine for his lapse. However large, it will be paid. Only give me Dinah!

Jacob's sons are in no way placated. Under apparent consent to the proposal, they contrive a proposal. A ruse. This—decree that you and all males of your clan will be circumcised like ourselves. Then we will hand over our sister and daughter, and enter this pact of intermarriage.

Hamor and Shechem return home, to persuade their people to the course proposed. Guile laces the argument: (If we consent), "would not their livestock, all the animals they have acquired, then be ours?" Sweet the uses of cunning communality!

They consent; all the males "who go out from the gates of the city" (an apparent reference to the able-bodied and warriors) line up for the rite.

✦   ✦   ✦

Meantime the avengers gather.

On the third day, while the Sechemites "are still in pain," the sons of Jacob arrive. They proceed to slaughter all the males, including Hamor and Shechem. Then they rescue their sister from Shechem's house, and vanish.

A second wave follows the first; these lay hold of the women and children, goods and chattels, and vanish.

✦   ✦   ✦

Jacob for his part is not pleased. One notes that his displeasure owes nothing to moral outrage; it is tactical. He fears enemy reprisal.

But his sons are adamant, unrepentant—no one may treat our sister like a whore, and go unavenged!

One notes too that in course of the entire episode, sordid and violent as it is, the deity keeps a discreet distance. No visions, no enticements—no reproofs either. No judgment on the slaughter.

✦   ✦   ✦

35:1 Only wait, and Jawe will enter with a flourish. He is, it seems, a great one for remembering and reminding.

Lest you, Jacob, forget, let me instruct in some detail. An altar is to be raised at Bethel to honor the God. Did he not grant you an epiphany when you were fleeing Esau?

✦   ✦   ✦

In remembrance is sanity, wholeness. Remembrance begets among other blessings, responsibility, gratitude. Through the raising of an altar, a noble mood is made permanent, generational. The stones, the rites of consecration, the yearly cycle urge—remember, be grateful!

A homily of departure therefore befits; let them cleanse the dwellings of foreign idols, handing over even the rings from their ears (apparently these bear idolatrous forms).

A "divine Terror" falls upon the surrounding towns; the departure is made without hindrance. In due time they arrive at Bethel, where Jacob constructs the altar. Later, a stele is raised and anointed and libations poured.

At least two epiphanies follow; in one, Jacob is named anew—Israel. In another, the promises made to Abraham and Isaac are verified; posterity and land shall be Jacob's.

And finally at Hebron, father Isaac dies, aged 180.

36:6–8   These priest–chroniclers and their dry, rather banal minds! They recorded the falling out of Abraham and Lot in purely economic terms.

"Hear no evil, speak no evil," their motto. They purport to know nothing (at least they choose to record nothing) of the dangerous conflict between Jacob and Esau. Nothing of that, this instead:

". . . their possessions had become too great for them to dwell together."

Which of course includes a measure of truth; great wealth tending to take possession of its possessors.

chapter eight

"Joseph dreams of greatness"
(37:1–42:5)

37–50   An astonishingly ample space, one third of our book of beginnings, is given over to the story of one patriarch—Joseph.

How comes this? Seeking a clue, one has recourse to events of exodus and subsequent history, the founding of the holy city, David and Solomon, those lightning strokes of glory.

For reasons beneficial to those who sit on the throne, it is of import to modify and amplify this saga, of Joseph the peerless.

✦   ✦   ✦

It will be recalled that our text of Genesis was edited and took final form at the time of David, or later. Markedly in the story of Joseph, we enter a form of history peculiar to an imperial era.

The record becomes highly secular; no more dreams unveil a deity present among his favorites, no more epiphanies, angels, visions.

When interventions occur, they take a highly indirect form; a claim of sorts, one thinks, set down by the chronicler and his royal patron. Through hints and whispers the deity, it is implied, favors such and such an enterprise or person.

Thus regal interests lay claim to the large history, and record it—straight-faced, dogmatic, final. They own the god who purportedly owns the story; or at least, dominates it.

And first and foremost—heavily bearing down, is the weight of imperial ideology. The shaping of the past, of its events, the advantages that accrue to a chosen (sometimes) virtuous ancestry—such is the task of these historians—indeed their primary task.

Did the patriarchs on occasion fall from grace? Undoubtedly they did. But the fall was never final; bruised but resilient, they rose and shone. Spoken for, preferred, chosen above all—this is the dominant note, the edge.

✦ ✦ ✦

The above being so, let a national myth be created, in accord with the interests of rulers and priesthood, justifying conquests and the seizure of world markets. All the while underscoring the choice from on high, as well as the perfidy of the adversary, the outsider—no matter whom.

Let his be the rule of thumb—the kings own the memories. They are free to define, shape, bend them about. And further; owning the memories, the kings mold the future.

✦ ✦ ✦

Thus the *labor limae*, the telling of the story with political correctness, requires scribes dedicated to service of temple and palace. Priests must oversee the task, as the ancestors, along with the current ruler, are duly placated, stroked, glorified.

Let the text conceal (even as it reveals to the close eye) certain details, highlighting other events and characters, for sake of national glory. Let the eye create and rest lovingly on the great beginnings, the nobility of key patriarchs.

✦ ✦ ✦

Those who own the memories, we have suggested, own the future. Continuity must govern the passing on of power and privilege. These are not merely the fruits of military victory or diplomatic skill. As implied strongly, they are forms of the blessing from on high. Again and again, through the long era of Kings, the blessing is underscored; the Promise arches like a rainbow above, in unbroken continuity. Every color in harmony and splendor! Behold, the deity hath done great things, the deity hath wrought our prospering!

✦ ✦ ✦

From the beginning, from the call of Abraham, the God singled this people out. Time and again the blessing was renewed. In adversity and breakup, even in defection and sin, it was woven into a tegument of communal hope.

And finally the blessing was incarnated in liberator and lawgiver Moses, initiating the parlous passage out of Egypt, into the era of Judges and Kings.

Thus, however indirectly, tribute is paid to a providence that with crooked lines, writes straight. And, let it be added; a providence that now and then, of crooked lives creates eventual, even unwilling, saints.

✦ ✦ ✦

To the task therefore, the collation of the great story. Grave questions must be dealt with. The ancestors have survived crisis after crisis—the Fall from grace, fratricide, a world-encompassing deluge, the scattering of the tribes, the malfeasance of the progeny of Abraham. Despite all, the blessing of land and descendants was renewed, given over even to the undeserving.

✦ ✦ ✦

Now, further questions arise, koans in a manner of speaking, for a resourceful eye and mind to puzzle over. Under what circumstance did the people of choice arrive in Egypt? And under what pretext or guile were they enslaved? And even more important, how did they eventually sunder their chains and wrest freedom from the oppressor?

Hence, a hero enters history. He creates history. His stature, his impeccable credential—this Joseph, immensely canny, endowed with ferocious ambition, wresting his stature and status from personal calamity, turning tables on his oppressors, eventually forgiving and reconciling.

The spectacular acts of liberation that follow, along with the announcement of the choice of the deity, require, if their grandeur and impact are to be grasped—these require a resounding, lengthy salvo, a blare of the shofar. No, more; a Beethovenian symphony, intricate and assured. The hero, give him ample space to rise and shine!

✦ ✦ ✦

37:2 Joseph comes on stage, in childhood. His initial deportment is, to say the least, unimpressive. He seems something of a spoiled brat, a tattletale. Regularly he bears to his father's ear ill reports against his brothers.

And, small fault of the child, foolish Jacob hears him out.

Down, down, the spiral of temperament and behavior. Jacob, we recall, was the darling of his mother and many suffered in consequence (including the favorite himself). Now Jacob inherits the malaise. To the despite of his other sons, a favoring eye rests on Joseph. No better (or worse) way, one thinks, to awaken liverish jealousies.

This favorite must also be prettied up, a little Lord Fauntleroy. So, doting father bestows on the child a coat of many colors, a garment fit for a small prince. Now he may preen and strut about and lord it over his brothers.

And their brows contract to a frown. Resentment yields to hatred outright.

✦ ✦ ✦

How many biblical episodes play out this theme of brothers, their frosty and torrid moods, their jealousies, the ambiguities that bind them close in affection and torment!

Cain and Abel became types of such ambiguous fraternities. Jacob and Esau compete from the womb. As adults, with the foolish connivance of their parents, they contrive—and break—an uneasy truce, turning murderous against one another.

Favoritism, that furnace of ambition and thwarting, brings forth flawed vessels. Thus in his last years Jacob grows fondly foolish, doting over his nestling.

✦　✦　✦

In the imperial record at hand, even dreams are secularized, psychologized, presented as little more than hunches, premonitions.

In this wise, even as a child Joseph is a great dreamer. Foolish and foppish and sure of himself, he pipes his dreams abroad. To his brothers.

One dream rankles beyond bearing. It is all of personal ascendancy.

The sentiment is laid on thick, with storied skill. Everything about Joseph is calculated to offend; his youth, the aura he wears, the child preferred, apple of a parent's eye—that and the gorgeous coat.

✦　✦　✦

37:5–11   And the innocent babbles aloud that noxious dream. It tells of sheaves of wheat, the sheaves of his brothers, how they grew animate and bowed to his own sheaves.

The message is odiously clear—they and he are no longer brothers, equals. No, he is a king, holding court. And they are subject to him, perhaps even enslaved.

Grandiose the dream, and he in no wise put down by their black looks.

Another fantasy. No mere sheaves in a wheat field now. In this dream Joseph is grandiosely himself. And the very heavens,

> ". . . the sun
> and moon
>
> and
> eleven stars,
>
> bow
> down
>
> before
> me."

The symbol "eleven"—and the eleven brothers. A remarkable, portentous dream. Spellbound he tells it, he half believes it.

✦   ✦   ✦

This it appears, even for besotted Jacob, is too much:
". . . Then I and your mother and brothers must bow before you?" (37:10)
The family reaction is complex; the brothers are further angered, the
father ponders in his heart. (Of the mother nothing is reported, she dwells in
the episode like her own ghost. By a different account she is long deceased.)

✦   ✦   ✦

We take note of the purported double source of the Joseph story, named
by scholars the "Yahvist" and "Eloist" traditions. The two are often rather
visibly stitched together, as oral traditions are finally set down; like Joseph's
coat, rich and diverse.

✦   ✦   ✦

37:21–24, 28–36   In the first of two versions, the brothers seek to kill
Joseph. But Reuben wins their consent to stop short of the crime. This,
rather—let the boy be cast in a cistern.
He will secretly return and save his brother.
Alas, a convoy of merchants aborts the plan; they come on the aban-
doned boy, draw him out, and take him along to Egypt.

✦   ✦   ✦

In **37:21–36,** a different set of details is offered. Here too the brothers
seek to kill the offensive one. But Judah demurs; he proposes rather that they
sell him as a slave, to a caravan en route to Egypt. Which is done. No great
matter the divergencies, one thinks. Either version is a horror.

✦   ✦   ✦

And let us, in a world grown ugly beyond telling, be grateful for a story
of even small mercies, two brothers who labor to mitigate a vast evil.
We linger over them, Reuben and Judah, and their stratagems. Are these
the first in the Bible to seek after a "lesser evil"? It would seem so.

✦   ✦   ✦

But why not refuse outright to have part in the crime? Would their resistance help succor Joseph? Or outnumbering the two, would the others proceed coolly with the murder?

Let us be compassionate, we omniscient bystanders. After all, we are privy to the happy outcome of a sordid affair.

Granted, the would-be saviors are no great heroes. They are more like antiheroes. The majority have contrived a vile conspiracy. And how shall a sorry duet salvage a tattered decency? Issues of life and death, innocence and guilt—how cut these neatly? Rueben and Judah would rescue something of honor, would balk at a most unnatural murder.

To our story. Blind, blind as a buried stone is aged Jacob. Could he not see how matters stood with his sons, how jealousies raged around the nimbus of his favorite?

Of this he took in nothing. So, on to a worse blunder. In sublime innocence, one day he sends the lamb to slaughter. Perhaps Joseph is bored, at home alone with his father. So, an errand—go, see how it fares with your brothers in the pasturage.

37:19   The brothers see Joseph approaching ("encroaching," do they think sourly?). And the mutter goes round, "Here comes the dreamer."

Worse then, the resolve:

> ". . . Let us kill him, and throw him onto a cistern here. We
> shall say a wild beast devoured him. Then we shall see
> what comes of his dreams!"

Ironies aplenty. Their vile act will turn about, serving to aid and abet "what comes of his dream."

Murder and its acolytes—duplicity, envy, larceny. How far across the centuries the arm of Cain reaches, what a grasp upon the throats of the fraternities of the Fall—upon fathers and sons and brothers (and in lesser measure upon mothers and daughters and sisters as well).

And, once again (sigh), how easily the bonds of the bloodline are torn to shreds!

These notes were set down in the autumn of 2001. We have endured the unthinkable, mass slaughter in downtown New York. The president is intent on a shadowy war against an adroit enemy. The American military (and the militarized leader) flexes. They are resolved on what must be accounted a continuum of carnage.

And in response, the Catholic bishops have hauled out the clanking casuistries of the "just war theory."

The pieties, the unreality of their counsels to the president, are beyond belief. Weapons of indiscriminate slaughter are put at ready—and with breathtaking illogic, the bishops urge that civilian lives not be put at risk!

To prepare the public for American losses, a public-relations blitz is underway. On the enemy and his projected losses no attention of course is expended.

Once again, the old wearisome scenario is played out to the end; hatred focuses on the demon–enemy, and his work of wickedness.

Of American works of wickedness, of the million Iraqi children, victims of a decade of American sanctions, not a word.

Few of the citizenry, none of the leaders, dare ask "why." Why this hatred of ourselves, reaching across the world, issuing in a daredevil blast of fury?

✦ ✦ ✦

The majority of Joseph's brothers are transformed to a coven of berserkers. They strip the boy of his robe, that garment of contention. Then they cast him in a dry cistern—dry, chosen by Reuben.

The task done, they sit and eat; a telling detail. Hardened hearts, a spurious normalcy? Two among them; and a gourd of milk and bread, one hopes, turns to gall on the tongue.

A caravan approaches, bound for Egypt. Seize the moment! Judah speaks up:

"Why kill our brother, and conceal his blood? Rather, let us sell him to these Ishmaelites. . . ." (37:26–27)

That blood, we are told earlier, would cry out from the earth.

✦ ✦ ✦

Deep waters, deeper blood. Sons of the Fall. Does Judah know that he hints at the word of Jawe to Cain, after the murder of Abel?

"... The blood

is

the
soul. . . ." (Deut 12:23)

And beware, cover your ears; the soul has voice.

✦ ✦ ✦

So Judah prevails, and the lesser evil. Money changes hands; Joseph is led off to bondage.

Appalled, we pause over the transaction. Predatory, ferocious, the sons of the Promise have come to this; selling their brother into slavery is accounted the lesser evil.

What the greater evil might be, is scarcely to be credited. They have come near to embracing it.

Has goodness fled the world?

✦ ✦ ✦

And no Voice from a cloud, no condemnation from on high. A moment of shameful betrayal—and the God might be thought not to exist.

In our story of beginnings, we are in a far different atmosphere than heretofore. We previously noted it—the highly secular tone, a text reeking of ascendancy, the ethos of empire.

Surely, the God signifies and is paid due tribute—there are after all, the temple and the Shekinah to be reckoned with. But the seat of decision, the setting of the drama of power, has soundlessly shifted. To the king's palace.

As for the "religious sense," such as it is, it has grown sophisticated, self-conscious, confident. The God dwells in his place, we, David, Solomon, dwell in ours. The prescribed rituals are performed with pomp and circumstance. And the chosen flourish, thank you, very much by their own wit and wisdom.

The God to be sure, wills this—our self-will.

If the deity is invoked, as he frequently is, one has a sense that the gesture is pro forma, tactical, even perfunctory.

Grammar too reflects a sea change. The address has turned indirect; the deity no longer speaks, he is spoken about, seldom if ever directly quoted. The divine-human linkage, one feels, is artificial, contrived by the royal scribe. Call it a rubric required by noblesse oblige, in no sense heartfelt, passionate—let alone disruptive of royal intent.

✦ ✦ ✦

One has only to compare these lukewarm nods in the direction of "religion" with the outbursts, spontaneous, calamitous, fiery, of a Jeremiah or an Ezekiel.

According to the scribes, our ancestral protagonists are hardly "undergoing, suffering the divine." They walk a middle road, temple- or palace-broken, meticulous as to rules, conventional, keepers of no flame. Somewhat boring.

✦ ✦ ✦

Prior to the era of Joseph, a vivid sense of the "godly" was at work. The human protagonists were constantly aware of the God, of a pressing presence—the great Interjector from on high. The deity engineered history; he instructed and issued commands and turned lives and institutions around.

Then after centuries, came the Kings. "And all, all is changed."

✦ ✦ ✦

Another point; the spirit of our story is suggestive of our own era. Of us Americans; whose deity is invoked, his (sic) blessing sought and to all appearances granted, as the military proceeds to cow Iraq or Kosovo or capture Ben Laden.

A caveat occurs. It is perhaps not expedient to go as far as obliteration; many across the world would disfavor such a move. Better, in the case of Iraq, terrorize, dislocate, and starve the enemy, allow the children and the aged to die in large numbers, reduce the country to economic slavery. And whether in the Fertile Crescent or Afghanistan, bomb, bomb the daylight into night.

With the God's approval? Consent by silence perhaps?

Or shall we take our ethical lead from Scripture? It is brothers and sisters, not strangers or enemies (the latter words forbidden) over whose bodies we vilely dicker; how much oil for how much blood?

✦ ✦ ✦

37:29 Reuben goes secretly to the cistern, seeking to draw the boy out. And he finds the well as empty of life as of water. He mourns aloud. The brothers are mum.

After the crime, the cover-up. To the boy's dazzling tunic they add another color, dipping the coat in the blood of a slaughtered goat. Let someone take the garment to father Jacob for evidence.

How skillfully told, with what care and apparent ease, as though an afterthought! The messenger is precisely that—a "someone."

Which brother shall go? Or shall it be none of them, but concealing both act and consequence—someone else, a friend or stranger?

A stroke of literary genius. The text leaves the matter uncertain.

✦ ✦ ✦

Nameless, shamed, a "someone" is dispatched on the sorry errand. (As those who contrive the errand are left nameless and shamed.)

Anonymous, the messenger bears a sorry burden, and a word from the far fields:

"Look, we have come on this. . . . See if it is not the tunic of your son." (37:32)

Not, be it noted, "the tunic of our brother." Nor "the tunic of Joseph." But "of your son." In a distancing phrase, a nameless messenger shrinks from naming names.

Joseph has become "the one we dare not name."

Anonymous, he is torn from affection, care, compassion. He is an amputation, no brother of ours. And shortly, as we know, he will be accounted nameless as the dead—a slave.

✦   ✦   ✦

The crime is done. And a veil falls. Crime (and possible consequence) demand anonymity, the absent, the former, the thrown away. Each brother is, in one way or another, complicit. It is as though they fled the text into a night of shame, a night of their own devising. No one is responsible; to their father they bear an ensanguined tunic and a message bloated with lies.

✦   ✦   ✦

The hateful stratagem! Why did they not go, each and all to their father, repenting? Did they argue among themselves, did someone propose casting lots as to who should bear the bloody robe, who utter the lie? Or would no one of them consent to undertake the errand?

Send "someone." Let the father conclude as he will. Our responsibility is other; we remain with the flocks.

Shepherds of the flocks, responsible. So the fiction, the cover-up. And what are they to their brother?

A touch worthy of Shakespearean oracles. Crime, the cloaking of crime, the distancing. Night "thickens"; the night of the lie that prevails. For a time.

✦   ✦   ✦

And Joseph, what of him?

The scene shifts. In Egypt we take up the tale, swiftly, skillfully told. The slave is passed from hand to hand, a chattel, invariably for a sum of money. Lastly, he is sold to a high official, Potiphar, courtier of Pharaoh and his chief steward.

✦   ✦   ✦

38   A shift of scene and actors.

Perhaps, as speculated by exegetes,

> . . . the sacred author inserted this independent account
> from the time of Juda . . . to mark the long hiatus during
> which Joseph's family knew nothing of his life in Egypt.
> (NAB)

And then again, perhaps not.

✦   ✦   ✦

In any case, we have what seems on the face of it a lengthy digression
from our "tales of Joseph"—an entire chapter that could well be named
"tales of Judah."

A clue. The Solomonic empire, we recall, is telling of its beginnings. Here,
with a bow to preimperial religion.

✦   ✦   ✦

The text is remarkable on several accounts. So long absent, the deity re-
enters history, summarily, as judge and executioner.

And it is a woman Tamar, daughter-in-law of Judah, who bests the great
founder of the tribe. She emerges, all unlikely, a nimble-minded hero.

Tamar risks all, even her life, to conceive a child, veiling herself as a temple prostitute. Her "prey" is none other than the great man himself. Through
a deception worthy of ancestor Rebecca, Tamar takes the sexual lead and
seduces Judah.

Then, threatened with capital punishment for harlotry, she turns the tables. Like a prophet confronting King David, she faces the father of her unborn child—"you are the man!"

A powerful recognition scene is condensed in two verses. She invites
Judah, one imagines with what scorn, to "recognize" the cord and staff, his
own, which she holds as surety.

He "recognizes" them as his own. How rare in the culture, how rare in
the Bible! Judah is forced to pay her tribute:

". . . She is more just than I. . . ."

✦   ✦   ✦

The episode has been called a diversion from the great theme of Joseph's
works and pomps. Still, there are subtle linkages; a like recognition scene
ended the previous chapter. There, we were told how Jacob "recognized" the
garment dipped in goat's blood as Joseph's own.

The initiative in the deception was Judah's. It was he who sought to mitigate the crime of his brothers, persuading them to cast Joseph in a cistern instead of killing him. And it may be inferred that he suggested the cover-up as well.

Perhaps our seemingly unrelated chapter is suggesting the point of the entire Joseph story. A kind of yin-yang of moral retribution is underway; Judah, the deceiver of his father is himself deceived, then unmasked.

And his sole credit in the disposal of his brother is his admission of no credit at all, but confusion and despair, as he returns to the well and reports to the others:

". . . The boy is gone! And I—where can I turn?" (37:30)

Thus the linkage.

✦ ✦ ✦

And more. In Judah's story there lurks a hint of things to come, as we resume the story of Joseph in Egypt.

Judah's dealing with his daughter-in-law is a tale of sexual irresponsibility, and its consequence. In contrast, Joseph will resist the blandishments of Potiphar's wife and, so resisting, will vindicate his honor.

In sum, it seems that the story of Judah is a rich variation on the story of his vastly greater brother. A literary principle is at work, and with what skill! From the lesser we are led to a larger setting and scope.

✦ ✦ ✦

39 Back to Joseph in Egypt. The authorial task is clear. Our hero must be shown untrammeled, pure, a model of every virtue. He is, after all, a close ancestor of the Davidic priests; closer than, say, his brother Judah, backsliding and shamed.

And of Joseph, shall we hear of human weakness? Nothing of the sort—at least not yet.

Strength upon strength. Enticed by the spouse of his highly placed patron, Joseph recoils. He improves the occasion moreover, offering a homily to the heated matron, reminding her of his rightful status in the household—and by implication, of her own.

Alas, the woman is relentless. Attempted seductions multiply. One day, the two being alone in the house and her advances proving hoydenish, Joseph flees.

But he leaves behind his outer garment, shed in haste.

A garment again, and evidence! First the coat of many colors, then the cord of his brother Judah. Now another proof of wrongdoing. In wicked hands, it will prove damning—to hope, to probity, to freedom itself.

✦ ✦ ✦

Up, then down, swings the pendulum of prosperity–adversity. In short order, the beldame denounces Joseph to her husband; before his furious eyes she waves the damning cloak. Potiphar, outraged, speedily consigns his fallen favorite to durance vile.

Be it noted too, the theological interjection. No less than six times, on prosperous occasion and ill, in episodes of Virtue Maintained against Vast Odds, it is stated that "the Lord was with Joseph."

Nothing of vision, epiphany, dreams, angels. We are in the hands of an omniscient scribe, at second or third remove from celestial headquarters. A kind of heavenly hearsay is in the wind—talk about talk about reinforcement from on high.

(And one is tempted to conjure up a modern equivalent of the scribe; perhaps an academic theologian? But hardly a mystic or prophet or martyr.)

✦ ✦ ✦

We are invited to admiration. What a convergence of grand gifts in a human frame! Surely Joseph is of the angelic company, among mortals a very paragon!

Only imagine, our hero has but to appear on a given scene, even a most unpromising one—here as a prisoner in custody—and lo! all bow low. Shall we say, like sheaves of wheat in a high wind?

Virtue, and more. Joseph is gifted—and presumably passes on through the bloodline to such as Saul, David, Solomon—gifted with striking good looks, "handsome in countenance and body."

Glowing phiz, splendid frame, unalloyed virtue—and alas, disgrace, lockup.

But wait. Once again failure is routed and virtue rewarded. The jailer, much in the manner of steward Potiphar, finds the panache of his prisoner irresistible. Shortly, hard and fast roles are reversed; Joseph is again, in the unlikeliest circumstance, placed in charge. The keeper hands his keys to the distinguished kept!

✦ ✦ ✦

40 The story moves apace. Our hero must not languish indefinitely. In prison, hard and close, walled and barred and locked, day follows upon dull day, a procession inducing acedia and waning interest. The attention, even of devoted advocates of the prisoner, tends to flag.

But wait, a break in routine. On a certain day, two prisoners are led to neighboring cells. The cupbearer and baker of great pharaoh have offended their liege lord—in what regard we are not told. In a hard place, with a thump they land, these two lugubrious ones, like Joseph, all said, much reduced in fortune.

✦ ✦ ✦

Dreams again. These two dream nightlong, as prisoners are wont to—dreams being a momentary escape, a distraction from the harsh realities of a world reduced to walls, bolts, bars, keepers, boredom.

We are not told whether in prison, Joseph too continued to dream. In any case, he has become a noted interpreter of dreams. Such gifts, as we shortly see, are greatly in demand in Egypt, a culture of avid soothsayers.

The new prisoners recount their dreams, seeking light from Joseph. He is quick on the code. This, in sum; the first prisoner, the cupbearer, will be restored to office and favor. But the second, the baker, will perish.

To his reassuring words to the former, Joseph appends a plea. May this lucky prisoner, once restored to freedom, even to his former honorable place, may he not forget his benefactor. Who, insists Joseph the upright, has committed no crime meriting this sorrowful plunge in fortune.

And thus matters came to pass. The outcome is cruel and arbitrary as, say, the edict of a pharaoh or Nebuchednezzar or Herod. Tyrants are much given to gestures of power, irresistible, irresponsible. In this instance, one prisoner is released, the other executed.

Bizarre—and acutely telling. Not a word concerning the delict for which the duet were jailed. And the outcome likewise—one walks free, the other perishes. Our canny storyteller knows it, and implies it; mortals are not to be made privy to the decisions of godlings!

A subtle critique of the misuse of power? The story is a mirror held to life. We rejoice for the cupbearer, we mourn the baker's doom. And we are instructed.

✦ ✦ ✦

But as to that freed prisoner, who, it is strongly implied, uttered a promise to his benefactor Joseph.

Once released, the cupbearer promptly forgot. Joseph is left high, dry, and locked in. Permanently?

✦ ✦ ✦

41   Joseph yields to no despair, though he must endure a cruel two years of confinement. And it could be more, it could be an indefinite sentence. . . .

Then an abrupt change of scene and of pace. One night, great pharaoh is invaded by a troubling dream. The palace is shaken. At dawn, the pharaoh summons his sages and magicians. To no avail; they are confounded—and he increasingly confused.

Presto! at that moment the cupbearer's memory revives. Why, two years ago a young Hebrew, a fellow prisoner, decoded brilliantly a dream of mine! Could he not help in the royal impasse?

Pharaoh is at wit's end. Let the prisoner be summoned.

Joseph, in a nice sartorial touch, shaves and arranges his costume, only then presenting himself.

This dreamer, like the prophet Daniel, is a good listener. Only in detailed recounting can the nocturnal burden of the king be lightened.

The pharaoh recounts a double set of invasive images—and for that, doubly dudgeonous. The images are vivid, shocking; they deride the logic of day. Sleek cows appear first, seven of them. Then a septenary of skinny, ravaged cows. And in a species of bovine cannibalism, the gaunt beasts proceed to consume the fat, alive.

Then a second nightmare; there appear seven ears of corn, glowing and golden in form. And after them, seven others, shriveled to cob. And the seven desiccated ears swallow the healthy.

Beyond doubt something dire is portended. Meat and corn, the staples of empire, are threatened. And the pharaoh, that emissary of the gods, undergoes a presentiment, a question that sets his bones quaking. What is the meaning of the fearsome images, what is to be done?

Our Joseph is equal to the moment; in a double sense, as will be seen. His third eye open on supersensible reality, he cracks the code.

Thus the purport. The images speak first of abundance; of seven years like seven cornucopias, of fat cows and flourishing harvests.

Then the dire images; a famine is to follow, also for seven years.

Thus certain facts of nature, sure to come in dire conjunction, must be faced.

Face them Joseph does. Strong of insight, he is also of practical bent, his skills honed in lofty service and low, from Potiphar to a chief prison warden.

Seize the moment! Responding to the warning visitation, in full flood of eloquence and will, Joseph outlines a vast project. The populace must garner the harvests of grain in the years immediately ahead, against the years of famine. (It would seem that there existed no equivalent facilities for storage, drying, pickling, or salting of meat.)

✦　✦　✦

41:37　Glory be for this portent in our midst!

In the space of an hour, an exile, a slave, a quondam prisoner, takes center stage in the empire. All glory to him, who has shown a way out of our plight!

Great pharaoh is quite beside himself with admiration; as are his courtiers, who might be heard prudently echoing the praises uttered by their lord. The Magians magnify the huzzahs, the moment belongs to Joseph!

The court is all ears, as practicalities tumble one on the other from the tongue of the neo-hero. Joseph outlines the steps to be taken, that the years of abundance may forestall famine.

Someone of vast prudence and skill, he insists, must be found and placed in charge of the national effort. Joseph is naming himself; that peerless "someone" is close at hand, as the pharaoh shortly recognizes.

✦　✦　✦

To be noted also. Without hesitation or sense of incongruity, here as on other occasions in Genesis, fealty to Jawe is placed on the lips of others than the chosen. Hence the pharaoh:

> "Shall
> we
> come
>
> on another
> such
> as this one,
>
> in
> whom
>
> dwells
> the
> spirit
>
> of
> God?"

And he turns to Joseph,

"Since
God

has
given
you

to
know

all
this . . ." (41:39)

Has sudden access of grace overwhelmed the regent, evoking the momentous confession?

Or is a far different force at work here? Shall we name it the imperial sensibility in the Davidic author(s), insisting that in the start of national history, Egypt too adopted the "true faith"? What more befitting than that the imperial deity prevail throughout the world?

Or perhaps this question arises: Is a far different aspect of the word of God commended to us—namely, that we take careful note of the drift of events as recounted here? As hinting at the common ideology and method of empire, whether Egyptian or Hebrew (or let us dare say, American)?

✦ ✦ ✦

We have suggested it before. In the Joseph story—detailed, plausible, skilled, above all polemical—the imperial method and motive are clarified. A national myth is in careful formation. Its final form will require the ethical cleansing of the ancestors, focusing on one among them, who surpasses in wisdom and ingenuity and power of improvisation all other patriarchs.

Let him appear as a kind of pre-Mosaic savior, a colossus of reconciliation. Betrayed and degraded, whether by foreigners or his own, against odds heroic acts of clairvoyance and reconciliation will turn the tables on his persecutors.

More, his story will legitimate the descent of his tribe into Egypt, will render the entrance providential—a divine presence and care to continue throughout the era of the Exodus.

✦ ✦ ✦

For the present, let there be heard frequent (though indirect) invocations of the deity, praise of Jawe issuing even from the tongue of a foreign tyrant. Thus the "true faith" is presented as irresistible in power and universal in principle.

Time will tell; why not say it plain? The deity of the chosen is the deity of Egyptians as well.

It is as though—albeit with far different intent—we were to hear the voice of an Isaiah thus early on, signaling the dead end of tribal religion, the dawn of the "God of the nations."

Still, we note a crucial contrast. Isaiah will envision (and his vision will announce) a far different deity than the god of Solomon—or for that matter, of the pharaoh. And the prophet will appeal (and plead on behalf of) a far different constituency than a claque of courtiers or imperial priests.

✦ ✦ ✦

Meantime, the time of our story—and all honor to Joseph! He is the appointed one, the savior of Egypt and in due time, of his own.

On the moment, due honors and emoluments are heaped, and fittingly. On his finger the signet ring, bossed with the imperial seal; on his person the finest linen, the collar of gold; at his behest the most splendid chariot after the pharaoh's own. And in public places let a cry of the populace be heard—"Take note who passes!"

And more, yet more, an Egyptian name, and an Egyptian bride. Truly Joseph's bejeweled cup runneth over.

✦ ✦ ✦

To the task, without delay. The imperial overseer must order wisely the years of plenty. He departs the court, to survey the land. In each city officials are appointed to oversee the local granary.

And plentiful the following seasons prove to be, the wheat "like the sands of the sea," excellent in weight and measure. Thus the years of plenty come and go.

✦ ✦ ✦

41:53–54 Eyeless, mindless, tooth and claw devour the land—the years of famine. A drought, a plague of locusts? We are told nothing; only that the threat of catastrophe, ". . . began, as Joseph had said."

From the people, a despairing clamor rises—"Give us bread!" And the pharaoh has but one reply:

"Go to Joseph, do whatever he commands!"

Joseph opens the granaries, and all are fed. And, with the merest hint of events to come:

> All the world came to Joseph to obtain rations of grain, for the famine had gripped the whole world. (41:57)

42   All roads lead to Egypt and its mysterious hero.

And another shift. We are back with the family of aged father Jacob. Lingering in Canaan, the patriarch grows exasperated with his sons. The famine has spread to their area. It worsens, he complains, and they stand "gaping about."

Let them bestir themselves, let them venture into Egypt, where, rumor has it, ample stores of grain are to be had.

The quill of the author, like the finger of God, writes crooked, writes straight. Sweetly, irresistibly, the long days' journey to reconciliation and healing is underway.

chapter nine

"I am your brother Joseph"
(42:5–50:26)

42:4   Regarding the journey into Egypt, a caveat is issued with all solemnity. Aged Jacob insists—in no circumstance is young Benjamin to accompany his brothers. No ill must come to the boy; he abides at home.

The story hurries us on. Without incident the brothers arrive in Egypt. Mingling with others seeking relief from the famine, they approach Joseph.

They see before them an Egyptian overlord, in whose hands the fate of their family rests. And he? Another recognition scene, a linkage. It holds. It is of the flesh, but it is strong as adamant:

> Joseph
> saw
>
> his
> brothers,
>
> and
> knew
> them. . . . (42:7)

Those brothers! Do hatred and love contend in his breast?

With an irony like a flash of lightning, Joseph's boyhood dream returns to him, their sheaves of grain bowing to his.

And years later, they kneel at his feet. Their quest is precisely for—grain. And the "sheaf" before which they bow is multiplied to a full granary—and more; a nation whose barns are bursting!

These are his brothers, yes—and no. They have betrayed him cruelly. Justice demands restitution, at least to a degree. He will humiliate them in the dust.

It is as though a minatory finger were laid against his lips. Quick. On the moment he contrives a strategy; a mix of severity and tenderness.

Repeat it—the recognition. And heap the irony high and higher, for the recognition is one-sided only:

>Thus
>Joseph
>
>knew
>his brothers,
>
>but
>they
>
>did
>not
>
>know
>him. (42:8)

✦ ✦ ✦

How could they know him? They do not know themselves or their crime; it is buried within, by a common despairing consent, it cannot be spoken of. Nor, in consequence, can it be exorcized.

He speaks; is it grain you seek? Nonsense, he waves the claim aside angrily:

". . . You are spies, you come to probe the weak points of our land!" (42:9)

No, no! They panic, they blurt their story, surely it will justify them! We are sons of a man of Canaan. The youngest remains at home, another of our brothers is no more. . . .

Joseph interrupts, his brows dark with thunder. Likely story! Spies they are; they stand revealed. There is but one way out. One among them must go fetch the youngest brother. The others will not depart until he is produced!

And he casts them in prison for three days.

Through their machinations, he was sold in slavery, far from home and family. Then, innocent, chained to misfortune, he was cast in prison—for two years.

✦ ✦ ✦

The sorry band is brought before him once more. The earlier decree is softened. One among them must remain in prison, for surety. The others may depart for Canaan with full sacks of grain. But the earlier order stands; they must return with their brother.

Only thus will their innocence be verified—and ominously—death avoided.

✦ ✦ ✦

42:21 Steely will, regal intransigence! They stand there, transfixed with remorse. Suddenly they are granted to see a connection that for years had lurked like a ghost in the mind, feared, unexamined, haunting.

And we ponder, and are granted to see. They see. Indeed, they confess in their hearts; we brought this misfortune on ourselves. Only remember—how the boy Joseph stood there all atremble, stripped of his garment, pleading for mercy.

Pleading with his brothers. Mercy? They were furious, turned to stone:

> ". . . Remember how treacherously we dealt with our brother Joseph. We shut our ears, we hardened our hearts against him. Rightfully then, this has befallen us."

Now, what remorse! Their hearts move to a new beat of sorrow and repentance.

Memories flare like a poked fire. Reuben's hands burn, he heaps living coals on the others:

> "Did I not urge you, don't harm the child? You would hear nothing of my plea; and now, his blood is being demanded of us!" (42:22)

And Joseph hears the entire exchange; he and they are speaking through an interpreter. He withdraws from them and weeps.

Again he enters and pronounces judgment. Simeon is seized and bound before their eyes.

✦ ✦ ✦

Departure is at hand. The sacks are filled with grain. By order of Joseph, payment for the grain is remitted. By his order as well, equivalent coins are hidden in the sacks.

Thus money clings to the story, an incubus. Years before, coins changed hands, in payment of a brother. They sold him outright. The memory scalds.

Is the covert act of prince Joseph a remission, or a reminder? Shall he repay them—and in their own coin?

Provisions are added for the journey home.

At the first night camp, one of the brothers opens a sack to feed the animals—there he finds the money. Awe seizes them all, and wonderment. Chastened, put to silence, they return to their father.

✦   ✦   ✦

We have seen it before. A charming feature of our story is the rather constant repetition, as two traditions converge in one—but hardly seamlessly. Has a given episode been recounted? No matter, we will dwell on it once more, and lovingly. We too gather about the storyteller; slowly, once again, dwell on each detail. Let the pace of event slow.

✦   ✦   ✦

43:1–10 The brothers have returned, they stand before their father; they must repeat the entire exchange between the Egyptian overseer and themselves.

They speak of the "lord of the country," and refer to "the other son." (They cannot name him "Joseph," let alone "our brother." Just as years before, overwhelming shame kept them from naming him, when they bought the deceptive coat to their father.)

In Egypt before the overlord, they explained:

> ". . . we are
> twelve brothers . . .
>
> the youngest
> is
>
> with
> our
> father. . . ." (42:13)

Then the fateful phrase that falls like a shroud, covering their crime against Joseph:

> ". . . and
> the
> other
> one
>
> is
> gone."

Now, before Jacob, they repeat the key phrase, but with a difference:

". . . one
is gone,

and
the youngest

is
at present

with
our
father. . . ." (42:32)

Their world is cleft, a gigantic disordered memory falls in two. At long last, can they name the name, can they not? Long ago, the name of their brother Joseph could not pass their lips, turned to stone.

And before "the man, the lord of the land," they do not name—Benjamin. What would that name mean to an imperial stranger?

Years after their befouled conspiracy, they cannot name their brother. Let the absent one, the dead one, remain nameless. Thus perhaps the crime is obliterated—or at least the memory becomes bearable.

Thus we too are compelled to ponder small points, implications, omissions, that in the full flood of narrative might sweep by. Attentive, be attentive!

42:36–38 The report to the father concludes on a dire note. The Egyptian vizier has put it plain:

". . . You must return with your youngest brother. Only then will I know that you are not spying out our land.

Once obeyed, and the youthful hostage before me, I will release your brother, and you may move freely about the countryside." (42:18–20)

The terms strike father Jacob like a thrust to the heart. He cries aloud:

"Must
you

234 CHAPTER 9

make me
childless?

Joseph
is gone

and Simeon
is gone

and now
you

would take
Benjamin?

Why
must

such
things

happen
to
me?"

Reuben offers a solace (of sorts):

"You
may kill

my own
two sons

if
I do not

return
Benjamin

to
you."

Hostage after hostage, one thinks, and not—"you may kill me, Reuben."
Always the young and innocent are summoned to requite the sins of the el-
ders.

The old man is adamant. His plaint pours out, grief upon grief:

"Joseph
is dead,
and you
would seize

the sole comfort
of my age.

If mishap
should overtake
Benjamin,

grief unending
would be
my portion

in
the world

to
come."

And there the matter rests—for awhile.

✦   ✦   ✦

43   The famine in Canaan is unrelenting. In time, the Egyptian grain is consumed. The Jacobeans must return to the source.

One matter is clear. If they are to obtain more grain (and of vastly greater moment, if Simeon is to be released), the boy Benjamin must accompany them.

✦   ✦   ✦

43:6–7   Jacob's other name, Israel, is here suddenly invoked. The name, it will be recalled, was conferred on him during the mysterious assault at Penuel, when Jacob and his angelic adversary wrestled nightlong.

Why here precisely, Israel? The name is variously translated; perhaps "May God prevail!" will do. Thus the distressed old man prays for relief of anguish. In prospect of another loss, he frets between pain and powerlessness.

Names, no names. The name has power; naming someone confers power. And what of a refusal to name someone? Fear of that latent power?

Since the name Joseph is forbidden among the guilty, so shall the name of "this man" (up to the present unknown) remain unmentioned by the grieving father.

> "What
> impelled you
>
> to tell
> this man
>
> that yes,
> we have
> at home
>
> a
> younger
> brother?"

How masterful and subtle, our author. Years after the crime, the name of their brother remains a forbidden word.

Joseph knows them, and conceals the knowledge. Recognition, also concealed. To them, the Egyptian lord remains an incognito. He is simply, perhaps contemptuously, perhaps fearfully, "the Egyptian," or here, "this man":

> "The man kept pressing us as to details of our family, of you. Was our father still living? And do you have brothers at home?"

They too grow fretful:

> "How could we have known that the Egyptian would hear us out, then spring on us? 'Bring me your youngest,' he cried, 'Or else!'"

✦ ✦ ✦

We take note of larger implications. With a kind of Greek inevitability, with clash of wills and emotional turbulence, through the sighted and blind, the story of the brothers moves toward a modest eschatology, the restoration of broken ties.

Joseph and his brothers; yet another story of siblings in mortal combat. From the first, the tales are brutish, primordial, murderous. Cain slays his brother; the descendants seize weapons and aim them at one another's throats. Jacob and Esau betray and lie.

Now to the time and place of Joseph. Brothers laid hands on an innocent, abandoned their brother to the unknown, to slavery. For years and years, his fate lay like an incubus on the family, unacknowledged. They plunged their crime in a dark pocket of memory (dark as that cistern . . . ?)

And to all appearances (appearances being to such as these, everything), they cared not a damn. The blood money is long spent; so, it might well be, is the blood.

They threw their brother away like a debris, then they consigned his memory to darkness. Was not this a sign of their moral estate—crime and no consequence?

No consequence, for awhile. Only a cover-up, a second crime—this one against the truth of the mind. They name evil good. Or at the least, inconsequential.

And Joseph? He survived and prospered. Unknown to his brothers, the slave was freed and rose in eminence. Stalwart, tender, commanding, blunt, he will seek by straight ways and byways of the heart, to reconcile.

Does he summon memory of his family, only to despise and fling them out of mind? Nothing of that. Slowly it becomes clear that like an Egyptian alchemist, ever so skillfully Joseph has mixed a draught of the elixir we name hope. He raises the cup, holds it out to his brothers. There is hope, even for such a vile fraternity as appears before him.

Reversal of roles, the toppling of some, the towering above, the accession of another! Victim has become protagonist; he will orchestrate event upon event, leading to a heart-stopping final scene.

Another image. Joseph stands at center stage. His hands, like hands on harp strings, summon an opening chord, magisterial. Then, severity and brio. By turns austere and grandly vast, he plucks at the heart. And the dominant theme, with what skill emerges. This—healing and reconciliation.

The brothers will become brotherly at last, united with one another, with their victim—and yes, with their better selves.

43:11 The raw grief of "their father Israel" yields to a resigned foreboding. He gives in. What must be, must be.

Israel:

> "May
> God
>
> then
> prevail."

He raises his arms, surrendering. In effect; take gifts with you, take double the money. Take even Benjamin.

And a prayer, addressed here to "el Shaddai," peculiar and solemn; perhaps "the One of the mountain."

An undercurrent also of anger against "the man," once more unnamed, that master in Egypt? (and brother Simeon, also unnamed).

> "May
> God
> Almighty
>
> grant you
> compassion
>
> in the sight
> of the man,
>
> that he
> may release
> to you
>
> your other
> brother,
>
> and
> Benjamin." (43:14)

✦ ✦ ✦

43:15 We must race to the end. In a single verse, they went again into Egypt; their mood is left to us to imagine. And they

> . . . stood
> before
> Joseph.

Joseph catches sight of Benjamin. A catch in the throat. Whatever the intended scenario—cancel it! He says abruptly to an aide:

"Conduct
them

to
my
house. . . ."

There, they are reunited with Simeon. Joseph enters. He beholds,

". . . his brother
Benjamin,

son
of

his
own
mother. . . ." (43:29)

He blesses the boy. Then, overcome, he retires to his chamber in tears.

✦ ✦ ✦

The scene is all of comings and goings, emotions unleashed, memories rife. A banquet is served. By instruction of the host, the brothers are seated in a row, eldest to youngest.

And they take note, struck with astonishment—how comes it that this unknown man knows our rank and age?

Not a hint proffered, expressionless, the master of the great house moves about, serving them. This strange majesty, to whom waiting at table is not a whit demeaning.

With this ictus, a break in the rank; it is like a crease in the smooth linens. Benjamin receives a vast portion, "exceeding by five, that of the others" (43:34). Honor heaped upon honor for the child!

And all drink deeply. Bewilderment and wild joy abound. What if, what if? But they cannot complete—.

✦ ✦ ✦

44   All good things have ending. They must depart for home.

The instruction of Joseph to his servants repeats that of the former visit. Fill their sacks with grain (with this addition—"as much as they can carry"). Then this fateful secretive note:

> "My own
> cup,
>
> the silver one—
> put it
>
> in
> the sack
>
> of
> the
> youngest." (44:2)

The procession has scarcely departed when Joseph orders a servant to follow, with contracted brows and an ominous word. He is to confront the brothers—How can this be? You have stolen something of great value, a cup of divination!

The servant overtakes them. All together, they commence to open the sacks in search. The order of the banquet is ominously followed once more, from eldest to youngest, open up!

And ruination. In the sack of Benjamin the child, a silver goblet gleams like a baleful eye.

Silver again, a talisman of doom. A brother sold for silver. Forbidden silver in the baggage. Now this. Silver again, a haunt, a quicksilver creeping into tents, sacks, into souls.

In grief and disarray they return.

There in the great house of "the man," it is Judah who speaks for them all. Simple, devastating, at last:

> "... God
> has
> revealed
>
> the guilt
>
> of
> your servants." (43:16)

"Revealed . . . the guilt."

It is left to ourselves. But he could hardly be referring to a theft they did not commit. Does his remorse refer rather to the "original sin," by which they sold their brother in slavery? The innuendo is there.

✦ ✦ ✦

Joseph, stony of face, meets them. His decision is awful beyond words:

> ". . . Only
> the man
>
> in whose hand
> this cup
> was found
>
> shall
> be
>
> my
> slave. . . ." (44:17)

The judgment falls on the brothers like a thunderbolt. Just such horrid outcome their father had envisioned.

Judah must make a last-ditch intervention, weighty, frantic, ironic. In this vein:

> ". . . my lord, you yourself questioned us as to our family. And we told you of our aged father, and of two sons; the one dead and gone, the other born in our father's old age. . . . And now, I do not wish to see the outcome of all this. . . . If I return without the child, my father will die of the loss. . . ." (44:18–34)

✦ ✦ ✦

45:4–5 Tearful and laden with pleading, his words overcome the last redoubt of Joseph's reserve. He waves his entourage out of the room, and commences to weep aloud. The burden of the years lifts at last. His words are a lament, an embrace, a pure and reconciling poetry:

> "Come
> closer

to
me,

I
am

your brother
Joseph
whom
you sold

into
Egypt.

Do not
be afraid,

do not
reproach yourselves.

It was
for sake

of
saving
lives

God
sent
me

here

ahead
of
you."

✦ ✦ ✦

45:8 What a moment, and what language to snare the moment! A paean of warrant and recognition, an unveiling of the inexplicable travail of life, an acknowledgment of the God of life.

Twice the man of fidelity invokes God:

"... who
sent me
here,

made me
vizier
of the pharaoh,

lord
of his household,

ruler
over
Egypt."

Does Joseph linger over titles and honors, dwelling on his lofty station, subtly pinking his brothers? Surely he is entitled to savor the moment, the past, the turning of tables.

✦ ✦ ✦

45:9 An epiphany. Disguise and concealment are laid aside; haste is the order of the day.

Feeble, advanced in years, father Jacob must be informed with all speed of the providential events now revealed. Joseph urges:

"Make haste
and go up
to my father

and say
to him,
'Thus says
your son Joseph . . .

Come down
to me,

do
not
tarry.'"

They have the pledge of Joseph their brother. And all manner of things will be well. . . .

More tears and embraces.

✦ ✦ ✦

The pharaoh himself deigns to enter the scene, in favor of his courtier Joseph. The riches of Egypt are placed at command of the brothers, together with a fleet of chariots to transport aged Jacob, the women, and children of the family. They are instructed to:

> "Waste
> no regret
>
> on what
> you leave
> behind,
>
> for the best
> of all
>
> the land
> of Egypt
>
> is
> yours!" (45:20)

Then, the ancient title of their father is invoked, a guerdon of reconciliation:

> The sons
> of Israel
>
> did
> so . . . .

Rich robes are bestowed, banquets set. Then a procession forms, and beasts are loaded with provender.

Finally, a triumphant departure. With this admonition from the vizier–brother, unaccustomedly stern:

> "And
> no
> recriminations
>
> on
> the
> way!" (45:24)

An abrupt command, and we are brought up short. Out of character? Hardly. He knows too well the sour clutch of their moods, how fragile too is change of heart, how easily they may revert to awful form.

✦   ✦   ✦

45:25–28   They arrive in Canaan with the Great News—Joseph lives! But the mind of Israel (that name again, for all is new) remains hazy. He cannot immediately take in this crashing impossibility. Had not child Joseph vanished years before, without trace except for a bloody garment?

The chariots of the pharaoh arrive on the scene, solid evidence of the truth, the munificence and prospering of Joseph. Like an old lion aroused, the patriarch shakes himself. No mistaking, let us name him twice:

> . . . The spirit
> of their father
> Jacob
>
> revived,
>
> and Israel
> said,
>
> "It
> is enough.
>
> Joseph
> my son
> is alive.
>
> I will go
> and see him
>
> before
> I
> die."

✦   ✦   ✦

46   They depart, this vast extended clan of seventy (which the priest–scribes are solicitous to number and name).

And who shall know, who live to see, the outcome of this hegira? No matter; after such travail, triumph at last.

The happy outcome includes a momentous epiphany, a summing up from on high, and a Promise renewed. Thus a continuum of providence oversees the journeys, the dislocating to–fro of the clan:

> "I
>
> am
> God,

the God

of

your

father . . . .." (46:3)

As Abraham had been led by an oracle into Canaan (12:1), divine intervention leads Jacob to depart the same land. But not finally, not forever!

Thus the book named Genesis nears its closure.

And the seeds of the Exodus are planted here, and the Promise renewed:

"Not only
will I

go down
to Egypt
with you,

I
will also
bring
you

back
here. . . ." (46:4)

Providential beginnings indeed—at least, as adduced by scribes hardly to be thought disinterested.

✦   ✦   ✦

46:28–34 The many-faceted personality of this Joseph, surely the most complex, as well as the most heartwarming of the patriarchs! As we have seen and marveled, at least for a time his image is of a peerless jewel, turning and turning before our bedazzled eyes.

Here in one brief passage is told the warmth of welcome accorded his father. And more—the perspicacious introduction of the entire clan to the pharaoh. How subtle the hint of prospects and perquisites!

To his family Joseph summarizes in advance the discourse he will shortly offer the pharaoh. They are to pay careful attention, and echo his words later, for the message will accrue greatly to their advantage.

To wit; the newly arrived people are shepherds. Let them settle in good grazing land, in Goshen, at the frontier.

✦ ✦ ✦

Joseph the farseeing, Joseph the provider! He would avoid two dangers. The first, that his people be assimilated with the Egyptians. And second, that they be assigned a kind of Bantustan, vulnerable and apart, in the center of the country.

Neither of these. Let them be granted free access to the length and breadth of Egypt. And (occasion requiring), equally free egress!

Thus, witting or not—but our scribe is witting indeed—the shadow of Exodus falls on the scene, like a cloud crossing the sun.

Momentarily, the cloud is pure gold, a falling shower of Danaë. But the sun? It is darkened.

✦ ✦ ✦

Interestingly, two versions of the audience with the pharaoh are placed vis-à-vis. In the first, Joseph and five brothers approach. They seek and are granted to dwell in Goshen. And a further honor; the flocks of the pharaoh are placed in their charge.

The second account is undoubtedly the work of priest–scribes; the words are sparse, precise, dry. Pharaoh takes the initiative. According to these acolytes of a later empire, it is as though the great ruler intuits a grand future, and praises accordingly. Glory shall fall to him and his people, as these renowned foreigners seek refuge in his land!

✦ ✦ ✦

47:7 We linger over the encounter, as great pharaoh bows to the greater patriarch. Awe, wonderment are in the air; the pharaoh gazes on his venerable guest. Perhaps at a loss, he questions him:

> "How
> many
> years
>
> does
> your
> life
> number?"

The answer is halting, words carefully measured, sorrow overriding all. It is as though Jacob grows prescient; his dimming eyes rest on the past, summing up the entire patriarchal era. He knows in his faltering bones, his slowing blood—how quickly, how sorrowfully the years have come and gone!

His age is 130 years; but,

> "my life . . .
> has not
> touched
>
> the age
>
> of
> my
> ancestors." (47:9)

Abraham, 175 years; Isaac, 180 years.

And a paradox; arrival in Canaan evaded these great patriarchs. In a sense, they never entered, but lived and died as outsiders, foreigners to the land of promise.

Still, in Egypt, consolations abound. Under the providential eye of one of their own, favored by the highest authority, the newcomers settle on the acreage granted.

And another paradox; it is as though the ancient promise has taken a foreign turn—and in permanence. Are the chosen, and the promise as well, to be stalled in Egypt? We shall see.

47:13 An interruption falls like a restraining hand across the narrative. And we are presented with a rather dry account of Joseph's "land policy."

The famine continues to ravage the land, a dragon with a fiery breath. Farmlands are stricken, crops shrivel, cattle falter and fall to the ground.

What to do? Joseph rises to the challenge; he adopts draconian measures. Step by astute step, he takes control of the economy. And always with one advantage in mind—the prospering of the pharaoh. First, through judicious sale of grain, he amasses from Egypt and Canaan an immense treasury. Time is on his side—time, whose other awful name is famine.

Public misery grows. In feverish panic people buy grain. Their stores quickly consumed, they have no wherewithal to buy more.

Bankruptcy. The flocks, such as survive, must be given over—to the pharaoh. Then worse—"bodies and farmland." As though whirled in a cyclone, landowners are swept from the land. Once prosperous farmers are reduced to serfs; their acreage passes into the estates of the pharaoh.

Was it all calculated beforehand by the pharaoh's adjutant? The dreamer, the skilled interpreter of dreams has hardened, his basilisk eye alert to the main chance. The ever so delicate balance between his double role, the pharaoh's man and servant of his people, has tipped.

And to this nadir, one thinks, the people be damned.

Both ruler and vizier are transformed before our eyes. The pharaoh—to a hard despot, and greedy to boot. And Joseph? A sedulous apparatchik, whip in hand.

Astutely, he exempts the lands of the priests from seizure.

A year passes, and no relief. Spring arrives. The farmers once more sow a crop. Joseph passes out seed, with a ruinous stipulation; one-fifth of the harvest must be handed over—to the pharaoh.

This monarch was once so solicitous of his people's welfare! So he credited a dreamer's dream of things to come.

Now all is changed. At work is a new appetite—for power and more power. Abstractions multiply; an imperial vocabulary flourishes like tares amid wheat. Our vizier has become a very demon of accumulation and centralization.

His decisions imply a stiffened resolve, a merciless will. The famine and the soul of Joseph are absorbed in the black hole named "empire."

And with brilliant indirection the author grants us a hint of things to come, in the Jerusalem of a later, domestic empire.

Solomon too will create a class society, with forced labor, a standing army, a ruinous economy of misery and vast wealth.

We, of course, studying the history of the Hebrews from our own point of view, can see the essential vice in the growth of Hebrew wealth; it was not widely diffused. Solomon's wisdom simply created a wealthy class and left the mass of the population as poor as it had been before.

> In the course of time, they became even poorer. . . . [The peasant] became a habitual debtor, and ultimately a slave. Ownership of land, once widely scattered, became concentrated in the hands of a few wealthy families. . . .

> The resources of the nation, since they were not widely possessed, were squandered on luxuries and not on the necessities of life.

We ought to notice that this state of affairs, which we would
call an unsound economic situation, was not limited to the
Hebrew community; it was normal in the ancient world, in
the medieval world, as it is normal in most of the modern
world. . . . (John L. McKenzie, *The Two-Edged Sword: An Interpretation of the Old Testament*)

✦   ✦   ✦

An Isaiah will appear, and assail the abomination:

"The land is full
of silver and gold,
there is no end
to their treasures;

the land is full
of horses,

there is no end
to their chariots.

the land is full
of idols;

they worship
the works of their hands,

that which
their fingers have made." (Isa 2:7–8)

✦   ✦   ✦

The roots of the abomination are here, early on, in Egypt. Joseph, vice-
regent of the pharaoh, has drunk the wine of tyranny. He takes in hand its
tools, his tongue grows ready in its threats—the whip, the treasury, domination, and seizure. And the inevitable miseries attendant—evictions, hunger,
shame, and resentment.

Thus the irony, the first arc of a circle that one day will close tight. Solomon will be a later wizard of the "pharaonic method."

Joseph tried it first, here. He found it a meat that fostered craving.

✦   ✦   ✦

To what end this disturbing, detailed episode in the otherwise immaculate record of Joseph the beloved, the wunderkind?

And a second question, no less disconcerting—why is the jolting inter-ruption inserted at this point? What light does the context seek to shed?

The contrast! We have seen in Joseph a behavior that merits only admi-ration. Ex-prisoner, clairvoyant, first of the patriarchs to forswear trickery and violence, to forgive and reconcile.

And now, behold the creator and enforcer of the pharaoh's absolute con-trol. The gears of the second-in-command ominously mesh with the su-preme will. A ferocious ambition grinds the people down.

Will this ethos, we wonder, be passed on to the pharaoh of Exodus and his merciless edicts, including the death of the Hebrew firstborn? Has this ironbound will to seize, dominate, control, taken its origin in—Joseph?

✦ ✦ ✦

On the vexing matter, the transformation of Joseph, NAM ignores com-ment; the Bible of Jerusalem sheds little or no light:

> It would be judgmental to attach to this "nationalization"
> a moral question mark which lies outside the intent of the
> author.

But of what that "intent" might be, we are told nothing. And yet the question nags—does not faith demand that we ponder that "intent"?

We have a few historical hints. The memories of the enslavement in Egypt are like an imprint on the national soul. Unexpunged, wounding, they live on, a patrimony of outrage. The memories endure, even to the time of Solomon. When, as we know, the present account was set down. Do we have here a latent historical resentment, dangerous as an embolism break-ing free?

✦ ✦ ✦

It is as though a long cycle were completed at last. Centuries after Joseph comes this strange convolution, this merging of history. With evident ap-proval, the scribes of Jerusalem set down the decisions of an ancestor—whose life brutally furthered the designs of empire.

More; in Egypt, Joseph is accounted far other than a native son—surely a crashing irony. He is an arriviste, a Jew. And more, a former slave. Do the scribes hint that when strong men (sic) and even stronger decisions are called for, a Hebrew slave can do a pharaoh one better?

✦ ✦ ✦

As to the context of the "land policy," it presents yet another puzzle. Prior to the encroachments and seizures, the Joseph saga is a positively dazzling success story. All goes well with the immigrants in Egypt. The good offices of Joseph, and indeed of the pharaoh himself, are at their behest.

Amid the misery of the indigenous people, there is plenty for the foreign few, a cruel triage:

> As pharaoh had ordered, Joseph settled his father and brothers and gave them holdings in Egypt on the pick of the land. . . .

> And Joseph sustained his fathers and brothers and his father's whole household down to the youngest, with food. (47:11–12)

✦ ✦ ✦

The dragon breathes fire. Famine eats the social fabric to tatters; splendid Egypt is reduced to a vast serfdom. The contrast must be driven home—the sordid theme of plenty amid misery, a stake in the heart of the undead:

> Thus Israel settled in the land of Egypt. . . .

> There they acquired property, were fertile and increased greatly. (47:27)

✦ ✦ ✦

Are we being warned? This Joseph whom we took to heart, this icon of forgiveness and reconciliation—suddenly he grows slippery, he escapes our net.

He shone on the page, immaculate, like a latter-day Daniel, an epiphany of unclouded virtue. A hopeful contrast to the ancestors, Cain the fratricide, Isaac the vacillator, slippery Jacob, boorish Esau. A shining contrast to those traitorous brothers, Reuben, Simeon, Levi, and worse.

Joseph, hero without blemish! The original fault left him faultless. He knew travail, scorn, betrayal, false charges, prison. Laboriously, by main force of intelligence and heart, he ascended to power.

Then, standing at summit, he shucks off his former mind. With fatal ease Joseph is suborned. Once the servant of an afflicted people, he becomes the lackey of a tyrant.

He goes further, he out-pharaohs the pharaoh. He sets in place structures of tyranny unknown before, seizing on the famine to destroy the social contract, degrade the economy, destroy the labor force.

✦ ✦ ✦

The septenary of misery comes to an end. Egypt is a vast lunar desert, a czarist landscape of serfs and owners. What was once unthinkable has come to pass—loss of land, loss of hope.

Behold our quondam icon, the architect and engineer of a would-be "new world order." The famine has ravaged more than the land; it has parched the soul of "Joseph the provider."

✦ ✦ ✦

Do we of the Christian book sense the shadow of a demon, whispering at the ear of the royal patron? Our Scripture offers a kind of "mutual midrash."

Only imagine—Joseph shows the pharaoh, or the pharaoh shows Joseph (why not, the two are one in ambition), as though "from a pinnacle . . . from a mountain top," the vast resources of land and labor that lie just beyond reach. The riches with a stroke of a pen, can be Joseph's own, to hand to his patron:

> "All
> this
>
> will
> I
>
> give
> you. . . ." (Matt 4:9)

Such are the methods of an absolute autocracy, a pharaoh and his spoliator. A duet of dishonor, the corruption of power.

And the perverting of rulers cannot be said to stop with themselves. One must ask, what of the citizenry and their fate, what of the descendants?

The Fates, as the Greeks knew, have a way of turning their darlings to prey. A successor of the pharaoh, we read in Exodus, will persecute the descendants of Joseph. And with a vengeance. In more ways than one, a vengeance.

✦ ✦ ✦

Is a kind of modified ancestor worship at work in our text?

The ancestor, in accord with the imperial "ethos of beginnings," must be

made useful to later designs. Therefore, let the bond be strengthened between Joseph, consolidating the economy of a foreign crown, and his descendants. A single dynastic design, across time and place—centralize,
accumulate!

Centuries later, the imperialists David and Solomon will make of Jerusalem the capital of the new empire. David will map the design; Solomon will
build for the god a gilded cage. And in matters economic and military, the
duet will play pharaoh to the hilt.

And let us add, in matters "religious" (sic) as well, will play the pharaoh.

Given the immense, unfettered power of the global economy in our day,
this wearisome report (1 Kings 6:21–7:50) of the temple in Jerusalem is a
warning of how religion can, and does, become a commodity.

> The practices of religious communal life are priced out ac-
> cording to an alien standard—money value, not theologi-
> cal value. . . . For all practical purposes, extreme and
> innocent acts of obedience, compassion, and generosity are
> eliminated. . . .
>
> Yet the "commoditization" of religion is only a symptom
> and sign of the greater commoditization, in which each
> person finally becomes an object of disputed value. In the
> process, we grow numb to neighbor and alienated from
> self. We can see this larger commoditization with Solomon
> in his policy of forced labor, which reduces thousands of fel-
> low Israelites to objects employed in temple construction (1
> Kings 5:13–16.) (Walter Brueggemann, "Faith with a Price,"
> *Other Side Online*)

✦ ✦ ✦

Joseph enters the counsels of the profane. Enters, and seizes command.
And are we not urged by this episode of power gone awry, to ponder the rot
of even the best intentions?

Joseph defies and violates conventional expectation.

The outcome is a livid question mark. Did we take for granted that a
sedulous satrap, enlightened by suffering and humiliation, would preserve
a pure heart, even as his fortunes rose? That he would move mountains to
assuage the plight of famine-stricken farmers and tradespeople, the lowly
and needy of his adopted land?

Would not the instruction of the pharaoh to the smitten people, "Go to

Joseph," have sounded in the heart of the vizier, a call to mercy and compassion?

In time, less and less of either. Until nothing remained. We have here, amid prospering and power, a severe hint and warning. There can be no guarantee that misfortune engenders mercy toward others.

Indeed, the biblical word is dire, and quite opposed to easy assumptions or cultural optimism:

> The rest of humankind who were not killed by these plagues, did not repent of the works of their hands nor give up worshipping demons and idols of gold and silver and bronze and stone and wood, which cannot either see or hear or walk.
>
> Nor did they repent of their sorceries or their immorality or their thefts. (Rev 9:20–21)

Another, far different guarantee, an awful one is biblically underscored in the Joseph story and elsewhere. Power corrupts.

47:27 Meantime, the newly arrived Israelites multiply and flourish. The announcement, heartening on the face of it, has a dark underside. Good news induces bad moods, a kind of Sauline malaise.

Does great pharaoh grow distempered? A report such as this, the Israelites' prospering (and Egypt the undoubted source of their serendipity), one day will lead to ominous rumblings from the throne.

Will lead—we have seen it—to a change of heart, to tightening the bonds of law, to outrageous decrees. The origins are here; the Exodus is not far distant.

48 We have a confusion of texts and traditions. It is as though the descendants cannot agree on the terms of Jacob's inheritance.

In any case, the tenderness of the episode (48:8) redeems its unclarities. Aged Jacob, dim of sight, is overcome at the news—Joseph has progeny. The patriarch, long resigned to the death of his son, had not dared hope for such gracious news. Now, quite beside himself with joy, he purposes to bless the children.

The ritual begins. And to Joseph's alert eye, the grandfather has gotten the rubric wrong. The patriarch rests his right hand on the head of the younger child, the left on the older. But surely the opposite is called for; surely the right hand holds more powerful medicine than the left!

Joseph intervenes, as though in panic. The blessing must fall on the child favored by correct gesture!

But no, the venerable one has things exactly right; he acts in accord with a larger wisdom. Memories, memories; Jacob and Esau and their conniving mother and the ancient reversal of fortune.

Here too let the unexpected prevail. The younger grandson is preferred; he receives the right-handed blessing.

And Joseph, aware that the interventions of God often stand human fortunes on their head—that the prosperous may go off to prison, that a slave may become a vizier—Joseph stands mute. And in silence, one thinks, he grows the wiser.

✦ ✦ ✦

49 Shall we speak here of the "benedictions of Jacob"? This is the traditional title of the chapter. But, in point of fact, precious few blessings are conferred. Not all descendants are of equal merit, not all tribes springing from the sons of Jacob are destined to flourish.

The so-called blessings are, in fact, more in the nature of solemn oracles; as though it were said, "Gather around, I shall reveal what shall be in days to come." The occasion is momentous, the air charged with prophecy. Alert of mind, the old man pierces a misty future. The moral behavior of his sons—what shall the consequence be?

On a noble deathbed, fully conscious, the patriarch waxes oracular.

We have seen it in the Bible, we have seen it in our lifetime; the spirit flares up, surpassing the dark, even as a flame feeds upon the failing body.

The father places evidence, pro and con, virtuous and wicked, on the scales of judgment. Is he playing God? Let us say rather he is paying tribute to a moral development apt to his time—(apt in degree, to our own as well). He speaks in detail of the fate of his sons. The words are like Sinaitic judgments. It is as though the future were set in stone.

Such is the power of the bloodline, of this bloodline and the final hour of the ancestor. His oracles become a form of *opus operatum*, a divine intervention on the human scene. They are by analogy "sacramental," they bring to pass what they announce.

The "blessings" exhaust, even as they attain, the high possibilities latent in human speech. Speech becomes the envelope of providence; like open arms, words embrace freedom both human and divine. A mysterious point is attained (a moment, a time out of time?) when human choice intersects the will of the Holy One.

✦   ✦   ✦

Alas, of all the tribes, all the sons, only Joseph is explicitly blessed. Judah for his part is—praised, a cool if not a cold comfort.

A different glance, frigid, rests on the others. They are spared nothing; they are summoned to judgment.

First, let a curse descend on Reuben. He was guilty of incest (35:22). Then Simeon and Levi, side by side, quail under the lash of the dying father; the blows land soundly, memory summoned in their despite. It stings.

These two played out the ancient, poisoned scenario of "Brothers of the Fall." Sons of Cain they have proved themselves. Together, they planned and executed the traitorous attack on Shechem. It is the first recorded instance of extermination polity; all inhabitants were destroyed (34:25–31).

And worse, if worse were possible. The assault placed in jeopardy the entire future of the tribes in Canaan.

We linger, we do well to linger, over the adduced "crime" and its punishment (of which, more later). In days to come, the wars of Judges and Kings will rage interminably—and be divinely blessed. Wars of extermination will multiply, as the "chosen" lay claim to the "promise."

The sanctioned violence represents an enormous scandal, an all but insurmountable stumbling block set against—what? Shall we say, against a confident, trusting biblical faith in God, self-revealed in those pages?

God self-revealed—or an ape of god, a confabulated god, in the image of those he serves and is served by?

✦   ✦   ✦

Of more than passing interest here is a judgment laid against such war as the brothers Simeon and Levi instigate. The war is accounted a capital crime, multiplied over and over.

If justice is to be attained, the crime must bring retribution both socialized and condign. The brothers' lives are spared. But the consolation is sorry and short-lived. Worse than death is decreed against them—the extinction of their tribes:

". . . I shall disperse them in Israel." (49:7)

✦   ✦   ✦

Slowed by subsequent awful events, we pause in wonderment. Is the atrocious assault on Shechem condemned because it is intrinsically wicked, or because (in a sense both narrow and morally frivolous) it is judged traitorous, running counter to the interests of the tribe? No answer; or an answer left to ourselves.

✦ ✦ ✦

49:8–12 The praise accorded Judah is as lengthy and fulsome as that bestowed on Joseph. And one surmises, perhaps soundly, that the paeans were composed as the two tribes became preeminent in the nation—in the era of David.

Thus does history shoulder some aside, nudge others to the fore. Given time, winners and losers emerge. And the winning descendants, as though in an adroit series of chess moves, reach into the past and adjust the ancestors accordingly; castles and kings swift and skilled, winners and losers. From the start, some blessed, others cursed.

Behold the winner—Judah. From him the Davidic dynasty arises. And of supreme import, and urging the necessity of forgiving much—from David the messianic Son, Jesus the Christ.

✦ ✦ ✦

49:13–21 We have passing references to six brothers, shortly disposed of. They are hardly to be accounted favorites—in effect, that chess game again!—losers.

✦ ✦ ✦

49:22–26 On to Joseph, the crowned favorite. Crowned indeed, and with a warrior's crown. The first blessings, as though conferred by a combative god, are all of combat. Joseph prevails, overcomes. He cannot be imagined at peace with others. His opponents "harrying and attacking," he harries and attacks. "Tit for tat" might be thought the motto of his escutcheon.

Some emerge from the nest of time, winged, beaked, and clawed. They seize the patrimony, nudging the less powerful out of the haven, over and down! Thus winners create and canonize the "correct" ancestors. Behold Joseph, the favored one—and his favoring God. How closely each resembles the other, these mirror images. Hence too a rather bizarre mélange of divine titles:

> "... the
> mighty one
> of Jacob ...

the shepherd,
the rock
of Israel,

the God

of
your
father. . . ."

It is as though the mightiest medicine of the divine must be mingled and supped by Joseph. What shall we name his magic—a concentration of light and heat, a spectrum white hot, a sword Excalibur?

✦   ✦   ✦

By implication, the world is presented in a single, dark image; it is an abode of mortal combat. Joseph must know this, and its consequence—surrounded by enemies, advancing to battle, emerging invincible! No other mortal is so enveloped, encompassed, fortified with blessing upon blessing.

Then all unexpectedly—at least to this ponderer—the blessing takes a more pacific, indeed an ecologically tender, poetic form.

". . . blessings

of
breast and womb,

blessing

of
fresh
grain

and
blossoms. . . ."

So, inevitably, the deity takes a like form, a pacific, sensitive lover of creation. And we wonder—whence this schizophrenic strain, in the favored human as in his god?

One suggestion; we have an implied evidence of the primitive calamity, the Fall. The blessing is bestowed by the god of the Fall, a title with ominous implication. The "blessing" is like a call to battle; it signals and summons division, angers, retribution.

Beware. It is also ineradicable, reaching forward from generation to generation. Those so "blessed" will wage wars without end, will revel in the analogues of war—racism, sexism, rancorous combat against the common good and the living earth.

The divisions defy resolution, dissolution—to the present millennium.

✦   ✦   ✦

More; those who claim the first of the great "divided blessing," victory in war—these hanker greatly after the second series of blessings. And the second is inevitably viewed as yet another form of war—the "conquest" of ecology, of "breast and womb, grain and blossoms."

✦   ✦   ✦

Today, technology would reach further, into alteration of genes and cloning. Technicians would be omnipotent; they seek to win and to bestow—

> ". . . the blessing
> of
> the heavens above,
> of
> the abyss
> that
> crouches
> below. . . ." (49:25)

✦   ✦   ✦

At length the pyrotechnics of our text near their end. Young Benjamin receives only bare—and unexpected, startling—mention. Nothing has prepared us for the imagery.

Imagine, this blameless stripling, the apple of his father's and brother's eye, the sweet prey of Joseph's sojourn in Egypt, of his longings for home and family. And now, in a single verse (49:27), the youngster leaps into the scene of his descendants, for all the world like a lupine fury! These Benjaminites will be a bellicose clan, morbid and guileful by turn, celebrated, denounced—and on occasion all but exterminated. Their blood and the blood of their enemies will stain the pages of the book of Judges.

Let it be to their honor; redemption comes at grievous cost. Nonetheless it comes, gratuitous, largehanded.

Their great descendant, Saul of Tarsus, will be stricken down as he proceeds on his horrific errand, an errand never to be resumed. And his sublime rhetoric will thrust to one side the bloody ghosts of his past, and the past of his tribe:

> "I ask then,
> has God
>
> rejected
> God's people?
>
> Of course not.
>
> I myself
> am an Israelite,
>
> descended
> from Abraham,
>
> of
> the
> tribe
>
> of
> Benjamin." (Rom 11:1)

✦　✦　✦

He could confess to no more shameful lineage; nor could he more openly glory in the surpassing of that shame. He was cast to ground by a fearsome visitation. And his former life? No more of that.

✦　✦　✦

49:29 Undoubtedly the pen of priest–scribes interjects here. Jacob's last charge, as to his place of burial, is legal and precise. He must rest in Hebron, in the grotto that Abraham purchased long before.

✦　✦　✦

50 Curiously, Jacob is embalmed in accord with Egyptian custom. Then, after a period of royal mourning, a magnificent cortege departs from Goshen for the burial.

The priests are heard once more, ensuring that all is right and rubrical as to placement; Abraham, Sara, Isaac, Rebecca, and Leah—the great ancestors repose together (50:14).

✦　✦　✦

Joseph and his brothers embrace in a final reconciliation. The gesture is tactical as well as emotionally fitting. Dread is in the air; with the death of Jacob, will Joseph take a retributive turn?

Nothing of the kind. Nothing has changed, his course is consistent; the benignity he showed them during the famine, he renews. Once for all, betrayal and dereliction are forgotten.

Thus Joseph reassures them. And we too are reassured, and granted a signal relief. Joseph holds his arms wide, welcomes his brothers. For once, the curse of Cain is annulled and voided. The brother embraces his brethren, unworthy as they are.

Joseph has reversed the downward spiral of sin, restored and strengthened the bonds of fraternity. In a fallen world, moral greatness asserts itself; an era of forgiveness dawns. The magnanimity of Joseph, underscored here, brings to happy conclusion the Book of Beginnings.

✦ ✦ ✦

And on this benign note, the grand era of the patriarchs closes, in a calm diminuendo.

Turbulent, tormented, morally ambiguous, tawdry, at times outright brutish was their story. But also now and again, valiant, ardent in affection, alight with a fugitive hope.

✦ ✦ ✦

The end is soon told. Joseph lives on, into a tranquil old age. His last words are heavy with a burden of prophecy. On a day known only to God, his descendants will depart Egypt and journey toward the land of Promise. Let them bear his bones along with them—those bones animate, electric with hope.

Death no dominion, and a new start.

✦ ✦ ✦

So. End with a poem, why not?

✦ ✦ ✦

THE WAY IT IS

Look; no one ever promised for sure
that we would sing. We have decided
to moan. In a strange dance that
we don't understand till we do it, we
have to carry on.

Just as in sleep you have to dream
the exact dream to round out your life,
so we have to live that dream into stories
and hold them close at you, close at the
edge we share, to be right.
We find it an awful thing to meet people,
serious or not, who have turned into vacant
effective people, so far lost that they
won't believe their own feelings
enough to follow them out.
The authentic is a line from one thing
along to the next; it interests us.
Strangely, it relates to what works,
but is not quite the same. It never
swerves for revenge,
Or profit, or fame; it holds
together something more than the world,
this line. And we are your wavery
efforts at following it. Are you coming?
Good; now it is time.

(William Stafford, *The Way It Is: New and Selected Poems*)

Works Cited

Baum, Markus. *Against the Wind: Eberhard Arnold and the Bruderhof.* E. Sussex: Plough Publishing House, 1989.

Berrigan, Daniel. *Uncommon Prayer: A Book of Psalms.* Maryknoll, NY: Orbis Books, 1998.

Brueggemann, Walter. "Faith with a Price." *Other Side Online* 34, no. 4 (July–August 1998).

Bruns, Gerald L. "Midrash and Allegory." In *The Literary Guide to the Bible,* eds. Robert Alter and Frank Kermode. Cambridge: Belknap Press of Harvard University Press, 1987.

Cohen, Abraham. *Everyman's Talmud.* New York: Schocken Books, 1975.

Dillard, Annie. *For The Time Being.* New York: Knopf, 1999.

Ehrenreich, Barbara. *Blood Rites: Origins and History of the Passions of War.* New York: Henry Holt, 1997.

Hopkins, Gerard Manley. *Poems.* London: Humphrey Milford, 1918.

Hunsinger, George. "Toward a New Confessing Church." Lecture, Bangor Theological Seminary, ME, 1986.

McKenzie, John L. *Dictionary of the Bible.* New York: Macmillan, 1967.

McKenzie, John L. *The Two-Edged Sword: An Interpretation of the Old Testament.* Garden City, NY: Doubleday, 1982.

Merton, Thomas. *Conjectures of a Guilty Bystander.* Garden City, NY: Doubleday, 1989.

Robb, Peter. *M: The Man Who Became Caravaggio.* New York: Henry Holt, 2000.

Schell, Jonathan. *The Unconquerable World: Power, Nonviolence, and the Will of the People.* New York: Metropolitan Books, 2003.

Stafford, William. *The Way It Is: New and Selected Poems.* Saint Paul, MN: Greywolf Press, 1998.

Von Speyr, Adrienne. *Three Women and the Lord.* San Francisco: Ignatius Press, 1986.

Wink, Walter. *Engaging the Powers: Discernment and Resistance in a World of Domination.* Minneapolis, MN: Augsburg Fortress, 1992.